EFFECTIVE CO

Applying public relatio

EFFECTIVE
CORPORATE RELATIONS
Applying public relations in business and industry

Edited by
Norman A. Hart
MSc, FIPR, FCAM, F Inst M

McGRAW-HILL BOOK COMPANY

London . New York . St Louis . San Francisco . Auckland
Bogota . Guatemala . Hamburg . Lisbon . Madrid . Mexico
Montreal . New Delhi . Panama . Paris . San Juan . São Paulo
Singapore . Sydney . Tokyo . Toronto

Published by
McGRAW-HILL Book Company (UK) Limited
MAIDENHEAD · BERKSHIRE · ENGLAND

British Library Cataloguing in Publication Data

Effective corporate relations : applying
  public relations in business and industry.
  1. Public relations—Corporations
  I. Hart, Norman A.
  659.2   HD59

  ISBN 0–07–084940–4

Library of Congress Cataloging-in-Publication Data
Effective corporate relations.
  Includes bibliographies and index.
  1. Public relations—Corporations. 2. Public
relations—Corporations. I. Hart, Norman A.
HD59.E33   1987   659.2'85   87–21520
ISBN 0–07–084940–4

2345   LT   8909

Printed and bound in Great Britain by
Latimer Trend & Company Ltd, Plymouth

To Kristie and to Jessica

CONTENTS

THE AUTHORS

Michael Arnott is Managing Director of Charles Barker Communications Limited. He joined Charles Barker in 1977 after a career first in advertising and then in management consultancy. He has close involvement with client business and has, since 1984, led internal communications projects with Barclays Bank, BET, Burroughs, CEGB, General Motors, Jaguar Cars, the Law Society, and Thorn EMI. His particular interest lies in the communication of organizational goals and in creating the environment that allows employees to make a full contribution to their achievement.

Arnott co-authored the 1975 benchmark study for the Confederation of British Industry, 'Priorities for In-company Communication', and the study 'Communications in the 80s', produced for the 1980 IPM Conference. He has also published articles on marketing and internal communication and has presented papers at ESOMAR. He is a graduate of Oxford University and a full member of the UK Market Research Society, the IPA, and the BIM.

John V. Cook, DAA, Dip. PA, is an independent communications consultant. He was formerly Manager of Corporate Market Communications at Atlas Copco AB, the Swedish international engineering group specializing in compressed air and hydraulics. His communications career developed in London advertising agencies, during which time, pre-CAM, he obtained, by examination, the diplomas of both the Advertising Association and the Institute of Practitioners in Advertising. For 15 years he was Publicity Manager of Atlas Copco (Great Britain) Ltd; in 1980 he moved to Belgium to be Communications Manager for the group's compressor division in Antwerp. He was then responsible for various international corporate communications activities of the Atlas Copco Group, including its advertising, literature, films, and, not least, its corporate identity.

Peter Gummer was educated at Kings School, Rochester, Kent, and Selwyn College, Cambridge, where he obtained a BA in 1964 and an MA in 1968. After a period of working on local newspapers, he joined the public relations department of Viyella International, then moved into consultancy work. In the mid-1960s he joined Industrial and Commercial Finance Corporation (ICFC) as Public Relations Manager. Later he was appointed Managing Director of the ICFC subsidiary, ICFC Communications Ltd. He left ICFC to form Shandwick in 1974.

Shandwick plc is now the largest independent PR Group in the world with offices in London and throughout the UK, in North America, Australia, Singapore and Hong Kong. The Group employs 800 people and acts for over 1000 clients.

John Hackett, FIPR, has been engaged in full-time PR practice since leaving the Royal Navy in 1958, and before that acted as PRO to the first Naval Jet Night Fighter Squadron of the Fleet Air Arm. For seven years he was Press and Public Relations Officer for Decca Radar, where he set up their first press and public relations department.

In 1965 he joined Rank Xerox where he initiated their PR department as Manager of Corporate and Financial Affairs, and saw the world-wide growth of this enterprise, travelling throughout Europe and the United States. In 1977 he joined Bulmers, cider makers of Hereford, where he is currently Group Public Affairs Consultant.

Norman Hart, M.Sc., FIPR, FCAM, F. Inst.M, is Managing Director of Interact International Limited and Consultant Director of Interact Communications Limited, a full service business-to-business advertising agency. He was previously Director of the CAM Foundation, a marketing manager with Unilever, a publisher, and a management consultant. As an author, writer, and speaker, he has concentrated on industrial marketing and advertising, and on public relations and training.

Hart is a Visiting Fellow of Bradford University Management Centre, a Visiting Professor of Public Relations at Fairleigh Dickenson University and a course director of the College of Marketing. His best-known books are *Business-to-Business Advertising, The Marketing of Industrial Products,* and *The Practice of Advertising.* He also operates a private consultancy and is a registered marketing consultant of the Institute of Marketing.

Roger Haywood is Managing Director of Roger Haywood Associates Limited. He has been marketing and public relations adviser to leading British and international companies in industries ranging from high technology to leisure and consumer products, and is also a lecturer, author, and broadcaster on marketing and communications in the UK, Europe, and the United States.

Haywood began his career as a copywriter in advertising agencies before moving on to hold marketing positions with Dunlop and Dexion International. He was European Communications Adviser to Air Products and Chemicals Incorporated, one of the largest US chemical corporations, before forming his own London consultancy. He has been a governor of the Communication, Advertising and Marketing Education Foundation (CAM), a member of the board of management and chairman of the education committee of the Public Relations Consultants Association, and a member of the national executive and past branch chairman of the Institute of Marketing.

Haywood is an accredited business communicator and one of the few practitioners in the UK to hold the CAM diploma qualification in both advertising and public relations. He is a fellow of the Institute of Public Relations, and has written the accepted management and training guide to business communications, *All about PR,* published by McGraw-Hill.

Angus Maitland joined the Weir Group as an economic analyst after graduating from Glasgow University, where he won the Singer Award in Management Studies. He spent several years with Weir, and also with the US-headquartered process engineering company Sybron Corporation, before joining Charles Barker City as the company's Director of Planning. He joined Valin Pollen in 1980, shortly after the formation of the consultancy, and is now a director of The VPI Group PLC, the holding company of the Valin Pollen Group. He has group responsibilities for investor relations consultancy, management and marketing consultancy, and research, and has ultimate responsibility for several of the group's largest clients.

A former winner of the Industrial Marketing Research Association's Gold Medal, Maitland is the joint author—with Professor Ronald McTavish—of one of the UK's basic textbooks on industrial marketing.

Patrick J. Nally left school at an early age and was soon running major accounts for Erwin Wasey's PR subsidiary. After five year's experience, just before he was 21, he was enticed into being MD of a new consultancy where he met the sports broadcaster Peter West. Very soon afterwards, Nally and West set up West Nally, specializing in the entirely new use of sport as a means of communication. In essence, it was the first company to crystallize into a specialist, international sponsorship consultancy. It has operated world-wide, and beyond the original sport concept, with subsidiary elements dealing with all forms of media and communications.

Len Peach is currently Chief Executive of the NHS Management Board. He was loaned by IBM to the DHSS as Director of Personnel in November 1985, became Acting Chairman of the NHS Management Board in June 1986 and Chief Executive in October 1986. He is also Chairman of the NHS Training Authority. Previously Peach had been Director of Personnel and Corporate Affairs for IBM UK since September 1975, and he wishes to pay tribute to B. J. A. Hargreaves, sometime Director of Public Affairs for IBM UK, with whom he worked for the early part of that period and whose thinking did much to formulate the ideas contained in the early part of his chapter. Peach had previously worked with IBM UK from 1962 in a number of personnel posts, becoming its Personnel Director in 1971; he was Group Director of Personnel for IBM Europe–Africa–Middle East, based in Paris, between 1972 and 1975. He was President of the Institute of Personnel Management between 1983 and 1985.

Douglas Smith read an honours degree at King's College London and the LSE. After a brief spell in Fleet Street, he joined Conservative Central Office as London Publicity Officer. Later he moved in general PR consultancy before forming one of Britain's early specialist public affairs companies, now Political Communication. He is also Chairman of Parliamentary Monitoring Services. He was a local councillor in London for 25 years, holding a number of senior posts.

Smith was Chairman of the UK Public Relations Consultants Association 1984–85. He is currently an elected member of the Institute of Public Relations Council and Founder Chairman in 1987 of the IPR's Government Affairs Group. He writes and broadcasts widely on government affairs and politics.

Kevin Traverse-Healy, FIPR, is Managing Director of Charles Barker
Traverse-Healy Limited. He spent three years in law before joining the public
relations and communications division of British Oxygen Company. During his
four-and-a-half years with BOC he was PR executive for the company's largest
trading division and spent one year overseas with BOC International. He entered
consultancy in 1976 and in 1980 was a founding director of Traverse-Healy &
Regester, a firm specializing in corporate and financial public relations and
investor relations.

Traverse-Healy was President of the Institute of Public Relations in 1985 and
recipient of the CERP Medal for contribution to European Public Relations in
1985; he is a member of the PRCA Consultancy Management Committee, Fellow
of the Institute of Public Relations, member of the International Association of
Business Communicators, member of the International Public Relations
Association, and member of the Investor Relations Society.

Christopher West, B.Sc.(Econ.), is a graduate of the London School of Economics
with an honours degree in geography. He subsequently obtained a wide range of
experience in marketing and planning through appointments held in London and
Paris.

He was with Industrial Marketing Research Ltd until 1984 and is now
Chairman of Business Marketing Services Ltd. Prior to joining IMR he worked in
the Economics and Supply and Planning Departments of Shell International
Petroleum Company, where he carried out a number of studies on the oil and
energy industries. He subsequently served as an economist with Eurofinance, a
Paris-based financial and economic consultancy where he carried out
European-wide industry studies and short-term economic forecasts for a group of
leading European and American banks. He was also engaged on projects for the
EEC and OECD.

West has edited two books: *Marketing on a Small Budget* and *Inflation—A
Management Guide to Survival.* He has lectured extensively for management
organizations in the United Kingdom, Scandinavia, the Netherlands, and Spain
and has broadcast on the BBC.

His project experience covers a wide range of product and service businesses and
he has specialized in the use of market research for corporate planning
applications.

Anthony Wreford was educated at Charterhouse and St Catherines College,
Oxford, where he obtained a degree in politics, philosophy, and economics.
Following a two-year spell with Leo Burnett he joined Cazenove, the leading firm
of stockbrokers. From 1975 until 1981 he was New Business Development
Manager at the *Financial Times* and was also Director of the *Financial Times*
Pension Fund. A large part of his role at the *Financial Times* was taken up with
promoting the case for corporate communications.

In 1981 Wreford set up McAvoy Wreford & Associates, which in 1984 became
McAvoy Wreford Bayley. The firm specializes in financial and corporate
communications and has a large number of blue-chip clients. Wreford is also a
member of the International Advertising Association and the International
Association of Business Communicators.

INTRODUCTION

Public relations developed as a separate discipline some 40 years ago, and since that time it has managed to acquire a rather negative reputation as being sometimes irrelevant, and often incompetent. This has not been helped by the fact that in the past much of PR practice often thoroughly deserved such a poor reputation.

The growth of PR in recent times as a management function has been rapid, as is indicated by the expansion of PR consultancies, which are more numerous, larger, and with more clients and bigger budgets than ever before.

Much of PR has tended to be no more than 'press relations': 'public relations' has taken second place. This is changing for sound business reasons, with the result that the need for effective two-way communications between an organization and its many publics is being accepted and even demanded. This 'total communications' concept, as applied to both publics and the media, is in fact little more than public relations as it was originally conceived. It has, however, been found to be expedient to apply a new term, if only to get away from the PR stigma, and this is 'corporate relations'. Hence the title of the book.

There are still too few practitioners with a knowledge and experience of corporate relations, in spite of a plethora of prestigious titles. For this reason, and with the growth in demand for corporate relations programmes, there seemed to be a need for a book that would demonstrate in practical terms what can be achieved by corporate relations, how, at what price, and over what period of time.

The aim of this book is to present PR practice in terms of strategic corporate objectives. As such, it follows that the primary target audience is chief executives and directors. Automatically it becomes essential reading for practitioners, and to a lesser degree for students and young executives.

Each chapter is complete in itself, dealing in detail with the primary PR disciplines and their associated key publics, communications objectives, and the media that might best be employed. Three particular media groups have been treated as subjects in their own right in order to avoid undue duplication: advertising, sponsorship, and press relations. Final chapters deal with research and evaluation and the emerging significance of social responsibility.

Norman A. Hart, 1987

1.

CORPORATE GOALS AND STRATEGIES

Kevin Traverse-Healy

With a few exceptions, the process of creating corporate goals and the strategies by which those goals may be achieved is the cornerstone of business success. In some corporate cultures this process is highly structured and formal, while in others, equally successful, it may be informal and intuitive. In today's commercial world, however, there are few organizations that can reasonably claim to be able to ignore the basic questions of 'Where do we want to go?' and 'How (and when) are we going to get there?'

There are many elements that have to be considered by management in constructing plans that incorporate realistic goals and feasible strategies: market forces, research and development, finance, and human resources are but a few. This book will demonstrate that the way in which an organization needs to be perceived by those whose decisions or opinions will impact on the achievement of its business goals has a no less essential case for recognition within the planning mix.

In the context of this book, 'corporate identity' and 'corporate image' are the elements that require definition if we are to understand their importance in formulating an organization's overall corporate plan and facilitating its progress. There is often confusion as to what these terms actually mean, and, in fairness, corporate communication specialists in the past have not been all that successful at defining their own terminology. The definition that I prefer is provided by W. P. Margulies in an article in the *Harvard Business Review* (July/August 1977):

> Identity means the sum of all the ways a company chooses to identify itself to all its publics . . . Image, on the other hand, is the perception of the company by those publics.

(Note that 'corporate identity' is not a term that is restricted to the visual element of corporate communication. The design industry has done a great deal to improve the manner in which companies project themselves in visual terms, but many have misused the term to imply only visual identity.)

It should go without saying that a company will have a corporate image whether or not it manages its corporate identity. Management almost universally has long since embraced—if sometimes with reluctance—the fundamental concept that it is going to have an image anyway so it might as well attempt to manage the development of that image through the communication of its chosen corporate identity. At last count, over 3500 organizations in Britain are currently using the services of a public relations consultancy in membership of the Public Relations Consultants Association. Many more are operating in-house departments or are being advised by non-member consultancies. Each of these companies or bodies is actively addressing the question of how it is viewed by its external audiences.

In the development of public relations over the past 40 years as a professional part of the management armoury, the function unfortunately gained in many organizations a 'bolt-on' status, as distinct from being accepted as an integral part of the overall management mix. This was due in part to the level of importance that managers, who were (and, some would argue, still are) largely untrained in this area, gave to the corporate communications process, although far greater credibility was afforded to marketing publicity. The blame must also be shared, however, by the PR practitioners, who were all too often well equipped to communicate but lacked the necessary parallel expertise of the other management processes they were seeking to represent.

While not totally removed from the management scene, this mismatch has been significantly eroded by the increase in the attention being paid to formal communications training for managers, coupled with the development of PR education and recruitment to encompass a broader understanding of other areas of management responsibility. The introduction of an MBA course at Cranfield in 1987 which concentrates on public relations, and the significant increase of PR electives at UK business schools over the past few years, are representative of the strength that the function has achieved.

The development of the corporate communications function within industry and its integration into the central stream of management is highlighted by a recent study, *The Practice of Public Relations* by Katie Arber, then of the Durham University Business School, and sponsored by my consultancy. From a sample of 179 of the 500 largest UK companies, 86 per cent of companies had a defined PR policy, and of these, 76 per cent said that the policy formed a fully integrated part of a public relations plan which required board-level agreement in the context of corporate planning.

It is particularly interesting to note from Katie Arber's research that, while marketing responsibilities (including marketing communication) are increasingly being devolved to individual business unit level, this is being achieved through the development and policing of corporate guidelines that keep the overall responsibility for the management of the corporate identity firmly within central control. This reflects the increasing understanding by management that there is little that cannot be devolved down to business unit level, provided central management retains control over the overall direction of the company and the role of each business unit in active support of clearly defined corporate objectives.

Later chapters will describe in detail the processes of constructing a framework for the integration of corporate communications into the corporate planning structure. However, in brief, what is needed is a process by which a company can first set for itself the identity that it wishes to promote. To do this, it must understand the commercial, social, and political environment within which it will be required to operate. A failure to understand these factors may well serve to nullify the effort that will follow in defining communications objectives and in developing communications strategies and programmes that will enable these objectives to be met.

All too often, management has looked first to the tools of communication—such as media relations or advertising—without considering the reasons for using them. It is rather like organizing a distribution system for a product not yet conceived, let alone researched and developed. Again, this has not always been the fault of management. Many corporate communicators continue to encourage management to concentrate on the 'How' and not the 'Why'.

The need for planning and control of the communications function extends throughout its major areas of influence. These are generally taken to include all the major 'stakeholder' groups:

1. Financial public relations
2. Investor relations
3. Government relations
4. Community affairs
5. Employee communications
6. Marketing communications

To these can be added 'Issue management', which, briefly, can be described as the understanding and influence of the significant commercial, social, and political factors that ultimately may impact the ability of a responsible company to meet its reasonable business objectives. While perhaps less immediately obvious in its benefits than investor relations or employee communications, issue management offers far greater potential for the determination by a company of the environment in which it can expand and flourish.

Too many companies tend to have PR programmes of a responsive rather than proactive nature, often without a background plan or policy, with little attempt to frame a strategy, and certainly unrelated to the company's overall business plans and corporate objectives. The thinking company starts with its corporate objectives and current business plans, and the PR programme that emerges is closely related to aiding and achieving these. In the sloppy, responsive company, by contrast, corporate objectives and business plans are handed down from on high, are seen more as a set of good intentions, and are never questioned until the post-mortem is held.

In the proactive company it is the responsibility of the corporate affairs professionals to question the validity of the commercial plans in the light of political and social trends that are likely adversely to affect their attainment, and of public and group perceptions of the company—since support depends upon perceptions. The secret lies in recognizing the nature of the external decision-making process, knowing who your friends and foes are, and having an early warning system in place. Simplistically, the process should be viewed as a quartered circle (see Fig. 1.1). The first quarter represents the phase where the topic is emerging, the second, that wherein it is being debated, and the third, the time when it is becoming codified. In the fourth quarter it becomes accepted and is sometimes given the force of law.

Historically—almost traditionally—industry generally, and individual companies particularly, enter the process in the final arc of the second quartile or later—far too late to have real effect on the majority of issues. The aim is to enter the arena as early in quarter 1 as is possible, when ideas and options are being formulated, the preliminary drafts are being concocted, and the small print is still negotiable. The currency of this sort of contact is information, and the price paid for genuine dialogue is, often as not, preparedness to anticipate and to enter into controversy. It is worth remembering that 90 per cent of the decisions made in the public domain affecting industry are taken at administrative and executive level, not at the political level. The chances of failure increase immeasurably if the topic is thrust or dragged into the political and social arenas.

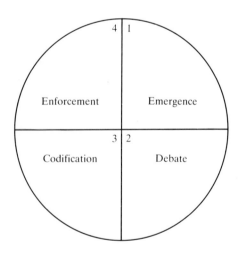

Figure 1.1   The external decision-making process

The selection of issues for corporate action is critical, and is a matter of management judgement against agreed criteria and the understanding of the 'likelihood/significance ratio' that takes account of:

1. Will or could this issue really affect our bottom line?
2. Is the 'bad news' scenario realistic?
3. Could corporate action halt/amend/modify/delay the progress of the issue?
4. Will our present policies and practices stand up to public examination?
5. Are the resources to act available?
6. Is the cost to the company acceptable?
7. Is the will to act present?
8. What would be the effect of inaction?

If the corporate objectives are to be achieved, then the company is likely to need varying degrees of support at various times from stakeholders. Implicitly, this support has to be for the company's present performance and programme, its future plans, and indeed even its problems, if the objectives are to be reached.

If a company needs support, then it has to possess that most maligned of factors on the balance sheet, goodwill. Goodwill is based upon understanding. Before understanding there has to be a reputation. And a reputation presupposes that a degree of awareness exists. Behavioural research has indicated that, all other factors being equal, there is a distinct relationship between familiarity and favourability—in other words, between the degree of public support a company might expect and the levels or awareness about it.

Awareness is based on the public's perceptions of an organization. These are created by statements (including visual) that a company makes about itself (or others make about it), by comments solicited or volunteered, by third-party endorsement (or otherwise) of its behaviour, and above all by the personal experience of individuals in their dealings with the company and its staff at all levels.

Perceptions may be right or they may be wrong, but because they exist they become fact. It follows that public affairs and public relations are all about issue selection and issue management, coupled with the management of the corporate perception process and the correction of incorrect perceptions. Only when the range of issues has been considered can those few that are likely to affect the achievement of bottom-line targets be isolated. Only then can the decision-making models be drawn and the specific role-players, junior and senior, be nominated.

Simultaneously, the company's position has to be set out, debated internally, and agreed. The perceptions of key external factors and factions need to be established, and sometimes existing internal policies and practices need to be modified and arguments reworked. Among the numerous items that remain to be considered under the heading of strategy are 'targets' and 'messages'.

By and large, the external role-players across all the selected issues become the target list for the company's contact-and-convince programme. Only when this point has been reached can a corporate communications strategy and plan be created and an effective programme be activated.

The selection and development of a corporate identity can be a most complex and exacting process, involving considerable analysis of what the company is and what it intends to be as well as what it would like to be seen to be. Statements of corporate identity include numerous value judgements (can a company be 'international' if it operates in only two or three countries? Can it be 'market-driven' if it fails to change with market needs?) which have to be thrashed out in a wholly realistic atmosphere. Often it takes outsiders to act as a catalyst to understanding the optimum corporate identity, and to produce a totally clear and concise definition of the organization that can, and should, be reflected in every detail of its communications effort.

I have often thought that the perfect example of a clear and concise corporate statement that says it all is 'The Best Little Whorehouse in Texas'. Can you think of anything relevant that it leaves out? For most companies, however, a more socially acceptable corporate identity will include elements such as 'innovative', 'market leader', 'well managed', 'profitable', 'responsive', 'responsible', 'creative', 'international', 'diversified', 'specialist' or 'prudent', and 'decent, honest, and truthful'.

The acid test of a corporate identity, once determined after hours, or even months, of agonizing over single words, is to go home and try it on your partner in life. If she, or he, rolls about on the floor in laughter, do not give up—you may not know if you have chosen the right identity, but you certainly know you have an image problem. For a corporate identity is a method of expressing a body corporate—machinery, products, factories, and effort—in human terms, and as such it must be within the boundaries of credibility of the audiences to which it will be communicated.

Once a company has defined where it wishes to go in commercial terms, the major external factors that might impact its ability to get there, and the corporate identity that will support it along the way, it needs to look closely at who it needs to be talking to in order to convert its chosen identity into a parallel image held by those who will ultimately make the decisions that will affect corporate performance.

In defining target audiences—traditionally called 'publics' by the PR profession—managers must distinguish between a variety of groups and individuals, who may or may not be interrelated or interactive, who have the ability either to take decisions that will impact the company or to influence the direction of the decision-takers through the respect in which their opinion is held.

To take a simple case by way of illustration, if a computer manufacturer wishes to sell its product, it will have key decision-taking audiences among the management of its potential customer companies, including data processing managers and possibly even their chief executives. In addition, however, a number of key external groups will exercise, to a greater or lesser extent, influence on the direction of the internal decision. In this case, these may well include external specialist consultants, the specialist computer journals and general management media, finance houses, and existing customers. All these have the potential beneficially or adversely to affect the decision that will eventually be taken by management. Since it is often impossible to predict precisely which individual or group is going to have an impact on each decision, it is generally necessary to communicate on a broader basis to target audiences that have been defined as closely as possible without becoming too limited.

Communication is, of course, a process that involves both the sender and the receiver of a message. It is fundamental in the management of the communication process that the company should understand the needs of its audiences, should use the language and media that the audiences understand and respect, should transmit messages that are believable to the target audiences, and, most importantly, should impart only messages that will motivate the receiver in some way—either to act, or to alter a perception of the company.

I apologize to those who find the above too obvious, but defend its inclusion on the basis of numerous encounters with managers who appear determined to communicate *their message* in *their words* through *their media*, apparently regardless of their lack of commonality with their target audience. The result has been described as 'cognitive dissonance' by communications theorists, and the suffering to corporate egos that accompanies this disease is well worth avoiding by simply following the military maxim of 'know your enemy'.

This book is unlikely, in itself, to convert any manager who still views public relations solely as some form of below-the-line marketing activity to an understanding of the breadth of contribution that it can make to the achievement of business objectives. There are some excellent publications that tackle this task, and guidance is freely available from both the Institute of Public Relations and the Public Relations Consultants Association. The book is of greater relevance to managers who have already accepted to some extent the value of managing their corporate relations and who wish to explore the processes and practices that they can use to ensure that their company will gain the maximum benefit from the professional application of this fundamental management skill.

In the end, no responsible manager can conduct the company's business without an eye to the impact on the bottom line of everything that is undertaken. Corporate communications is no exception, but with the added difficulty that here the manager is often dealing in areas of activity that defy measurement in terms that would be regarded as acceptable in other management functions. While corporate communications professionals continue to seek acceptable methodologies by which they may be able to justify, not unreasonably, the value of their activity in financial terms, there is one truism in corporate communications that has rarely been faulted: of the thousands of companies that have decided to manage their corporate identity and annually spend hundreds of millions in corporate communications activity, there are few, if any, that have found the function of so little obvious value that they have not consistently increased the resources allocated to it—often while cutting expenditure in other areas.

Given the respect I hold for both British management and the public relations profession, I have to assume that they are not redistributing wealth from one to the other just for the sake of a 'bolt-on' service or corporate amusement. The simple fact is that effective corporate communications is neither difficult nor necessarily expensive to achieve. Rarely has its value been questioned except by those who have failed to plan and operate their corporate communications effort in a professional manner—and a number of other management disciplines have suffered to the same extent in their time.

2.

PLANNING FOR CORPORATE COMMUNICATIONS

Anthony Wreford

The first task for the individual responsible for planning the corporate communications activities is to gain the acceptance of the senior management, almost certainly the chairman and managing director, to the principle of an active corporate communications programme. Even today, there are many companies that simply do not accept that a corporate image needs to be planned with the same business disciplines as other functions.

This resistance is often based on the false belief that corporate communications activities will provide yet another drain on the company's bottom line and hence be an unnecessary overhead. The first golden rule for initiating any corporate communications plan, therefore, is to stress to the senior management of the company that the purpose of the programme is to help improve the bottom line, not the reverse.

Many industrialists are very firm on this view, including Sir John Clark, the Chairman of Plessey, who defines the role of public relations much more narrowly as 'making more profit for the company'. Conversations with other industrialists, including Sir John Harvey-Jones, former Chairman of ICI, confirm a similar view.

Part of this negative attitude reflects the way that an ever-increasing number of companies are now structured as decentralized organizations, leaving the profit responsibility to the operating units. This inevitably means that there is a greater resistance to add head office costs, and, of course, this affects corporate communications budgets, as well as staffing levels in the central communications department.

At the time of writing, the United Kingdom and the United States are experiencing one of the biggest waves of take-over battles in corporate history. One of the effects of this level of activity has been the demonstration of the need for a good company image, particularly among the investment community. Indeed, a survey conducted by Korn Ferry among company directors in the United Kingdom in 1986 showed that the issue of greatest concern to those directors was company image. Measured against other issues like cash flow, future growth, and employee relations, company image obtained 56% of first mentions.

Looking further ahead, this resistance to corporate communications programmes should decline, not only because of fears of a predator around the corner, but because companies inevitably study the activities of others operating in the same sector. With an increasing number of companies engaged in active corporate communications programmes, many more reluctant communicators will be drawn in on competitive grounds alone.

This chapter has been structured as a series of steps derived from experience in planning programmes with clients, where the problems of company structure, culture, and personalities can often get in the way of sensible progress. Ten steps are suggested. Some might argue that many of the actions proposed can take place at the same time, but the real point of addressing corporate communications planning as a series of steps is to progress it as a structured plan. The great danger with corporate communications is that all the company directors will have different and preconceived ideas as to the preferred company image and the sort of techniques that should be employed. If it is possible to sell the company management the concept of a structured programme, there is one major benefit: it buys time. In other words, you will not be hurried into a particular programme of activities. It also ensures that proper and more objective thought is given to the sort of techniques that might be relevant for the audiences that need to be addressed. It further provides time to research attitudes outside the company.

The ten steps are therefore by no means commandments, but are tips based on bitter experience of what can go wrong.

Step 1: Understand the business objectives and strategy

The objective of any corporate communications programme must be to help build the profitability of the company, so it is essential that the business objectives are understood before any corporate communications planning takes place.

All business plans differ and inevitably have varying priorities. For instance, the priority might be to move into new geographic areas; it might be to move into product areas where the company is not associated; it might be more narrow, in terms of ensuring that the company has a good image among the investment community prior to, say, a rights issue. Whatever the priorities, it is vital that the professional communicator is able to set the firm's objectives based on its overall business plan and priorities.

Most companies have rolling three- to five-year plans, and it is these longer-term objectives that should be taken into account. There may in addition be short-term objectives set for, say, three to six months, and these will also need to be considered but may require a separate communications programme.

A good company image usually takes several years—indeed, often generations—to build, but there is an old saying that a good image can also be destroyed overnight. In some cases images may need to be built in a much shorter period. Take-over battles are a good example of a situation that may confront the company and where a good image has to be created in a very short period. In this situation, where the company is in the limelight, there are many more opportunities to put across the company's strengths, and it is surprising how much can be achieved in a short period. Typically, those responsible for planning the corporate communications will be expected to achieve far more in a much shorter space of time than is possible. It is important, therefore, that the board of the company recognize the limitations as well as the possibilities of an active corporate communications programme.

Unless the communications adviser has direct access to the board of the company, it will be very difficult to carry out this most important first stage of planning. Senior management who recognize the importance of communications will be only too willing to share these broad business objectives with the adviser; the more cynical will not see the need.

It will be necessary to hold individual meetings with the directors responsible for the different parts of the business. These meetings should bring the business objectives to life. For example, the finance director's main concern will be the company's reputation in the financial community, and therefore his objective may well be described in terms of 'I want a higher share price for the company' or 'I want a good image so I can raise some more money.' The directors responsible for operating divisions are more likely to talk in terms of the image of the company in their particular markets. The director responsible for international activities will have a very different view, and often the most difficult request for the communications expert to achieve; this is often described in terms of 'achieving the sort of image overseas that the company enjoys at home'.

An ideal planning process must enable the communications expert or adviser to talk to all the board directors and to as many of the senior management of the operating companies as possible. Only in this way will the business plan be brought to life and the potential conflicts and the objectives be identified, and only in this way will the communicator get a proper feel for the characteristics of the company that might be promoted and those that may need to be played down.

Step 2: Agree on realistic communications objectives

Before any further planning is done, it is essential that the business objectives are interpreted as corporate communications objectives and are agreed with the company's senior management.

There is an old saying that you can sell anybody anything once, but the trick of a good salesman is to be able to go back and sell the same product to the same individual again and again. This maxim can also be used in corporate communications because it is very easy, indeed tempting, to promise the chairman a better reputation among any of the relevant target audiences in a short space of time, but, as those who have worked in this area will know, very much more difficult to achieve, and in particular to prove! So be realistic in the goals that you set for the communications programme, and resist the temptation of trying to promise something that is unlikely to be achieved. There is so much that can happen to the company during, say, a 12-month period that is totally beyond the communications expert's control, and the setting of unrealistic goals can only damage the function and reduce its credibility in the eyes of senior management. Building a good image like that enjoyed by ICI or BP in the UK, and on an international basis by companies like IBM and Coca Cola, takes a considerable amount of time and effort. Good images cannot be created overnight: they have to be built through a realistic commitment by the company to all aspects of its activity.

The very process of sitting down and discussing the broad communications objectives with the company management will provide an opportunity for discussing the time scale for the business, and should provide the right sort of forum for determining the priorities of the company. As such, this contact should be regular. In the process of obtaining the views of the company management, the communicator should be able to develop communications objectives and test them with the individuals concerned, so that, when the formal process of agreeing on objectives begins, all the individuals concerned should have agreed on the broad principles.

The process to date has been exclusively an internal one, in obtaining the views of the key individuals and developing a broad plan. The next step is to ascertain the views and perceptions of those outside the organization to determine the extent to which they differ from the internal view.

Step 3: Understand your target audiences

Many companies are reluctant to look in the mirror and conduct market research. It is important that the professional communicator overcomes this problem, for without the help of market research, some of the key information for the planning process will be missing. The key issues to be researched will include:

1. How the various target audiences view the company
2. What the perceived strengths and weaknesses are
3. Whether the company has a high or low level of awareness
4. How the competition is viewed
5. How well the management are regarded

6. What characteristics are ideally sought in a company operating in this sector

Only extensive market research can answer these and other questions. In many cases it may be necessary to conduct several studies among the specialist target audiences. Issues that may be relevant to customers, for example, will not be those that may be relevant to the financial community or indeed other opinion-formers.

There are a number of benefits to be derived from this type of research. These include:

1. An objective view of the company
2. A better understanding of the values and characteristics that are perceived as important by the target audiences
3. A check on whether the business objectives are consistent with the needs and views of the various target audiences
4. A benchmark from which to measure progress in the future

One of the most helpful aspects of some research studies is the analysis of how key audiences evaluate companies. The market research should not therefore restrict itself simply to how the company is perceived, but should study the very communications process that the target audiences go through in making their evaluation. In this context, there may be existing research studies that are available to answer some of these questions. So before embarking on any research programme, part of the planning process should be to identify all market research studies that have been conducted in the sector to ascertain what is already available, where gaps exist, and what information needs to be updated.

Some research studies are available for general use, and in many cases companies or their trade associations are willing to share market research findings with friendly or member companies. Although the topic is covered later in this chapter, it is important that the individual or group that is allocated the task of planning the corporate communications has relevant experience of market research, not only in terms of interpretation, but also for briefing the market research companies. A regular part of the corporate communications planning process is to keep these research data up to date and to use them to measure the effectiveness of the programme.

Step 4: Develop an intelligence system—information is power

Market research is vital to determine how the company is viewed from difference perspectives. But these attitudes need to be looked at together with information on the company's markets, the competitors' activities, and the other issues that may be of importance.

To plan the company image effectively, the communicator needs to be able to understand all there is to know about the sectors in which the company operates and the information needs of the target audiences being addressed. This means putting together as much published information as possible about each sector, how it is viewed, and what are regarded as the key issues. Such information is likely to come in a variety of forms. To illustrate the breadth of possibilities, the following lists contain some of the sources from two typical audiences.

1. Customers

● Industry and sector projections, e.g. CBI, IOD
● Trade press comment
● Information through trade associations
● Industry image studies
● Comparative data from overseas markets
● Reports and accounts of competitors
● Industry seminars and conferences
● Advertising expenditure figures

2. Financial community

● Business school studies, e.g. Henley, Manchester Business School
● Stockbroker write-ups
● Industry reviews
● Press cuttings
● Reports and accounts of domestic and international competitors
● Sector newsletters
● Corporate brochures and videos

In collecting information from these various sources, the communications adviser will quickly build a picture of the sort of attitudes and issues affecting not only the company, but also the industry or sectors in which it operates. One of the roles of the communicator is to be able to collect this research and to interpret it for the benefit of the company management. This analysis will help in finalizing the communications objectives, and in highlighting the particular aspects of the company that need to be researched in greater detail.

Companies whose market intelligence is thorough and up to date will often have the cutting edge in the targeting and planning of the corporate communications programme. A familiar component of today's corporate communications department is a computer with sufficient storage capacity to hold all the data required. Information must be readily available on the target audience so that it can be called up at short notice.

A regular part of this information process is to ensure that names and addresses of customers and other target groups, such as investors, are kept up to date, along with other relevant information, including their attendance at various meetings, invitations to hospitality events, special interests, etc. For this reason, the corporate communications department should be staffed with an information officer or librarian, whose sole responsibility should be to ensure that the department has access to all the information on the various markets, and that this information on the specific target audiences is kept up to date. This process has become more time-consuming with the many changes taking place among a range of target audiences. Customers, investors, and journalists move from one organization to another more frequently than ever before, and there is nothing more embarrassing for the company than a mail shot or an invitation sent to the wrong individual.

A well briefed researcher in the corporate communications department will also need to read all the newspapers and trade publications to ensure that speeches by industry leaders and commentators are picked up, that new market research information is filed and analysed, and that information on the competition is up to date and competitors' annual reports are obtained. It is not unusual, therefore, for a part of the corporate communications budget to be devoted to subscriptions. Indeed, some companies now buy shares in their competitors to ensure that all published information is obtained, ranging from the company report and accounts to corporate brochures and corporate videos, which are now sent to shareholders on a regular basis. Subscriptions to trade associations are frequently centralized with the corporate communications department to help control this information flow.

Information *is* power, therefore, but it needs to be analysed so that it can be used and acted upon. A vital part of the corporation communications planning process is to provide this interpretation.

5: Establish priorities for tasks and target audiences

In developing the set of objectives, the communicator will need to identify the most important audiences to be addressed, for the objectives for each audience will differ according to their information needs and requirements.

In the early 1970s, most corporate communications programmes took a 'shotgun' approach in preaching a similar message to all target audiences. As the levels of knowledge and understanding towards business and companies have grown, so it has become necessary for companies increasingly to segment their programmes. Today an effective corporate communications programme may have four or five separate strands with specific objectives and goals. A message, for example, that may be of relevance to the financial audience will not necessarily be of the same relevance to government officials, and will certainly not be of relevance to the local community.

One of the frustrations in the planning process is trying to reach agreement on the priority tasks and the priority audiences. Inevitably, short-term considerations may often override the longer-term objectives, and one of the permanent dilemmas that will be faced in the planning process is how to reconcile the short-term considerations with the longer-term requirements. In practice, it is probably better to allocate sufficient funds behind achievable short-term tasks than to scatter insufficient funds across longer-term objectives.

It is the setting of the priorities against the various target audiences that is one of the hardest tasks in the planning process, for it can often end up as a personality debate. The finance director, for very legitimate reasons, may want to use a substantial proportion of the funds to talk to the investment community. The sales director, on the other hand, may have other ideas about a particular opportunity to talk to customers, and what can often follow is an internal debate with the communications department caught in the middle, probably being lobbied from every side. It is to be hoped that this can be avoided; a regular process to review the communications activities should ensure that these conflicts are identified long before they become an embarrassment. Ultimately, the setting of priorities has to be agreed by consensus.

Step 6: Agree on the communications strategy, an outline programme, and the budget

By now all the relevant information should be at hand, and the communications planner can put forward a recommended strategy to achieve the agreed objectives, against the agreed set of priorities and target audiences.

In many ways this is the most difficult process of all, for committing strategic recommendations to paper inevitably brings back the structural considerations within the company. A decentralized organization will inevitably face a conflict if further corporate initiatives are suggested and if money is to be taken from operating units to fund these activities.

There has been much debate over the years as to the most effective way of funding a corporate communications programme. Operating companies recognize how management charges are set up, and a heavy loading in a particular year is unlikely to escape their notice. The other route, of asking operating companies to give up a proportion of their product promotional budget, is not really an acceptable alternative when in most cases they are being asked to achieve a bottom-line target and should be allowed the freedom to do this. There is therefore no perfect way of setting a corporate communications budget. The experienced communicator will know that any strategic recommendations will have to be digestible; and, whatever the inadequacies of the corporate structure and philosophy, unless a strategy can work in practice, there is little point in putting it forward to the management board.

The board of the company should be allowed to comment on the outline programme of activities, and on some communications activities, such as corporate advertising, they are likely to have very strong views. It is potentially dangerous at this stage to allow the board to get into too long a discussion on the precise nature of the activities, as this will need to be worked out by the communications department with their own advertising agency and PR consultancy.

The main purpose of discussing an outline programme is to sort out the monetary considerations. A not uncommon practice is effectively to split the elements of the communications programme between those parts that are truly head office considerations (for example, communications with the financial community and government) and those that are likely to benefit the operating companies (in other words, initiatives to improve company image amongst customers). The former category should be funded out of head office costs, and with the latter it may be possible to ask operating units for a contribution.

A not uncommon practice, particularly in the United States, is for the head office to start the ball rolling by putting in some money in the first two years on the basis that the operating units will pick up the costs in subsequent years. This practice is also found in the overseas operations of multinational companies, where the head office may well put in some money as 'pump-priming' in order to initiate a programme.

Step 7: Involve the operating companies

For most companies, one of the important roles of the corporate communications programme will be to help improve and develop the company's image with customers. It is therefore sensible at a relatively early stage to involve the relevant individuals from the operating companies. This has to be a good principle, if only on the basis that early involvement with these key persons is more likely to provide the prospect of acceptance of a programme than if the individuals were presented with a *fait accompli*.

Most programmes are intended to help the operating companies and to supplement the existing brand or product promotions already in place. The level of involvement will depend upon the company and the type of products that are sold. Companies with a strong brand orientation will need to involve their marketing directors, whereas companies selling to industrial markets are more likely to involve their sales directors, who should be in tune with customers' needs.

There are other considerable advantages in this process of consultation. Operating companies may at some stage have to pay for part of the corporate communications programme, and they are more likely to be willing to participate in this budget if they feel they have had some input. There may also be other market intelligence or information which they can feed into the planning process. However, the most significant reason why this process is necessary is that the individuals concerned will have their own views as to what the corporate image should be and what communications techniques should be employed.

This consultation process with operating companies is a necessary part of the overall planning process if the programme is to work, be accepted, and have any chance of life beyond year one.

Step 8: Allocate responsibilities

One of the fundamental differences between the corporate communications departments of European companies and their counterparts in the United States is the number of personnel. It is not unusual in the USA to find a corporate communications department with between 20 and 40 personnel: with the exception of the oil majors, this is not the case in Europe.

With fewer human resources, the company must decide how best to implement an active corporate communications programme. The problem is exaggerated by the inevitable front-loading that most programmes require. The sort of issues that will have to be addressed include:

1. Which board directors should be actively involved in the programme?
2. Who should be the prime spokesman on financial issues, on government related issues, and on strategic issues?
3. How much of the programme can be handled internally and to what extent will external services be needed?
4. How much involvement or help should be expected from the operating companies?
5. Should the firm use the services of agencies currently working for operating companies, or should specialist corporate communications agencies be employed?
6. Should the company buy different services from different agencies, or find an agency that can provide an integrated approach?
7. Does the company need to take on temporary staff during the early phases of the programme?

One of the principal reasons why corporate communications agencies have grown so rapidly in the last few years is due to the poor staffing within companies. The specialist corporate communications agency can be very helpful to the company, particularly in the early stages, when new systems have to be set up and where internal resources do not provide adequate depth. Indeed, with the move towards decentralization and with an increased availability of external resources, it is quite possible to keep a relatively small internal office and supplement it with services from outside.

An important consideration in allocating responsibilities is to ensure that the left foot does know what the right foot is doing and that regular meetings are held between the various consultancies, agencies and personnel who are involved in the communications programme to ensure a co-ordinated approach. Even today, when the cry for co-ordination is all too familiar, there are too few examples of companies that practise what is so often preached.

Senior management, who are inevitably very busy, will respond to precise instructions, and there should not be a problem in allocating responsibilities if the early part of the planning process has been carried out properly. Typically, the finance director will concentrate on the financial community, covering in particular the investment analysts in stockbroking firms and institutions. The chief executive and chairman will supplement the finance director, particularly when it comes to direct contact with major institutional shareholders and with the more important financial journalists. On government relations, the chairman or chief executive is more likely to play a key role except where there may be a specific scientific or technical issue, where the board director who is responsible for that operating unit is more likely to do so.

Allocating responsibilities is perhaps the simplest of the tasks. Persuading those who have been allocated responsibilities to report back on a regular basis on the outcome of their discussions and the impressions seen and created, or indeed to pass on other relevant information, is altogether another problem. Some form of regular debriefing must take place if the programme is to be adequately policed once the individuals have been allocated responsibilities.

Step 9: Sell the programme internally

This chapter has so far ignored the employees and any consultation process wider than either the board directors or key operating personnel. It is time to redress the imbalance, for employees are important if the programme is to have maximum impact.

Most employees appreciate why their products or services have to be promoted through advertising, on television or the press, or through other communications techniques. What is often more difficult for them to grasp is why the company should spend substantial sums of money on promoting its name and its image. This can be a particularly sensitive issue at a time when the company may be engaged in negotiating either the closure of a plant or the annual wage review.

Very few companies take time to pre-sell the corporate communications programme to their employees and keep them informed about its activities. If the programme is to be accepted and, more significantly, supported by employees, however, it should be sold to them before it appears externally. This is not an exercise in damage limitation, but goes back to the basic premise that the best (or indeed worst) form of corporate advertising for any company is the employees themselves. This is supported by many research studies and shows why a well briefed employee can often be the most effective communications tool the company possesses.

One example demonstrates how this should work. Several years ago, when Dunlop were starting their corporate advertising programme, a short video was prepared explaining the reasons for the campaign. A sample of customers and members of the public were shown being interviewed and asked what they thought of Dunlop. The results were presented on the video as background to why it was important that major customers and the buying public have a better understanding of the range of Dunlop products. The video was shown in all Dunlop offices several days before the first television commercial appeared. Coupled with the video presentation were details of the viewing times of the TV commercial in the relevant ITV regions. The response was very encouraging. Employees reported back to their families and friends and were proud to be able to discuss the reasons behind the new corporate advertising for Dunlop.

Although Dunlop has now been taken over, this does not invalidate the process that the company went through to pre-brief its employees. This is a principle that has since been followed by many companies and is essential if the corporate communications programme is to gain internal support. It is particularly important if the company is embarking on corporate advertising or any form of sponsorship which may be highly visible and not immediately understood by the rank-and-file in the company. Regular updates are also important, preferably with simple research findings, such as new customers or press comments. All of this can be a very helpful way of demonstrating the value of the corporate communications initiative.

Step 10: Don't stop planning

It would be easy to form the impression that the communications planning process is a once-and-for-all process. This is far from the truth, for communications planning is a regular process. Discussions with senior management need to take place on a regular basis to ensure that the communications department is up to date with corporate planning, changing market conditions and, indeed, the economic, political and social issues that inevitably face every company.

Part of this regular planning process of course can be linked with the market research programme which has been discussed and which is covered in greater detail later in the book. Customers' attitudes change, so do those of investors, and it is important that these changes are fed into the planning process so that it can be fine-tuned.

Time scales inevitably differ between companies, but a regular review process at least twice a year should ensure that the programme remains in touch with external developments and is consistent with the company's own corporate plans.

Remember, the purpose of any corporate communications programme is to help the company be more profitable.

Concluding remarks

In many ways this subject is not an easy one, since the corporate communications function is relatively new, certainly to most European companies. The resources put behind corporate communications have not been as great as many have felt desirable, and the commitment of the company management has in many cases been, at best, questionable. We are all still learning the best way of approaching this area, and the ten steps that were outlined above should be taken as guiding steps rather than a definitive approach.

I have deliberately avoided reference in this chapter to what is often known as the communications audit. I feared that to discuss the communications audit would in many ways detract from the practicalities of planning the corporate communications function. The audit, which is described elsewhere, is a very useful process to take account of all the communications activities that a company is engaged in, and as such it should be part of the overall corporate communications planning process. Indeed, the approaches that I have advocated are in themselves some form of audit.

The success or failure of the communications planning process will at the end of the day rest upon two key factors: the commitment and energy of the top management, and the willingness of other individuals to share their experience and expertise towards a common interest. Too often, these factors are sadly missing, because the corporate communications function either is not high enough on the chairman's agenda or, alternatively, is in conflict with the interests of the operating companies.

Corporate communications planning requires determination, common sense, a little politics, and a great deal of patience!

3

MARKETING COMMUNICATIONS

Norman A. Hart

Considerable confusion exists concerning the roles of public relations and advertising in relation to the marketing function. This stems largely from the ambiguity of the term 'public relations', which has two distinct interpretations, one conceptual and the other practical. The former is well stated in the definition given by the Institute of Public Relations:

> The deliberate planned and sustained effort to establish and maintain mutual understanding between an organization and its public.

Clearly, the achievement of such a broad objective implies the sending and receiving of messages along the most appropriate channels of communication to reach the many diverse publics upon which the success of an organization depends. And the publics include customers and prospects just as much as employees and shareholders, while the channels of communication include advertising and direct mail just as much as editorial publicity and sponsorship.

In spite of the very clear definition given above, practitioners and top management alike continue to interpret PR in its practical application as being little more than press relations leading to editorial publicity. What is overlooked is that advertising and editorial publicity are both 'media', and are as relevant to the achievement of marketing objectives as they are to the achievement of public relations objectives. Advertising, then, is a subset of public relations, and not a competitor. It carries messages that may relate to financial matters, personnel, purchasing, or indeed marketing. The same can be said of editorial publicity.

The purpose of this chapter is to identify and discuss briefly all the various messages, sources, and channels that are likely to impinge upon the minds of customers and others who might have a role to play in the purchasing–selling interface. For convenience, these are all brought together under the term 'marketing communications'. Here, alas, there are a number of definitions giving alternative interpretations, from a narrow perspective to a broad one.

The generally held view is that marketing communications is simply the promotional activities of advertising, personal selling, sales promotion and public relations. While in practice this is exactly right, for the purposes of this chapter it is necessary to move a little further into the ultimate objective, and here another definition helps: 'Marketing communications are normally across-the-board communications ... to help move a potential customer from a state of ignorance towards a position of decision and action.'[1]

In other words, a prospective customer goes through a series of stages of acceptance in the process of adopting a new product, and it is the purpose of marketing communications to facilitate and accelerate that movement. This procedure is referred to as the 'adoption process' and can be broken down into five stages:[2]

1. *Awareness*: the individual becomes cognizant of the innovation but lacks information about it.
2. *Interest*: the individual is stimulated to seek information about the innovation.
3. *Evaluation*: the individual considers whether it would make sense to try the innovation.
4. *Trial*: the individual tries the innovation on a small scale to improve his estimation of its utility.
5. *Adoption*: the individual decides to make full and regular use of the innovation.

Clearly, marketing communications encompasses any form of communication that contributes to the conversion of a non-customer to a customer, and subsequently to the retention of such custom.

A model that has stood the test of time comes from a classic text.[3] Here, as can be seen in Fig. 3.1, are not only the stages of the adoption process, but also the positive and negative factors which will accelerate or decelerate the rate at which the process will take place.

Message cues

Within the marketing mix, provision for marketing communications may seem to reside in the fourth of the '4 Ps':

1. Product
2. Price
3. Place
4. Promotion

This, however, is now regarded as inadequate, since by compartmentalizing 'promotion' a number of other important opportunities can be missed. One authority makes this point:

> The promotional mix has long been viewed as the company's sole communications link with the consumer. However, this kind of provincialism can often lead to suboptimisation of the firm's total communications effort. Because if viewed in

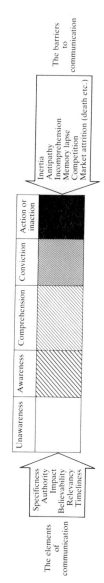

Figure 3.1 The communication process

isolation, promotion can actually work against other elements in the marketing communications mix. Other communications elements with which promotion must be co-ordinated are price, product, retail outlets, and all other company actions which consumers might perceive as communicating something about the company's total product offering.[4]

Before examining the role of promotion as such we should look at the message cues that might be transmitted by the other 3 P's: product, price, and place.

PRODUCT

The fundamental marketing concept postulates that a customer does not buy a product but rather a product performance, or more to the point, a satisfaction. In the consumer field it has been said that a customer does not buy soap, but rather hope; similarly, in industrial marketing the customer buys holes rather than a drill. Furthermore, the customer bases his purchasing decision upon the perceived benefit that he will receive as against the actual physical product attributes.

The total product offering is not what the supplier offers, but what the customer sees to be on offer. It may well be that packaging and presentation constitute the key factor in a purchasing decision, particularly with the increasing number of undifferentiated products. Indeed, with some of these—for instance, cigarettes, cosmetics, and drinks—it could be argued that the package is the product. Increasingly, what comes inside the pack is identical as between one brand and another, and that where that is so, the package is the single most important purchasing influence. With products that sell in supermarkets, this is particularly important.

An interesting example of packaging and presentation concerns a range of divan beds where the mattresses were finished in a variety of fabrics from the traditional to the very modern. A further variable was that the finishes on offer were of a soft plain surface, a quilted finish, or the rather old-fashioned button-type fixing. The customers unhesitatingly chose a quilted finish in the traditional fabric, notwithstanding the fact that all the mattresses were physically identical.

Research evidence shows that the buyer is influenced to a critical degree by the size of a product and its shape, colour, weight, feel, typography, and even smell. The successful package is the one that appeals to both the conscious and unconscious levels of the consumer's mind. The conscious mind recognizes just the product, whereas the unconscious mind is motivated by the package.

It must not be supposed that 'presentation' of product applies only to the consumer field. The study of 'organizational buyer behaviour' shows clearly the many subjective factors that enter into a purchasing decision. Gone are the days when a handful of components was bundled into a black box, and all that mattered was that the performance matched the specification. The appearance of an industrial product sends out signals. The design, shape, colour, and so on, all combine to create an impression on the one hand of a dynamic, innovative, go-ahead company, or on the other of a traditional or maybe a backward one. It is important to realize that it usually costs no more to put a conscious effort into good product presentation, whereas to create the same effect by means of conventional promotional media is often very expensive.

Consideration must further be given to brand name as part of the total product offering. Any product is going to be called something by its customers and users, so it might as well be a name of the company's own choice, and one that brings with it certain positive attributes. Does it have or imply a favourable connotation? Is it short and memorable? Can people actually pronounce it? Does it support the claims being made of product performance? And then there is the graphic symbolism or the associated logotype; a good brand name can evoke a feeling of trust, confidence, security, strength, durability, speed, status, and the like.

PRICE

For many if not most products, the signal given by price, and thus the effect on purchasing, follows the normal economist's law of demand. As price falls, so demand increases. With everyday products, where price levels are common knowledge, the message conveyed by price is indicative of good or bad value for money; hence the success of supermarkets in being able to offer heavily branded products at a lower price than the local grocer, and, going one stage further, the success of own-label products which undercut the established branded ones.

For some products, however, the normal rules do not apply, as is shown for instance in Fig. 3.2. In this case, price is taken as signalling quality or prestige, and within limits creates a desire to acquire which increases as the price increases. Without delving into the ethical considerations, the fact is that in some circumstances a reduction in price will signal a reduction in quality and vice versa. This is particularly so where the customer is unable to make a judgement on any other basis—a watch, for instance, or a hi-fi set, or cosmetics in general. There are other factors, of course, such as appearance and availability, but in the main, the assessment of quality in such items will be based heavily upon price.

The same price–demand relationship is found in products that are purchased as gifts. Here a higher price may be paid largely as a compliment to the receiver of the gift, or for that matter to enhance the prestige or satisfy the ego of the giver. Once again, it is a matter of perception on the part of the

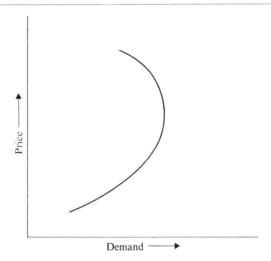

Figure 3.2   Where price is taken as signalling quality or prestige

buyer. It matters little what message the seller intends to convey; the purchase will be determined by the way in which the buyer interprets the message.

An example in the field of services was in a programme of seminars where, in order to attract larger numbers to a particular subject area, the price per day was dropped progressively over a period of years: the numbers decreased. The sponsor in desperation offered the seminar free of charge. No one attended. At the other end of the scale, an advanced course of instruction was offered at a much higher price than hitherto, and higher than the competition: the number of registrations went up.

Over and above simple price levels, there are many price offerings that can give positive signals without involving the price-cutting that leads to a price war. Credit facilities, quantity discounts, prompt payment discounts, special offers, trade-ins, free delivery, sale or return, and so on can all provide a competitive edge without necessarily incurring a high cost.

PLACE

Physically, of course, there is a well defined correlation between market share and the number of outlets. This can be seen in car hire firms, for example, or petrol service stations. But there is also a psychological factor, and that is that every retail outlet has a perceived reputation or image, and if this is positive then it is likely to bear an influence on the sales of the individual products it carries. The products will stand to benefit from what is known as the 'halo effect' of the store.

The store image or personality will vary from one group of people to another. So an expensive high-fashion store might evoke a feeling of confidence, reliability and comfort to people in the higher-income bracket, whereas to people on lower incomes it might communicate extravagance, waste, and snobbishness.

The location of a store is perhaps the starting point. It may be situated in either an up-market or down-market part of a town. Furthermore, the exterior of the building will signal ancient or modern, small or large, elegant or drab—even the name and facia will convey an impression. The interior of the store is even more important. The size of gangways, displays, colour, sound, smell, temperature, decor, and lighting will all play a part. Added to this is store personnel, all of whom will be transmitting messages depending upon their age, sex, colour, speech, product knowledge, friendliness, and helpfulness. In the personnel field it is most easy to swing from a very positive perception to a very negative one just for lack of staff selection, training, and motivation.

In putting together a marketing communications mix, the question here is, To what extent might 'place' be important in enhancing a product perception in such a way as to increase sales? Let us take an example of two extremes. In one case take a new Russian wristwatch being offered by a soap-box salesman in Woolwich market. He claims that its accuracy is greater than any other watch owing to the application of new technology. The price is at a bargain knock-down level of £49.00 including gold bracelet. Now take the same watch and the same claims and price, and put it in the window of Harrods in Knightsbridge. Which 'place' is likely to be most successful? An interesting reflection on the reputation of Harrods is that, referring to the previous section, if the price of the watch were put up to £149.00, the sales might well increase.

PROMOTION

It is unreasonable to discuss promotional media before first examining the nature of the market with which it is intended to communicate, the people that go to make up that market, and their purchasing motivations.

In the first place, there is very little evidence to support the contention that any purchasing decisions, even those of consumers, are largely irrational. Purchases are made to provide a perceived satisfaction, and as long as they do just that, such an action can hardly be held to be irrational. What they are in fact is subjective, but that is quite a different matter. The confusion arises out of the basic purchasing motivation. What we have had drilled into us is that people buy things to satisfy their 'needs'. This is not so. They actually make purchases for the most part to satisfy their 'wants', a fundamentally different human characteristic. What a person 'wants' is a highly subjective matter and varies from individual to individual regardless of whether the decision is within the framework of a family purchase or a company (organization) purchase. Indeed, since the number of people known to be involved in the latter is so much larger, so also is the likelihood of decisions being all the more subjective and complex.

The change from a philosophy of 'needs' to one of 'wants' can be quite profound throughout the marketing process—in product design, in market research formulation, in pricing strategy, in selling, but above all in promotional propositions and promotional media. This is not to argue that objective factors do not enter into purchasing decisions. Quite the opposite: they enter into all such decisions to a greater or lesser extent. What is argued, however, is that there is also a high degree of personal motivation—to satisfy the self in all purchases, whether for company, family, or indeed self.

Consumer behaviour
'Consumer behaviour', whether personal or organizational, is governed by what might be termed internal and external factors. The former are largely outside the control of the marketer and comprise innate personality factors plus early acquired behavioural patterns such as attitudes, beliefs, cultural and social mores, ego deficiencies, and the like. External factors are much more current and dynamic influences; they contribute to people's continuous development in terms of preferences, aspirations, activities, and indeed their perceptions of themselves—how they would wish to be seen by their contemporaries and their peer groups.

Thus, in terms of buying behaviour, the messages reaching them will be from a vast variety of sources, some of which will be acceptable and others not, but all from one standpoint: the buyers themselves. And this must be the key to successful marketing information formulation. The starting point, then, of the buying process is the buyer and the buyer's perceived wants.

The media mix
All markets are amenable to segmentation, especially industrial ones. And in each market segment there will be a multitude of quite different decision-making units, each comprising a number of individuals having their own particular egocentric motivations. Not only will the selling message need to vary from one to another, but, even more important, so will the media necessary to reach any target group. And a target group may vary between a few tens of people to millions. For effective communication, therefore, it is unlikely that just one or two media can be relied on; rather more likely is the need to select by methodical analysis an optimum combination of media categories to achieve the desired effect on the buyer in the form of any of the

classical marketing communications models such as attention, interest, belief, intention, desire, purchase. All the indications are that, in order to make a thorough and positive communication with all the purchasing influences in a particular market segment, what is required is a 'media mix'.

Inter-media comparisons

To arrive at an effective media mix presupposes the availability of data upon which to make comparative judgements. In consumer advertising there is a relatively wide range of research material available to assist the media planner, but, even here the task is not easy. In the industrial sector it is difficult to obtain even the most elementary information. Thus, if guesswork is to be avoided, some form of logical grid should be devised against which each possible medium can be evaluated and given a comparative rating.

Figure 3.3 is an example of a typical grid. The list of promotional media is by no means exhaustive, and will differ from one company to another. In the same way, the criteria for media choice may vary depending, for instance, on whether the target market is a consumer or an industry. The following 12 factors and the use of a matrix are regarded as no more than an aid to planning for the marketing communicator.

1. *Market size*   The total size of a market segment and all of the people within it must influence the choice of media. With a market size of 10 units, there is clearly not much room for anything more than personal contact and whatever back-up might be required. Move to 100 units and the situation hardly changes. At 1000, the personal contact must become selective: here one can add direct mail, specialized press, editorial publicity, literature, and perhaps sponsored films and audio-visual (AV) material, local demonstrations, or telephone selling. At 10 000, the value of personal selling lessens and press advertising and other non-personal media take over. Exhibitions have a particular merit here, combining unit economy with the benefits of face-to-face contact. At this point, direct mail sometimes becomes difficult to handle, but editorial back-up is well worth full exploitation. At 100 000 it is possible to move into the mass media, with television, radio, national newspapers, and posters replacing, or heavily supplementing, the media already listed.

2. *Impact*   The extent to which a promotional message is transmitted, received, stored, and can then be recalled with accuracy is vital. Each medium has its own intrinsic impact potential. Clearly, a medium that facilitates two-way communication is top of the list, so personal selling, exhibitions, demonstrations, and telephone selling are all worthy of a high rating. Direct mail, properly conceived, can expect to perform well here, as can editorial publicity, sponsored films, and literature. All the research evidence we have on page traffic and Starch (USA) measurements would

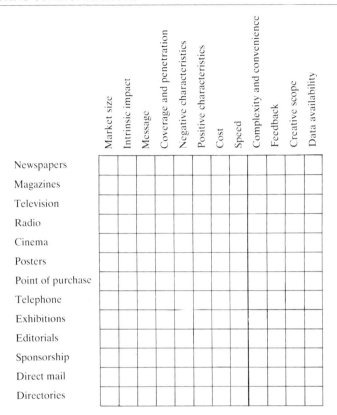

Figure 3.3   Promotional media grid

indicate that press advertising performs least well in achieving impact. Television, on the other hand, has a high, if transitory, impact potential.

3. *Message*   What is the nature of the selling message? Is it simple, or a reminder? Is it complex, technical, or innovative? In the former case television, press advertising, point of purchase, posters, and radio will do well. For a complicated message, however, the need is for demonstrations, seminars, feature articles, literature, sponsored films, and for the efforts of the sales force.

4. *Coverage and penetration*   This is the breadth and depth of a medium's capability. In breadth the question is, What proportion of the target audience (i.e. people within a market segment) is covered by readership as opposed to

circulation (in other words, will have an 'opportunity to see')? In direct mail this could be 100 per cent; with a national newspaper, perhaps 60 per cent. Commonly, an in-depth coverage of around 80 per cent is aimed for. Turning to penetration, certain media are known by long-standing practice to penetrate decision-making units even where the people involved cannot be identified—a major trade fair, for instance, or a weekly trade magazine that has to be seen by anyone who is anyone in order to keep up to date.

5. *Negative characteristics* Some people resent advertising, and it is as well to check before using a particular media group whether this could be in any way counter-productive. Most people in the UK dislike advertising messages on the telephone or salesmen at the front door or on the street corner. They also dislike loose inserts, and direct mail that is too intensive or repetitive: for many, radio and television commercials are intrusive. It depends on many factors—just check it out.

6. *Positive characteristics* Is there an added plus which comes over and above the basic medium itself? Examples are with an advert in a very prestigious publication, where to be seen in good company lends an extra credibility to an advertising proposition. With an exhibition stand, a comfortable lounge can be a welcome oasis after the formal business has been completed. An in-house exhibition or seminar might draw together people with common interests who have not met for some time and welcome the chance of informal discussion almost as much as they appreciate the event itself.

7. *Cost* There are two costs to be considered, and also price. The first cost is the total capital investment involved and whether this is compatible with the cash flow position and the other major expenditures in marketing activities. Second, the cost per contact must be evaluated, ranging as it does from the latest estimated call cost for an industrial salesman of over £100 to just a few pence for a mass medium. Media planning decisions are often made on the outcome of aggressive media buying, and this is where price comes in. All rate cards have their price, and 10 per cent off quoted rates can be a lot of money.

8. *Speed* Television, radio, newspapers, direct mail—all, under pressure, can transmit messages within 24 hours or less, and to very large audiences. The sales force can respond even more quickly, but at a rate of just a few people a day. At the other extreme, it might be two years before an appropriate trade fair takes place. Thus, if the time for activating consumer/ customer behaviour is a critical factor, the choice of media must be influenced by this.

9. *Complexity and convenience* Nothing could be simpler than to advocate

a half million pound appropriation to a single commercial network on television, and the balance to full pages in national newspapers. Such a media strategy may even be right. This is in stark contrast to the complexity of a multi-market multi-shot direct mail campaign, coupled with regional presentations and tied in with local PR, back-up sales visits, regional press, supporting literature, and posters with a culminating business gift. The choice of media just might be influenced by ease of use (idleness), coupled with such other non-professional factors as good or bad agency commission: is there any possible justification for some media nominally paying commission and others not? Media choice within an agency, therefore, must have some regard for the amount of effort required to service each medium (a cost) in relation to the income and aggravation it is likely to receive.

10. *Feedback* Examine any advertising medium and you will find that the greater majority of advertisements invite no explicit response in the way of a direct feedback, and so receive very little. Hence press advertising, and television, are essentially one-way communication systems. Since impact is greater where a dialogue can be established, there must be an intrinsic advantage in all the face-to-face media, and even with direct mail and editorial publicity where there are some instances of feedback. It is worth noting that many of the popular sales promotion techniques heavily involve the customers' participation.

11. *Creative scope* Should a medium be chosen for its creative scope? This is increasingly regarded as a major factor, but within the rather strict limits of availability of colour or movement. What is meant by creative scope is the opportunity for some quite novel or extraordinary approach that could be made entirely as a result of the medium being used. In press relations the creative opportunities to set up an extremely newsworthy event are limitless, and needless to say this would be done in such a way as to involve the product or company inextricably. With direct mail there is complete freedom on material, size, shape, colour, smell, timing, audience, and frequency. Exhibitions also have an almost infinite variety of creative opportunities. Particularly where the product itself is mundane, the choice of media for creativity is especially relevant.

12. *Data availability* It is inexcusable that large sums of money should be invested into promotional media which in turn cannot be bothered to provide basic data on the audience they are reaching. A good deal of information is available regarding television and the press and their coverage of the various consumer market segments. It follows that the more a marketing company can feel sure of its facts about a particular medium, the safer it will feel in using that medium.

In general, as audiences become narrower and more specialized, so the data available become less reliable. In technical journals, for instance, and in exhibitions there is usually very little information available.

Other promotional activities
In any marketing textbook, the promotional ingredient of the 4 Ps will be shown to comprise four elements: advertising, personal selling, sales promotion, and publicity (the latter being the American term for editorial publicity and the like). There are a number of items which should be added to those already mentioned, and most of these come under the heading of sales promotion:

- Coupons
- Premiums
- Trading stamps
- Contests
- Incentive travel
- Discounts
- Branded offers
- Samples
- Co-operative advertising

Message sources

A new concept in planning for marketing communications is to consider incoming messages from the perspective of the receiver. Just how does a prospective customer learn about a product or a company, and what are the message sources that lead to the forming of an attitude and eventually to an intention to buy, followed by an actual purchase? Clearly, all those activities listed under 'promotion' play a major part here, as do the important message cues received from product, price, and place. But where, for instance, does 'personal recommendation' come in? In many purchasing transactions, particularly first-time buying, this can be more important than any amount of advertising or packaging.

The fact is that there are tens or even hundreds of other message sources which have been neglected in the past and are now emerging as important contributors to the development of perception by customers. They can be considered under three headings: outside message sources, people message sources, and passive message sources.

OUTSIDE MESSAGE SOURCES

Opinions about you or your product expressed by what might be called 'third parties' are always more powerful and credible than your own claims. Messages from customers and/or users of a product are possibly more effective than any other message source, and yet the main thrust of any promotional campaign seems to be at prospects to gain new business rather than encouraging recommendation by reassuring existing customers that their purchasing decisions were right ones. Recommendation by a retailer, agent, or distributor is equally important. Such people are seen to be largely unbiased as well as perhaps slightly better informed than oneself. The value of considering the messages transmitted by people outside the organization is that in the first place they exist, and to ignore them is foolish, and in the second place they will be regarded as credible. What *is* being said, then, by one's competitors, suppliers, and local communities? And what also by relevant trade associations and institutions and special interest groups whose point of view can have a major effect?

PEOPLE MESSAGE SOURCES

Obviously, the sales force is in the forefront of sending messages about a company and its products, and it is worth while examining these messages to make sure they are in every way positive and supportive. To a greater or lesser degree, however, every employee develops an attitude, good or bad, and has the opportunity at least occasionally to express a view.

What impression does the chief executive give when speaking in public? Indeed, is there a proactive programme of speaking engagements to help raise the company's visibility and the regard with which its top management is held? How about other senior management? Are they encouraged to be seen and heard in public, and do they give a good account of themselves? Are they trained to do so? Receptionists and telephonists are in the front line and are recognized as being so, but is the same consideration given to the public interface of service engineers and delivery drivers? How are complaints and enquiries handled, and (to take an extreme example) what kind of an impression is given to applicants for jobs, and in particular those who are eventually turned down? Shareholders are a potential source of good news about an organization, but to what extent are they cultivated and informed so as to ensure that they transmit favourable messages?

The answer to all these questions is that in the past much has been left to chance: if anything, the involvement of employees in outside activities has been regarded as being of dubious value. There is now a growing realization that, not only is there a benefit to marketing, but also, the benefit can be greatly enhanced if a properly planned programme of participation is produced and implemented. Membership of trade associations, learned bodies, chambers of trade, CBI, etc., can all contribute to the overall corporate perception.

PASSIVE MESSAGE SOURCES

Every company has a company cheque, with its name printed on it. As such, the cheque serves its purpose of making payments to its creditors. But, like it or not, it is also a message source. A well designed cheque costs no more to print than an indifferent one, and even though the potential audience is both small and specialized, it can surely only benefit the company and its products that they are seen in the best possible light. There are many other objects and activities whose functions are not remotely connected with marketing as such but which inevitably contribute to the total marketing communications offering: obvious ones like sales letters, or indeed any letters, house magazines, labels, house styling, business cards, and annual reports; less obvious items such as instruction manuals, price lists, delivery notes and invoices, calendars and diaries, wall charts, notice boards, showrooms, and the appearance of the factory.

Then what about the company name and logotype, the reception area, the way visitors are received and entertained? Each company differs in its range of relevant message sources. It is simply a matter of taking action to capitalize on a much under-utilized resource.

MEASUREMENT OF MESSAGE SOURCES (MOMS)

The value of one particular message source as against another can vary widely, so it is necessary to give some kind of weighting to each. Taking each source in turn, we need to ask, Does this message source create an impression that is favourable, passive, or unfavourable? This is not a difficult or expensive exercise, and it can result in a profile that shows clearly where attention is needed.

Going one stage further, a check-list can be produced in which each item is classified according to its importance. An overall measurement can then be obtained which can act as a benchmark for comparisons in the future. Such an example is given in Table 3.1. The 'rating' number is the maximum that should be scored against a particular item if it is thought to give a good impression in every way. If on the other hand it is thought to give an inferior impression, then the score allocated should be marked down accordingly as far as zero. In this example, if the score is above 100 then the company image is well above average; in the range 70–100 the image is fair to good; below 70 calls for some action, and from the score sheet it is obvious which particular elements need attention.

Table 3.1

Item	Rating	Score
1. Company name	5	____
2. Letter heading	6	____
3. Head office building	2	____
4. Reception area	4	____
5. Sales literature	7	____
6. House style/logo/trademark	5	____
7. Switchboard response	6	____
8. Price list	2	____
9. Company car	2	____
10. Notice boards	2	____
11. Entertaining guests	3	____
12. Product performance	8	____
13. Product range	5	____
14. Product appearance & packaging	4	____
15. Distribution & agents	3	____
16. People outside your business, e.g. trade associations	4	____
17. Chief executive speaking in public	5	____
18. Salesmen	6	____
19. Sales service	6	____
20. Delivery times	7	____
21. Applicants for jobs	2	____
22. Advertising	7	____
23. Press releases	4	____
24. Exhibitions, displays, receptions	5	____
25. Visual aids, films, photographs	3	____
26. Business gifts	2	____
27. Direct mail & letters	3	____
28. Charity support	1	____
29. Directories entries	1	____
30. Invoices, delivery notes, documentation	1	____

Notes

1. J. Wilmshurst, *The Fundamentals and Practice of Marketing* (Heinemann, London, 1984).
2. Philip Kotler, *Marketing Management* (Prentice-Hall, Englewood Cliffs, N.J., 1976).
3. L. W. Rodger, *Marketing in a Competitive Economy* (Associated Business Programmes, 1974).
4. M. Wayne Delozier, *The Marketing Communications Process* (McGraw-Hill, Maidenhead, Berks., 1976).

Further Reading

Bernstein, D., *Company Image and Reality* (Holt, Rinehart & Winston, New York, 1984).
Broadbent, S., *Spending Advertising Money* (Business Books, London, 1984).
Broadbent, S., *Twenty Advertising Case Histories* (Holt, Rinehart & Winston, New York, 1984).
Davis, M., *The Effective Use of Advertising Media*, 2nd edn (Business Books, London, 1985).
Director's Guide, *Choosing and Using an Advertising Agency*. (Director's Guide, London, 1985).
Farbey, A. D., *The Business of Advertising* (Associated Business Publishers, London, 1979).
Hart, N., *Business to Business Advertising*, 3rd edn (Associated Business Publishers, London, 1983).
Hart, N., *The Marketing of Industrial Products* (McGraw-Hill, Maidenhead, Berks., 1984).
Hart, N. and O'Connor, J. *The Practice of Advertising*, 2nd edn (Heinemann, IM, London, 1983).
Haywood, R., *All About PR* (McGraw-Hill, Maidenhead, Berks., 1984).
Howard, W., *The Practice of Public Relations* (Heinemann, IM, London, 1982).
Olins, W., *Corporate Identity* (ISBA, London, 1984).

4.

FINANCIAL PUBLIC RELATIONS

Peter S. Gummer

Introduction

Financial public relations has done more for the respectability of PR in general and the PR practitioner in particular than any other single factor. The success of financial PR has forced many chief executives and their financial officers to reconsider the role of PR in their businesses and, in many cases, to accept that public relations today is as important a corporate weapon as media advertising, market research, or any other modern business skill.

This re-evaluation has taken place against a backdrop of intense activity in the City of London. The Big Bang in October 1986, a long bull market with an unprecedented string of corporate take-over battles, and the development of secondary and tertiary markets have all put communications and financial PR in centre stage. The markets in which this acceleration has taken place, however, are now played by a new set of rules. The Big Bang has thrown traditional roles of market-making, dealing, and banking into confusion, and it will be a long time before the public is really clear about who does what.

For financial PR to grow up in this context is both good and bad. It is good because the traditional rules and ways of the City have been broken, providing an opportunity for those with the reputation and entrepreneurship to have a go. The financial PR practitioners have been able almost to write their own rule book. On the other hand, these executives have been able to move into areas that are not by rights their own preserve. For example, certain aspects of the role of the merchant banker and the financial PR executive are too blurred and confusing to the market being served.

The chief executive, therefore, who is reviewing the firm's current financial PR advice or, more importantly, is bringing financial PR on board for the first time, must be perfectly clear about what the PR role is to achieve for the company and how it will interface with other advisers.

There is only one satisfactory way into and through this problem. Chief executives (and 99 per cent of the time this role cannot be delegated) must set down clearly what they believe financial PR can achieve in the normal course of events—particularly in handling the financial calendar. This should be

agreed with the other advisers—the merchant bankers, stockbrokers, etc.—
and with the internal finance director, company secretary, and PR officer. It
is only when this has been agreed that the more high-profile roles in flotation,
take-overs, and mergers can be considered.

So who are financial PR people trying to influence, and what would a
typical programme of financial PR consist of?

The key targets for financial PR

In most PR activities, and financial PR is no exception, detailed attention
and an analysis of the key target groups to be influenced bring great benefit
to both the evaluation of the programme and its cost efficiency.

Key targets that would be included in any list for a financial PR
programme would be:

1. Financial journalists
   - Newspapers/electronic media, etc.
2. The City
   - Stockbrokers
   - Merchant bankers
   - Analysts
3. Shareholders (existing and potential)
   - Private
   - Institutional

The priority given to these targets will depend somewhat upon the programme being written and the objectives to be reached.

Let us consider how these target groups relate one to another when
planning a financial PR programme to support the financial calendar.

The financial calendar

GENERAL

Every public company of whatever size, from the smallest USM to the largest
multinational, must provide information for the Stock Exchange for public
digestion at certain times during the year. Ideally, many substantial private
companies, particularly those planning flotations or take-overs, should be
disciplined to undertake a similar programme of disclosure. The more
effectively this is undertaken, the better the communication between the
company and its existing and potential shareholders is likely to be.

The basic schedule of work is outlined below. It provides a useful step in
establishing a PR programme, whether a company is using its internal
department, external advisers, or a combination of both. It is the basis for an

identifiable set of tasks which can easily be evaluated on a qualitative basis. Most important of all, it establishes personal relationships between a company's chairman or chief executive and the key people in the PR department or PR consultancy.

For the PR team, the financial calendar provides an opportunity to understand in detail how the public company operates and therefore ensures that, in times of crisis such as take-over bids or defences, the PR team can hit the ground running.

HALF-YEAR RESULTS/INTERIMS

Generally speaking, the half-year figures are a low-publicity item unless a public company is in the FT 100 or is itself a very high-profile business. There is little advantage in holding a press conference to present these results.

The PR agency/internal department should fulfil four key functions:

1. It should be responsible for the preparation of the relevant press release and should be prepared to argue about detailed content to ensure that it properly represents what the journalists wish to know. This is not always an easy matter. Company chairmen often wish to make different points in a very different way!

2. After providing copies of the press information to the Stock Exchange, the PR executives are responsible for further distribution. The circulation of a financial press release should not be limited to the media, although they are very important. The release and any supporting information should also be delivered to banks and brokers—both those of the company and those of other interested parties—and in some circumstances to key institutional shareholders.

3. The company must be thoroughly briefed on likely questions and answers from any of the above target groups. There is nothing more embarrassing for the chairman of a company, having released information and indicated at the foot of the release that he is available to answer questions, than to find that he is inadequately briefed. It behoves PR advisers to ensure that this never happens.

4. Ideally, the press release should go out as early as possible in the day. The good PR executive will ring around the key journalists to ensure that any questions which can be answered can be dealt with quickly, thereby gaining a position to advise on likely questions and model answers. The cardinal rule is that access to the chairman of the public company should be facilitated by the PR executive, not hindered.

PRELIMINARY RESULTS

The publication of the preliminary results of a public company is the highlight of the financial year. It is the moment at which the City, the shareholders, and the media can all evaluate the company's performance. It therefore has high publicity value for all listed and unlisted public, and large private, companies.

To the chairman and chief executive, this is what it is all about! They and their teams have worked very hard to make the results happen; the tendency—particularly if they consider the results good—is to expect them to have a higher publicity value than in fact they merit. The pressure is often put on the PR people to arrange press conferences, run advertising, and do all manner of other things to make these results a media event.

It should be remembered that the results of a public company are usually announced on a day when plenty of other public companies are also active—not just with results but with news of take-overs, personnel changes, etc. PR executives must give due warning that preliminary results can fall on good or bad days and should encourage the client to plan accordingly. The media, as will be shown later in this chapter, will discuss results with the brokers. If the results are good (or even bad) but in line with market expectations, they will tend to receive more modest coverage than if they are really hot news—i.e., unexpectedly good or bad.

Try not to have a press conference. Instead, try to encourage individual journalists to follow up the detail on a one-to-one basis or on the telephone. There is no point in planning a press conference, which will always take up more journalistic time than is readily available, unless the company news really justifies it.

The PR agency or internal department have some very important tasks to perform when the preliminaries are due.

1. Obviously, as with the interims, they are responsible for the preparation of the press documentation. This will include the press release and a statement of the figures, together with whatever the company and its auditors consider relevant to a real understanding of the press statement. Financial PR people are reliable professionals, and they should be involved early in the preparation of this information with other advisers such as auditors, merchant bankers, and stockbrokers. If a company does not feel that it can involve the PR people on this confidential basis, then it has the wrong PR team; any doubts about their ability to handle such information should immediately result in their dismissal or resignation.
2. A similar circulation should be arranged for the preliminaries as for the interims.
3. The client briefing should be as thorough as possible. A review of recent press coverage and brokers' circulars, particularly the interims and the

previous annual results, will help to prepare for likely questions. Those are the sources, coupled with the annual report, to which most journalists will refer in order to update themselves before interviewing the chief executive.

4. An early circulation to the Stock Exchange, the media and the brokers is recommended. Most key journalists will talk to the brokers in order to gauge the City reaction before writing their own articles. These are intimate relationships and feed off each other. They are mutually supportive.

5. Most public companies tend to talk to the media before they talk to the brokers. Experience suggests that this is incorrect. Briefing brokers early in the day before the media start compiling their articles is to be encouraged. The message will then be the same in the City and in the next day's press.

THE ANNUAL REPORT AND ACCOUNTS

Normally this is a very low-interest item. The annual report simply confirms what the preliminaries have already indicated. It is around this time that some public companies choose to implement corporate advertising. If there has been a failure to get the message across in the editorial columns at the preliminary stage, then there is a case for advertising the annual results, highlighting that key message if only to put the record straight. Advertising the annual results through the purchase of space usually does little more than repeat what the media have already covered in the editorial columns and what the City already knows and is therefore reflected in the share price. It should only be used when it is necessary to correct facts or ill-balanced reporting. The PR role regarding the annual report could normally be considered as follows:

1. PR people are inevitably involved in the design, layout, and content of this document. Indeed, their input and knowledge is very considerable, and they should be encouraged to help in any way possible.

2. PR has a unique role in the preparation of the chairman's statement, and yet PR executives often are not consulted or involved until too late. However, they should have their ears close to the ground and should advise their chairman on particular announcements and points to emphasize in the annual report.

3. The chairman and the PR adviser should decide between them whether they want a high-profile annual report or not. By introducing items that will interest the City or the press, the PR executive can present the chairman's statement in such a way that it will make news or not as the case may warrant.

4. The circulation list for the annual report should be as comprehensive as possible. This is the document to which all commentators will refer, whatever their interests, in preparing future articles, brokers circulars, etc. The fullest possible circulation list should be maintained and updated year by year to encourage wide and informed comment.

THE ANNUAL GENERAL MEETING

For most public companies, the AGM is an anticlimax. This is a sad reflection on the owners of the business, the shareholders. It is only when matters are at crisis point that meetings are well attended. PR people believe, in general, that shareholders should be encouraged and invited to take an active part in the interests of the company which they own. For the company secretary and the finance director, therefore, the AGM is an important PR platform. Their main tasks are:

1. To establish a time and date which allows shareholders to attend from around the country; if there is a strong geographical concentration of shareholding members, it is better to hold the AGM in the centre of that conurbation.
2. To establish the format and timetable. This is, of course, the company secretary's domain. PR people should be a party to those discussions and should undertake to arrange the entertaining of guests in an appropriate manner.
3. To review carefully the circulation lists for the annual report, and the interim and preliminary results, when inviting people to the AGM. In most cases the merchant bank, accountants, stockbrokers, and other company advisers will wish to send representatives. This is an ideal opportunity for the board of directors of the public company to meet these advisers and discuss plans for the future.
4. To advise on the impact of any proposed statements that might be made at the meeting. There is great pressure on the chairman to make statements additional to those included in the annual report. Inevitably, the AGM takes place at the beginning of a new financial year, and therefore it is too early to make statements which later events may prove ill-founded or hurried. The impact of any such public statements should be discussed with the PR people before they are made to ensure that they are going to have the desired effect. Company chairmen often feel the need to talk before it is necessary so to do.
5. To provide some basis for staff, pensioners, etc., to attend. With wider share ownership among employees, this is now an important company event.

The ongoing financial PR programme

GENERAL

Although the financial calendar provides an ideal opportunity for a public company to develop its relationship with its public relations advisers, there are three main areas of ongoing work which should be thoroughly undertaken throughout the year.

First and foremost there should be a scheduled plan for communicating with the City, including the brokers and institutions. Second, the area that usually receives most attention is the communications programme with the press. Third, the area that is least considered is the need to ensure that the staff, whatever their number and wherever their location, are fully informed of the financial statements that are being made about their company and its financial stability and growth upon which their employment depends.

Let us consider each of these three areas in turn.

COMMUNICATING WITH THE CITY

The principles
When establishing the policy for a public company's communication programme with the City, it is important that the public company adheres to certain key principles.

First, the City hates surprises. As a community, the requirement is for a public company to move inexorably through its financial calendar, meeting or significantly exceeding the brokers' forecasts and therefore supporting the share price upon which they are predicated. Of course commercial and financial life is not like that. In effect, however, this idealistic scheme really requires the existence of an orderly market. The responsibility of the public company is to be prepared to adopt an honest stance, particularly with the stockbroker and analyst who follow its shares.

Second, a public company must be prepared to share both the good and the bad news with the brokers and the institutions, either in face-to-face discussions or through selected intermediaries such as merchant bankers or PR people. This places a very heavy burden of responsibility on the PR people.

Third, it is only very rarely that public companies get away with being less than honest with the City. Occasionally this may be possible, but in the vast majority of cases misleading the City means that your card is marked. The City has a long memory, and often the share price will suffer for many years to come.

Recognizing the needs of the key targets

There are three key targets for the majority of public companies: brokers, institutions, and private shareholders.

Stockbrokers live on a steady flow of information, both planned and rumoured! This is the basis for their circulars and the analyses upon which they wish to recommend shares for purchase or sale. Similarly, since the Big Bang, attention should be given to the market-makers responsible for the shares in the public company. These probably number only two or three firms.

Institutional shareholders wish to see a return on their investment based on an ongoing relationship. Full information of a detailed kind is vital. Institutions tend to become disenchanted with those companies that consider their needs as shareholders only in situations of crisis. Many public companies could have spurned unwelcome take-over bids with ease if only they had developed relationships with those key institutions who own their shares. Nobody likes being called upon for support only when trouble is brewing and their help is urgently needed.

Private shareholders rarely own the business in which they invest. It is the institutions that invariably carry most shareholding muscle. However, the programme of privatization, the marketing of the stock market, and the Big Bang have all made the private shareholder a very important element in the mix. A regular, but not excessive, flow of information from a public company to its private shareholders, over and above that required by the Stock Exchange in the form of annual and interim returns, is an essential part of the communications programme.

Establishing lines of communication with the City

Most of the financial PR community would argue that an open door policy is a cornerstone of a satisfactory relationship with the City. Willingness to deal with questions and devote time to nurture relationships is essential.

Invariably, public companies become concerned about the number of requests they receive to give brokers' lunches and similar City platforms. They also complain, simultaneously, that they do not obtain an adequate City rating. The truth is that, with the exception of the very large public company, one person at main board level must be prepared to devote some time and effort to these City events, in order to present the company's case. Moreover, as the City buys the future of a company and not its past, such presentations should be forward-looking and, above all else, honest.

These events, and particularly the stockbroker lunches, are really selling exercises for the stockbroking firm. They provide an opportunity for the broker to introduce an interesting public company to a number of institutional investors. It is the task of the public company to enable the stockbroker to do deals as a result of such a lunch. This is a selling opportunity; it should be prepared for on exactly that basis.

The relationship between stockbroker and the media has already been discussed. If brokers find the share of a particular company and the style of its management attractive, and if they believe that the share is undervalued, then inevitably the company will receive sympathetic coverage in the media. The role of the PR team in preparing a complementary message for stockbrokers and the media is therefore essential.

Institutional communications

A regular analysis of the shareholder register will indicate the numbers of institutional shareholders in any company. It is the responsibility of the company secretary to note changes in the register, usually on a fortnightly basis. Such an analysis will lead most public company boards to the conclusion that they are owned by City institutions. A regular programme of meetings with these institutions on a face-to-face basis, therefore, will bring considerable benefit in creating shareholder loyalty in good times and bad. This is a task that should never be delegated or put on one side simply because of the pressure of other short-term obligations.

Communication with the private shareholder

It has long been argued that the private shareholder is disinterested in the annual report—all that he looks at is the salary of the chairman and highest paid director! While this is clearly not the case, there is more than a germ of truth in the thought. Most private shareholders do not understand, and have limited interest in, the flood of company material that pours through their letterboxes, particularly during crisis situations such as take-overs. Their real interest is in the dividend or capital growth of the stock.

However, shareholder loyalty cannot only be bought: it should be sought. A regular flow of press clippings and interesting information helps to bring life to the shareholders' investment. If the company produces products, gifts, and services at a discount which may be of interest to a shareholder and can be offered at a preferential rate, then this too may create longer-term loyalty.

In general, however, there is no substitute for good financial performance and making the shareholders feel that they are part of a company that cares.

COMMUNICATING WITH THE PRESS

The principles

Most PR activity is unfortunately reduced to media relations. It has already been demonstrated that financial PR entails much more than simply dealing with a few financial journalists. This is not to denigrate the role of media relations—it is important and vital. However, it is not the only role of financial public relations.

Professional communication with the press involves a time commitment. Above all else, public company spokesmen must be accessible. Whether chairmen, chief executives, or finance directors, they must be accessible not only as far as their own diaries are concerned, but also as far as the journalist is concerned. The journalist has different priorities, different deadlines, and different schedules to meet. These must be recognized and accepted if good media contacts are to be established.

Being accessible is the keynote of all that follows.

Second, public company spokesmen should ascertain from the outset of a conversation the exact status of the discussion. Is it on or off the record? Is the quote attributable? Most journalists will abide by these conventions, but only if they are clearly stated at the outset. For some reason, many people who talk to the media are self-conscious about establishing this at the beginning of a conversation. This is precisely what the less scrupulous journalists want! They do not ask the question themselves, but will assume that everything is on the record unless told that this is not the case. All spokesmen should establish the status of the conversation before discussing an item which, when the paper appears the next day, they may regret.

Third, know exactly who your friends are. Help good journalists to do their job better; give them the direct line that rings on your desk, your home telephone number, your weekend number. Expect them to do the same. Reciprocate their attention. Invest in that trust.

Awareness of the media role

The financial journalist has a responsibility to his reader, not to the chairmen of the companies about which he writes. This is an oversimplification of a complex relationship. However, in essence, journalists want a good story which preferably no other newspaper is carrying. They want their readers to make, or at least not to lose, money. Where situations are going wrong, they want to ensure that their readers sell stock before the losses become really damaging. Remember that this is what keeps the financial columns of the national press alive. Providing financial journalists with information to help them fulfil their role is a key part of the communications programme.

Journalists are not their own masters. They are always subject to the editorial position of the newspaper that employs them. The *Daily Mirror* clearly takes a different political line from *The Times* or *Telegraph*. Contentious issues will have an effect on the way a newspaper positions a story.

If any public company spokesman ever reads a story about his company or watches it on television or video and then sits back and says, 'I did not mean to say that', or 'She did not understand what I meant', then that spokesman has not yet understood the role of the media in reporting a public company's activities.

Building on existing contacts
Accessibility to journalists will inevitably develop relationships which will spill from a business into a social environment.

Trying to persuade people through a vigorous exchange to give their individual endorsement to your point of view requires an investment of time. Only superficial commentators require limited attention—and their opinion is hardly worth the paper on which it is written. So, if you are going to persuade leading financial journalists to take up your case, you must know and respect their points of view. These journalists may well become close allies or even close friends.

As the relationship develops, you will find that it may become relaxed and easy-going. A word of warning, however. Many company chairmen have found that, in developing the relationship, they have forgotten that their confidants are journalists. They have not remembered to establish the status of their conversation, and the result has sometimes been the breaking of a confidence. It is then too late to shout, 'I did not mean to say that' or 'That was not for publication.' Never forget that the journalist is a journalist. As in all matters, remember the status of every conversation you have.

Question of timetable
Press relations is ultimately about copy in the paper, pictures on a screen, or words from a radio. Serving the journalist therefore entails understanding in detail the timetable that leads up to that deadline. It is not enough to know roughly when the copy goes down: you must know whether it is going down at 6.10 pm or 6.30 pm.

Why is timing so important? In situations of crisis a late comment can often be very useful. For example, in a take-over bid a late statement from a predator may just make the morning editions, but there might not be time for the adversary's point of view to appear in the same edition. Nothing confirms this as finally as the journalistic line stating: 'Mr XYZ was not available for comment.'

How and when to use a press conference
A press conference provides, in financial PR terms, an opportunity to promote a single message which can be clearly put forward to a number of people who will then be able to ask good questions in lively debate.

Press conferences, however, have one drawback, which is often catastrophically underestimated. There are now far fewer financial journalists on national papers than there were some years ago. The pressures on their time, the variety of companies they need to follow, and the lack of specialization that has resulted mean that the mix of journalists who appear at a press conference vary, from the very good to the very bad. This means that a good question from a good journalist can be heard by everybody else present and is often misinterpreted by the less able media representatives. In addition, if the chairman of a public company makes an error in answering a particular line of questioning, it is not just one newspaper that is being told, but ten or twenty different media representatives.

If conversations are usually or always conducted on a one-to-one basis and are carefully reviewed with the PR advisers directly afterwards, there is always the opportunity of putting right a particular point in conversation with the next journalist with whom one speaks.

Sometimes a press conference is vital, but it should be held somewhere easily accessible for the journalists rather than the public company board. Even a press conference at 3 pm in the Hyde Park Hotel, Knightsbridge, London SW1, is likely to have a low unqualified turnout unless the content is of earth-shattering importance!

Formulating a financial press release

A financial press release has to be newsworthy. There is financial news that is important to the boards of public companies but has little or no significance to the majority of journalists. The PR adviser must be ruthless in identifying what should go out and what should not. Infrequent but newsworthy press releases give a much higher standing to any public company than regular, low-news-value stories which are spiked as often as they are read.

Always ensure that, wherever possible, the press release can be easily subdivided into short and long stories. Some newspapers have little financial space and one or two paragraphs is all they can use. Other more specialist publications, such as the *Financial Times*, may be able to use seven or eight paragraphs. Long or short, however, better stories include a quotation which adds colour and quality to the release.

Any financial release will usually have an effect on the share price, and therefore it has to be right in every respect—a decimal point can send a share price through the floor or the sky. Proofreading should never be left to one person or simply to the word processor operator. The cardinal rule is for the final draft release to be signed off by an officer of the company, preferably the finance director or company secretary.

Broadcasting

It is now a truism that nobody reads any more! Most people receive most information from a screen, a little from a radio, but hardly anything through the written word. If a public company is to make itself understood in a colourful and lasting way, then it is vital that its spokesman learns to use broadcasting media.

Training, training, and more training is the sine qua non of success in this area. Doing mock interviews for the annual report or in preparation for crises helps enormously when the real event arises.

If television or the radio invite you to appear, grasp the opportunity with both hands. Take it and use it to the best advantage. If in the midst of a take-over bid, make sure that the take-over panel is content with the decision to appear. What can and cannot be said in these circumstances is divided by a very fine line. Whenever possible, go on live; prerecorded programmes can suffer quite a lot in the hands of editors.

Keeping the initiative

In all that is done in financial press relations, it is necessary to be open and to keep the initiative. A defensive position under scrutiny from the financial media invariably leads to disaster. Keep coming forward in the discussions and sharing with the media the problems and opportunities in which your business is placed.

There are many PR people who unfortunately still indulge in dirty tricks. This reprehensible behaviour may lead to short-term gain, but experience suggests that those who play dirty tricks fall by dirty tricks!

COMMUNICATING WITH THE STAFF

The principles

There will be only very limited disagreement about the principles that apply when communicating with employees at all levels. Unfortunately, the acceptance in theory is rarely carried out in practice.

The fact is that staff know very much more about the financial situation of the company than the chairman and board ever believe. This is hardly surprising. Staff have to deal with suppliers that do not get paid or are kept waiting; staff hear rumours of lay-offs or short working. They have a sharp-end understanding of the ebb and flow of business life and often a simple housekeeping approach to financial matters which runs close to the truth. Any communication with employees therefore must assume a very high level of pre-knowledge, albeit of a rather unsophisticated kind.

Always communicate with staff by preparing answers to the questions *they* want answered. The temptation is to present a case to employees which boosts the ego of management but leaves a feeling of dissatisfaction among the staff. Think carefully what questions need answering, and even try them out on two or three groups before wider circulation.

It is essential that management makes every effort, however expensive and difficult it may prove to be, to inform all employees before they read about their employer or company in the press. It is *their* company; they work in it, and they should be given a priority. To allow them to read in the press or see on TV stories about their company before they have been consulted or informed is asking for trouble.

The order of the day is clear: get to those who work with you first; deal with them honestly, and be prepared to view the financial performance of the business from their point of view rather than your own.

It is an ongoing process
The temptation to regard financial communication with employees as a once- or twice-yearly exercise is, of course, too easy. Financial communication is really about having an ongoing dialogue on the financial performance of the company. The financial timetable is obviously helpful in this. A video, house newspaper, financial seminars, and so on are all helpful in getting the information across.

Consider structuring these activities by using journalists, who approach problems in the same way as the workforce. Invite the City editor of a national daily to interview the board on the financial results so they can be circulated to the workplace. Video the interviews. Encourage discussion. The sharing of financial information rarely does any harm and greatly helps in disposing of rumour and defusing situations.

This is particularly true when dealing with the trade unions. Keeping them informed encourages a genuine understanding of the decisions that have to be made to keep businesses moving forward in the light of new technology, reducing workforces, and so on. Frank discussions with employees' unions, employee committees, etc., help in planning major changes in a company's fortunes.

Special situations

Most financial public relations professionals will enjoy developing an on-going programme with a public company. The special situation, however, sends blood coursing through their veins. Mention the words 'flotation', 'take-over', or 'defence' and they know that their skills will be tested to the full.

These special situations are always best handled by PR advisers—internal or external—who know a company's business, have good relationships with its officers and other advisers, and know the media, stockbrokers, etc., who follow the company's fortunes. Hence, establishing the relationship with PR professionals is best initiated with a commitment to the ongoing financial calendar. Then they are up to speed for the special situation.

The three examples chosen—flotation, take-over defence, and attack—require skills peculiar to only a handful of agencies and even fewer internal departments. Make sure that your company employs these skills, whether you need them now or not. If yours is a professionally run business, you will almost certainly need them in the future!

FLOTATION—A PUBLIC RELATIONS PLAN

In the following section a PR programme for a company flotation is identified. Naturally, it is general rather than specific, but it provides a check-list for the PR tasks that need to be considered.

1. *AN Company Limited—Background information*
   1.1 *Name*   A statement of the name of the company before and after listing must be clarified, particularly where a new company is being formed and the business of this operating company is subsumed in a new entity.
   1.2 *Details of the issue*   A clear statement of the intention to float the company, either by placing or by tender, needs to be presented. The timetable is important in establishing the target date as early as possible.
   1.3 *History*   A detailed statement of the history of the company needs to be agreed with the client so that PR advisers can talk with authority when briefing journalists, brokers, etc. This should include details of main products and services provided, main offices throughout the UK, export and other trading details, etc.
   1.4 *Competition*   Details should be provided of any competitive company, particularly if listed, so that comparisons can be made, dates identified, and satisfactory explanations given to intermediaries.

2. *Public relations objectives*
   A clear statement of the PR objectives needs to be agreed between the company, its PR people, and other advisers.

3. *Target groups*
   Although these groups will vary depending upon the nature of the industry and the size of the company involved, a list of probable targets will include the following:

3.1 *Media*
   ● National and regional financial and business press
   ● National, local, and provincial press
   ● Specialist trade press
   ● Financial and business correspondents on national and local radio and television

3.2 *Investment community*
- Stockbrokers
- Market-makers
- Investment analysts
- Institutional investors
- Banks
- Finance houses

3.3 *Employees*
- Management
- Staff

4. *Methods*

4.1 *General*   In view of the fact that these notes are intended as a guideline towards the launch, for purpose of clarity a section is included with a timetable of activities in which the week of the launch is nominated as 'week X'.

4.2 *Media*   A balanced and informed media is of prime importance to any company planning either a full or USM listing. Effective media relations involve the development of mutual respect and confidence between the individuals concerned, which necessitates the devotion of time by senior management in making itself available to the media both in face-to-face meetings and on the telephone.

It is always to be recommended that any company in this situation undertakes a carefully orchestrated programme of media liaison in order to establish awareness of the company's activities, its history, successes and future potential as an investment medium. It is important to guard against the dangerous effects of overkill in such a programme, and so it is recommended that a limited number of quality editorial features be sought in the appropriate media.

5. *Programme and timetable* (Week X = week of launch)

5.1 *Introduction*   The programme that follows assumes a period of notice of up to three months. In some cases it could be much longer, probably up to a year. The longer the period, the more opportunities are presented to control the weight of publicity, particularly in the company's own trade and technical media.

5.2 *Week commencing*

$X-10$
- Carry out in-depth briefing with AN Company Limited
- Establish existence of, and obtain current market research relating to, the Group's activities and markets
- Liaise with company and brokers on preparation of corporate brochure and prospectus
- Prepare press information folders and press release paper

X−9
- Continue liaison on preparation of corporate brochure and prospectus
- Start preparing brief company profile and biographies of key directors
- Arrange photography of key directors for press purposes

X−8
- Continue liaison on preparation of corporate brochure and prospectus
- Prepare detailed media distribution lists
- Prepare list of selected financial journalists for individual interviews and start scheduling meetings for week *X−6*
- Continue preparation of corporate brochure and prospectus
- Arrange press cuttings' monitoring service

X−7
- Identify appropriate brokers' investment analysts for company's sectors
- Obtain current brokers' circulars on company's sectors, if available

X−6
- Start programme of press interviews for feature stories
- Start making arrangements for investment analysts' presentation in week *X−1*
- Agree final proof of corporate brochure
- Identify, in conjunction with brokers, appropriate potential institutional investors
- Press information folders and press release paper ready

X−5
- Prepare first draft of press announcement for circulation by company and brokers
- Make preparations for potential institutional investors' lunch in week *X−2*

X−4
- Assist company in preparing 'box' advertisement for one newspaper or as required for full listing
- Company to book advertising space for ('box') advertisement
- Continue liaison on preparation of prospectus
- Continue arrangements for investment analysts' presentation in week *X−1*

X − 3
- Issue invitations to selected journalists for press conference during week *X*
- Issue invitations to investment analysts for presentation in week *X* − 1
- Prepare draft press announcement of launch
- Corporate brochure ready
- Continue to liaise on preparation of prospectus
- Submit proposals for ongoing corporate and financial public relations support

X − 2
- Finalize press announcement
- Finalize contents of press folder, including photographs, biographies of key directors, corporate brochures, etc.
- Prepare list of likely press questions and answers at press conference
- Prepare list of likely analysts' questions and answers
- Liaise on final proof of prospectus
- Agree final copy for ('box') advertisement
- Arrange for *Financial Times* and other appropriate newspapers to carry share price in New Issues/USM column
- Lunch for potential institutional investors

X − 1
- Prospectus available
- Investment analysts' presentation
- Distribute press announcement of launch with press (information folders, under embargo if appropriate)
- ('Box') advertisement appears in selected press

X
- Monitor and assess all press comments
- Monitor and assess brokers' reactions/circulars
- Monitor share price at start of dealings
- Prepare report on first day's dealings
- Assess required level of press follow-up

X + 1
- Prepare report on public relations aspects of launch
- Undertake agreed corporate and financial public relations programme
- Continue to monitor share price movements
- Establish new shareholder profile

DEFENCE OR ATTACK — SOME KEY RULES

Every take-over attack or defence is different. Much of the earlier discussion on developing a strong financial PR programme on an ongoing basis will stand most public companies in good stead when these crises occur.

There are nine key areas, however, which every public company should consider with its PR people, whatever its own plans or size:

1. *Define the audiences* Always review the audiences—media, investment community, and staff—and be certain there is clarity among them as to the company's intentions and long-term plans.
2. *Evaluate image* Perceived reality is far more important than reality. Spend time and money researching the key audiences so there is genuine knowledge—up-to-date knowledge—of how the company is perceived.
3. *Clear channels of communication* Make sure that the lines of communication are known and open—particularly throughout the organization to the staff.
4. *Form a control group* Always have at the ready a control group with board authority to react to any given crisis. This group should include seconded advisers from the bank, brokers, and PR firm.
5. *Logistical aspects of communications* Crises rarely happen in office hours! Does the switchboard operate late at night? Is it easy to gain access to the office outside office hours? Is there a full list of directors' home numbers? Is there a duty secretary who can work the fax and telex machine? These, and many other questions, must be asked and answered in preparation for a crisis.
6. *Tone of voice* Every company has a character—an image, if you prefer. In crisis, panic can set in and result in behaviour that is 'out of character'. Determine and understand how to behave in character at times of crisis.
7. *Review strengths and weaknesses* The control group should always review the company's strengths and weaknesses, as these will change with the market and the perceptions of the key target groups.
8. *Analysis of predator or target* As the company's strengths and weaknesses change, so does the view taken of a predator or a target. Remember it is the perceived strengths and weaknesses that are more important than the reality.
9. *Assess political factors* The Monopolies Commission, the employment effect in marginal constituencies, and many other political facts can make or break a major bid situation. Analyse these in relation to each situation, whether as target or predator.

Conclusion

Financial public relations is here to stay. This chapter has illustrated its role in handling the financial calendar, its ongoing role, and some key elements of communication in special situations.

In the final analysis, however, financial public relations is about the quality of people who do it. Essentially, it is a creative function at general management level with all the financial discipline that implies. It is the duty of every public company to ensure that it enjoys the quality of financial PR help it deserves.

5.

EFFECTIVE EMPLOYEE COMMUNICATION

Mike Arnott

Employee communication is all about running the organization effectively. It is about making sure people know what needs to be done, understand why it's necessary, feel committed to achieving it, and have a chance to use their own knowledge and skills to do it better if possible. Said like that, it sounds easy. If it *is* so easy, why have managers been hectored, exhorted, lectured, and preached at non-stop for the last 25 years on the subject? Why has no one come up with a straightforward answer? Surely there must be some models about that can be copied?

In their best-seller, *In Search of Excellence*,[1] Peters and Waterman identified 43 'excellent' companies which could provide model behaviour, much of it concerning communication. In the subsequent four years, about half of those companies had quite serious problems. Some have bounced back, the future of others is still in doubt. It's possible to go back through the literature and find case after case of the good example made dubious by time. Today, for example, the sureness of political touch ascribed to Jimmy Carter and Margaret Thatcher in a 1977 book about employee communication reads with less conviction. If all organizations were the same and stayed that way, then perhaps a model could be found.

However, some organizations go back 50 or 100 years, while others were set up yesterday. Some have been bought and sold two or even three times in the last decade. Situations alter, people retire or die, new managers come, individuals develop different points of view. In one part of the economy there is growth, in another decline, while in yet another there is massive technological change. There are organizations employing over 100 000 people and organizations employing one or two.

Work carried out by Stewart and Stewart[2] shows that, of the characteristics that differentiate between an effective and an ineffective manager, about one-third relates to the personality of the manager and the other two-thirds relates to the specific situation the manager is operating in. In *Designing Organisations for Satisfaction and Efficiency*,[3] the point is made that 'organisational systems must be designed contingently so that they are appropriate to specific organisational circumstances and objectives'. In other words, there's no such thing as an all-purpose manager or a best organizational design. Given all this diversity, how can there be a model that ensures successful employee communication?

Of course, there is no prescriptive answer that lays down for any organization precisely what it must do and how to do it. But there is by now a considerable body of knowledge about the process involved and some of the factors that can either help or hinder. The best place to start is by looking at what the employee wants, at what the organization wants, and at how best to bring these together.

What organizations want from their employees

What most organizations want from their employees is simple and reasonable. Take the 'simple' part first. Organizations want their employees to come to work at the appointed time, work for the due number of hours, and then go home. While they are at work, the organization wants them to carry out the job they have been assigned, to a required level of performance, and within a given time. Furthermore, the organization expects employees not to cause problems, to keep to agreements, and generally to behave in a responsible fashion. Given this, the organization expects to be sufficiently successful, provided it has taken the right strategic decisions, to be able to provide acceptable wages and conditions. However, few organizations are able to get all their strategic decisions right all the time, and no organizations can survive without change.

Change inevitably puts additional strain on the way the organization works and on its employees. When this happens, the organization asks more than the simple straightforward 'fair day's work for a fair day's pay' arrangement. It then expects employees to be flexible, to be understanding, and to be co-operative in the acceptance of change. In short, it expects them to be 'reasonable'. New technology, economic and social trends, political or legislative decisions at national or international level, and, often the most powerful of all, competitor actions, are the engines that drive these changes, and these engines are never still.

The more successful organizations who thrive over the long term go further than that. They expect their employees to be highly committed to their values and to be deeply involved with their work and to the part that their work has to play in the success of the organization as a whole, and to accept that change and adaptation are everyday and normal procedures in the pursuit of those values.

Obviously, whatever an organization wants from its employees demands some form of communication, but communication must relate to the overriding needs of the organization. It cannot be an end in itself.

THE BASIC ORGANIZATION NEEDS

The needs of an organization are multiple and complex, and there are many models that attempt to provide a structure that makes this complexity more tractable.

A basic structure of corporate needs, helpful in relation to mapping out associated communication needs, is provided by Pearson.[4] It is useful because it provides a framework that can be used across a number of contexts. Pearson used the Maslow hierarchy as his model. Maslow[5] recognized that different people have different needs, that these may be either clearly conscious and articulated or taken for granted or even not consciously realized at all, that there can be many motivations at work at one time, and that different motivations have differing degrees of strength. In short, the structure allows for the very wide variations that exist between one individual and another. This recognition of diversity is necessary also for dealing with organizations.

The Pearson model says that an organization has needs at five different levels and that these levels can be placed in a hierarchy where at least adequate performance at a lower level is necessary in order to begin to get genuine or lasting performance at a higher level. Thus, as shown in Table 5.1, there is little hope of getting active approval of shareholders if the share performance is poor. Equally, it is impossible to maintain a leadership position if there is a chronic high level of dissatisfaction among employees.

There are many organizations today in which employee communications practice appears to relate to this model, but all too often still at only the first two or three levels. In these organizations there is a considerable concentration on information concerned with output and with survival communica-

Table 5.1

Level	Organizational need	Typical requirements
Lower		
1	Output	Money, machines, manpower, materials
2	Survival	Cash flow, profits, share performance, customers
3	Morale	Basic employee job satisfaction
4	Acceptability	Approval by main external stakeholders, e.g. shareholders, voters, customers, suppliers, society
5	Leadership	Strategies delivering a developed and respected position in one or more chosen
Higher		fields; high customer satisfaction, high employee involvement

tions, mainly of a financial nature, and communications about pay and conditions are given a high degree of importance, although they are not always handled particularly well. This may well be because these organizations are still fighting output and survival battles; others may have won the battle but may not have got out of the habits formed during their struggles; yet others may never have considered going beyond level 2, because essentially they view the achievement of output and an adequate financial performance as sufficient. However, there is also an increasing number of organizations today who have recognized the importance of performing well at the two higher levels—either over a long time, such as Marks and Spencer or IBM (UK), or more recently, such as ICL or Jaguar.

HOW ORGANIZATIONAL NEEDS ARE SATISFIED

Although Pearson's structure is descriptively helpful, it does not suggest what organizations have to do in order to satisfy their needs. For this it is necessary to turn to organizational analysis and management theory. This goes back a long way, but generally it has been characterized by emphasis on specific points, for example Xenophon (428–354 BC) on leadership, Machiavelli (1467–1527) on power relationships, Adam Smith (1723–1790) on functional specialization in the pin mill, Robert Owen (1771–1858) on the responsibilities between the enterprise and its employees, Frederick Taylor (1856–1915) on productivity, or Alfred Sloan Jr (1875–1966) on strategic planning and decentralization. Recent work has concentrated more on the pragmatic analysis of successful organizations, and this has led to a holistic approach. Waterman, Peters, and Phillips[6] in 1977 began to develop the 7-S model, which suggests that organization effectiveness stems from the interaction of a number of factors that are interconnected and none of which has any hierarchical dominance. At any one time one factor may be most critical, depending on the specific challenges facing the organization. However, change in that factor alone will not lead to success unless responsive change takes place in the other factors as well. The seven factors are:

1. *Structure* Task division and co-ordination, probably with a simple basic form and the use of temporary devices, such as programmes, project groups, etc., to meet current strategic needs
2. *Strategy* The actions an organization plans in response to or in anticipation of changes in its environment
3. *Systems* The basic procedures, formal and informal, that make the organization work
4. *Style* The way that an organization communicates its values and priorities, both internally and externally
5. *Staff* All the people in the organization and the way in which they are selected, trained, developed, managed, and rewarded

6. *Skills*   Those things that an organization does, or needs to do, best in its circumstances; examples might be innovative research, development, product management, financial control, or customer service
7. *Superordinate goals*   The guiding values of the organization. The point is made by the authors that most organizations do not appear to possess superordinate goals, but that superior performers, such as AT&T, IBM, GE, and 3M, do. (In later writing, the term 'superordinate goals' was translated into 'shared values'.)

The authors conclude that 'Our own experience with the framework has convinced us that it can be a powerful aid to senior managers seeking a better understanding of the forces at work in their enterprises and a more reliable command of the real levers of organisation change.' This conclusion appears to be being borne out in practice because the 7-S approach is now being used extensively not only by McKinsey, Waterman, Peters, and Phillips's parent organization at that time, but by many others as well. Much of its underlying thinking is also to be found in the subsequent Peters and Waterman book, *In Search of Excellence*,[7] and in Peters and Austin's *A Passion for Excellence— The Leadership Difference*.[8]

Pragmatic analysis of successful organizations also provides the basis for sociologist Rosabeth Moss Kanter's book *The Change Masters—Corporate Entrepreneurs at Work*.[9] The book concentrates on examining how the better use of people in organizations can lead to necessary improved performance at a time when economic, social, and competitive demands are greater than ever before for organizations in the developed economies. Part of the research identified and matched, size by size and sector by sector, 44 organizations with 'progressive systems and practices with respect to people' with 38 organizations not identified as such. The performance of the 44 was significantly higher over a five-year period on bottom-line criteria such as return on equity, return on capital, and growth in earnings per share. The main theme of the book is that 'when a company innovates in practices which ensure that more kinds of people, at all levels, have the skills and opportunity to contribute to solving problems and suggesting ideas, then it is establishing the context for further innovations.' And in an interesting extension of the ideas outlined in the 'structure' component of the 7-S approach, Kanter outlines the need for a parallel structure to be created in order consciously to manage organizational innovation while at the same time preserving the basic systems and structures that allow the organization to function. The key tasks she outlines for this parallel structure are:

1. *Encouraging an atmosphere of pride*   By highlighting the achievements of the organization's own people, by applying innovations across internal boundaries, and by using innovators as 'consultants'
2. *Providing suitable vehicles*   By setting up organizational mechanisms that

allow innovatory proposals to be made and projects, especially cross-boundary projects, to be set up and managed successfully

3. *Improving lateral communication*   By instituting cross-functional links, exchange of people, joint project teams

4. *Cutting down layers of hierarchy*   By allowing people more direct access to their key resource needs, by pushing decision-making down the organization, and by creating 'diagonal slices' cutting across functions and levels to improve information flows

5. *Increasing and getting earlier information about company plans and projects*   By reducing secrecy and by getting greater involvement of those who have to carry the plans through prior to their final formulation

6. *Ensuring that the leadership understands that running the organization from the top can never be as effective as deploying as fully as possible the capacities of all the people in the organization*

All of this stream of thinking presupposes, however, that people at work actually want to be involved more fully with their job and with their organization. There are many managers who dispute this and whose point of view is that the majority of people at work are merely interested in their pay packet. Is there any evidence to the contrary?

What employees want

The philosophical differences between people with an open and optimistic view of human nature and those with a rather pessimistic and authoritarian view go back at least to Socrates and Plato. But only in the last 50 years have systematic studies of people at work in organizations set out to determine which approach is most effective for the people concerned. A large number of social scientists have addressed this question. Mayo,[10] in his commentary on the Hawthorne experiments, identified the importance of the working group rather than the individual and described how an open and consultative relationship led to a considerable number of improvements in work organization and output. McGregor,[11] in his Theory X and Theory Y analysis, called Maslow's[12] hierarchy of human needs into play as part of the evidence to demonstrate that work can be a source of satisfaction, that people can strive to attain organizational objectives, that rewards at work are not restricted to the financial, that people enjoy responsibility, that the ability to solve organizational problems is widely distributed among people at work, and that the potentials of the average human being at work are only partially utilized. At the same time as McGregor was developing the Theory X and Theory Y approach, Herzberg[13] was examining the motivation of people at work and coming to several important conclusions. The first was that underlying job attitudes appear to be fairly universal, and the main thing that makes, say, hourly paid workers different from managers is the actual day-to-day experiences they have at work. The second was that human needs at work can be broadly split into two: the hygiene or maintenance factors and the motivating factors. The hygiene factors include questions of pay, working conditions, job security, status, company policy, and administration and supervision. By and large, these factors contribute to dissatisfaction at work but are not intrinsic motivators. The motivators are achievement, recognition, responsibility, and the actual work itself. Herzberg refers to Jung, Maslow, and others and to how their work in personality theory relates to the motivating-hygiene theory.

Maslow, in developing his theory of human motivation, set out five main levels of need: the basic physiological needs, such as food and drink; the safety needs, such as security and freedom from fear; belonging needs, such as a place in the group or the family; esteem needs, such as feelings of competence and achievement and also recognition and appreciation; and finally, self-actualization or self-fulfilment, where people are developing the full use and exploitation of their talents and capabilities. Maslow was very aware of the dangers of approaching his model naively and carefully outlined many of the variations which occur owing to individual differences. More centrally, he also pointed out that

> [we] may have given the impression that these five sets of needs are somehow in such terms as the following: If one need is satisfied, then another emerges. This statement might give the false impression that a need must be satisfied 100 per cent before the next need emerges. In actual fact, most members of our society who are normal are partially satisfied in all their basic needs and partially unsatisfied at the same time. A more realistic description of the hierarchy would be in terms of decreasing percentages of satisfaction as we go up . . .

Communications have an important part to play in this model. Maslow argues that 'secrecy, censorship, dishonesty, blocking of communication threaten *all* the basic needs', and he suggests another hierarchy which parallels the basic needs, one where the lower level is knowledge and the higher level is understanding. This basic model has been adapted to reflect what people want out of their work by a number of people working in the employee communications area, including myself.[14] These adaptations (see Table 5.2) usually combine the top two categories because at work, which is only part of human life, the esteem needs and self-fulfilment needs are virtually inseparable.

The communication needs associated with each of these levels can be mapped on appropriately. Job instructions obviously go with level 1, an adequate procedure for handling grievances with level 2, consultation between the organization and the employees with level 3, an award scheme with level 4. It may be argued that some of these examples do not fall into the category of employee communications. However, from the point of view of the employee, all of these and many more activities are seen as communica-

Table 5.2

Level	Employee need	Typical requirements
Lower		
1	A job	Reasonable pay and working conditions
2	Security	A predictable and felt fair working environment
3	Belonging	A sense of identity at least with the work-group but more generally with the organization as a whole
4	Involvement and recognition	The opportunity to contribute one's own knowledge and skills and to have these rewarded
Higher		

tions. To the employee, what the organization does is much more important than what it says. And even how it says what it says is often more important than the apparent message conveyed by a cold analysis of the words themselves.

What the employee wants from an organization is a *mixture of words and actions* and a consistency between the two. This opens up into the whole field of employee experience at work and accordingly includes all the areas of organizational activity covered by the 7-S framework. It begins to sound as though employee communications is a superhuman task. Obviously it is not, but to be performed well it does demand an appreciation of how the needs of the organization and the needs of the employee come together. What is needed is an integrative holistic structure that takes into account the fact that, *unless* some needs are met reasonably well, activities aimed at answering other levels of need are not going to be effective.

Matching organizational needs with employee needs

Combining Maslow and Herzberg and adding in the idea of the predominant type of activity at each level gives a framework that is useful in examining existing communications practice in an organization. It is also helpful in diagnosing gaps or inconsistencies, and pointing the way to improvement. Furthermore, it fits with Pearson's description of organizational needs.

Table 5.3 shows how this can be done. The first column shows Pearson's description of organizational needs. The second column shows the adapted Maslow level relating human needs to the workplace. The third column describes the basic nature of the organization's 'words and actions' taking place at that level, and the fourth and fifth columns give examples of words and actions split into hygiene items and motivating items.

Table 5.3

Level	Organiza-tional need	Employee need	Predominant nature of activities	Typical examples of associated 'words and actions'	
				Hygiene	Motivating
Lower				Instructions,	Goals and
1	Output	A job	Top-down or telling	regulations, materials, or equipment necessary to do the job	objectives, basic 'reasons why' feedback on performance
2	Survival	Security	Bilateral or dealing	Bargaining, pay structures, grading systems, appraisal, grievance procedures	Benefits, training, single-status schemes, ombudsman schemes
3	Morale	Belonging	Bottom-up or listening	Consultation, formal or informal	An open management style, suggestion schemes, attitude surveys, 'open door' schemes
4	Leadership	Involve-ment and recognition	Mutual or working together	Profit-sharing, share ownership	An active 'involving' management style, information about the environment, customer needs, and the competitive position; joint action planning, quality circles, award schemes, using shared values/business goals as common basis for action
Higher					

What the model shows is that employee communications consists of a large number of things, and that getting employee communications right— that is, making it effective both for the organization and for its employees— means doing a number of them well and doing them well simultaneously. That is why many people working in this field are now talking of employee communications as an integral part of the management process.

One of several similar studies that I carried out in a wide range of organizations shows this hierarchical process at work (Fig. 5.1). The analysis was conducted among a homogeneous group of workpeople. It is worth noting that, even in the worst case (A), there is still a proportion of people feeling positively involved with the organization. Indeed, the first four columns show how little you have to do to get comparatively high levels of involvement. It is also significant that wide variations in employee perceptions of what management might think are standard common systems not

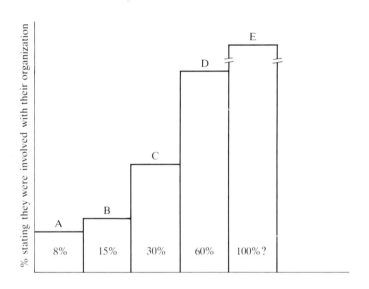

Figure 5.1   Building involvement

A = *dissatisfied* with pay, conditions, job security, knowledge of job objectives
B = *dissatisfied* with pay, conditions and job security; *satisfied* with knowledge of
     job objectives
C = *satisfied* with pay, conditions, job security, knowledge of job objectives;
     dissatisfied with communications from management
D = *satisfied* with all the above
E = The other 40% is going to be gained mainly from level 3 and level 4
     activities

only exist, but significantly affect employee attitudes to their organization overall. For instance, in the case given above, people with identical terms and conditions and job security in fact had widely differing perceptions about their own circumstances. In this organization there were no regular formal communication channels except for a joint consultative committee that had fallen into disrepair, meeting on an *ad hoc* basis and discussing rest-room and car parking issues, predominantly. It was therefore not surprising that further analysis of the results showed that what made the difference to people's perception of how the same set of conditions affected them was how good a communicator their immediate boss was. People who had an open and communicative manager were three to four times more likely to feel satisfied with their jobs and twice as likely to be committed to the organization.

Communications thus can be seen to play a vital role in the dynamics of the model outlined in Table 5.3. Not only is it important for actions not to *undermine* words, as has already been suggested: communication has a positive role to play in that words must be used to *underline* actions. It is no good putting in a new programme of equal status on pensions and sick-pay if you don't make sure that everyone knows that the change has been made, why it has been made, and how it is going to affect them.

Roger d'Aprix, who developed internal communications for many years in the Xerox Corporation before becoming a consultant, translates the Maslow-based model into a simple set of six questions split into two parts. These look at communications strictly from the employee perspective. The first three he calls the 'I' questions:

1. What's my job?
2. How am I doing?
3. Does anybody give a damn?

and he says people need adequate answers to these before they start wanting answers to the second three, which he calls the 'We' questions:

4. How are we doing?
5. How do we fit in to the whole?
6. How can I help?

Active involvement doesn't really come until people start asking question 6.

Who should communicate—manager or shop steward?

The traditional British view of the traditional British trade unionist was expressed by Ken Gill, at the time General Secretary of AUEW TASS: 'If employers are serious about improving communication in their firm, then the first step is to help trade unions communicate with their members.'[15] One can see his point, but that is surely the second step. The first has got to be to get managers to communicate with the people they manage. Thus, the proper formula should perhaps be: management have a duty to communicate with their employees, and unions have a duty to communicate with their members. In fact, taking the country as a whole, neither side is seen to be doing a particularly good job. This seems to have come as more of a shock to the unions than to management, perhaps because it is only recently that unions have begun to examine the issue as it applies to themselves. For example, unions have recently conducted surveys among their membership and have discovered dissatisfaction with communications between the average individual members and the leadership. The introduction of compulsory balloting has obviously given this gap much greater significance for many union leaders because the consequences of being out of touch with the membership and vice versa are potentially now much more damaging. However, even given this and the many other factors arising out of the high levels of structural unemployment and the labour law changes that have taken place since 1979, a 1985 survey of the 25 major unions in the UK showed that only just over half were doing anything about improving communications with their membership.[16] A study carried out at the same time analysed the quality of response made by 100 UK companies in reply to Section 1 of the Employment Act.[17] This obliges companies with more than 250 employees to include in their annual reports a statement describing the action taken during the previous year to introduce, maintain, or develop arrangements aimed at:

1. Providing employees systematically with information on matters of concern to them as employees
2. Consulting employees or their representatives on a regular basis so that employees' views can be taken into account in making decisions that are likely to affect their interests
3. Encouraging the involvement of employees in the company's performance through an employees' share scheme or by some other means
4. Achieving a common awareness on the part of all employees of the financial and economic factors affecting the performance of the company

The study concluded that only a minority of British companies appears to be committed to any systematic or reasonable programme for employee involvement. It quotes the Industrial Participation Society estimate that only 600–700 firms in the UK are committed to employee involvement to any extent; and it sounds the warning, quite justifiably, that unless further advances are made the current voluntary framework for consultation and involvement will be overcome by legislation, particularly through the employee participation aspects of the EEC Fifth Directive on Company Law. Finally, it warns against the unthought-through single and inadequate response to the challenge, such as those who for example [use] 'the wide distribution of the company report as an indication that the spirit of the legislation is generally being met. Exaggeration of this sort can be a dangerous tactic if the employees know that the report bears little relationship to reality.'

If it is the manager who should communicate with the organization's employees, there is a lot of evidence to suggest that not many organizations are pursuing this goal wholeheartedly.

Why don't organizations use their human resources more effectively?

A basic psychological inclination rules some organizations out immediately. Those run by people who at heart believe that management by fear is the most effective method will never be able to use their human resources to best effect. Attempts to improve communications in organizations that are run like this, in a distant, punitive style, will be seen as a charade. The use of language in such organizations is often a good indicator. You will read staff notices that begin 'It is imperative that . . .' You will find factory gates locked immediately after starting time so that late-comers are highlighted, or gates locked until finishing time to demonstrate company ownership of employee time, whatever wash-up agreements may be in force. Managers will feel embattled, some responding with a macho air, others by passivity. You will find an anthology of stories among employees instancing cases of double dealing, unfair dismissal, and favouritism in promotion or work assignments. You may even come across the extremities of double-think when, for example, a worker is told that his job has been 'saved' only to discover he has been made redundant. For these, there is no hope.

But there are other obstacles. One obstacle to progress often raised is the legacy of the past—the entrenched warfare between management and union, capital and labour. Certainly, there are ideologues on both sides. Of course, there are organizations with appalling histories of mismanagement by conveners, blunders by managers, and cynicism and lack of trust on all sides. These exist, but luckily they are decreasing in number, and not just because of failures, decline, or redundancy. In the Midlands motor industry Talbot and Jaguar have both fought back from the precipice by concentrating on the basics of making a good product at a reasonable price and building communications at all levels in the organization. Nor is there any widespread opposition to change. A recent study, for example, examined the introduction of new technology into 1200 factories in the UK:[18] in only 5 per cent was there any opposition from shop-floor or unions. The old truism that management gets the industrial relations it deserves is just as valid today as ever it was.

There is also the problem of our national culture. UMIST research has compared British and Japanese management attitudes and their perceptions of each other as managers.[19] The Japanese view of the British managers (an external mirror is worth a lot of self-diagnosis) is that typically they are conservative, authoritarian, take decisions without much consultation, protect the status quo, and have little respect for subordinates—hardly a recipe for success in providing the active and enthusiastic leadership required to reverse our poor overall performance. Corelli Barnett has chronicled the worst of our failings in this respect.[20] And it is not only the British, with their widely touted talent of muddling through: it is a problem of the Old World in competition with the New, and indeed of the Newest, the Pacific Basin countries such as Japan, Korea, Hong Kong, and Singapore.

An in-depth study of nine major French and Belgian companies with some 340 subsidiaries between them showed that only a few had begun to meet adequate corporate management criteria set out in the first three of the 7-Ss.[21] And without competence in strategy, structure, and systems there is little opportunity or possibility of succeeding in the last four of the 7-Ss—staff, style, skills, and shared values—where employee communication is centred. Apart from discovering numbers of top managers who actively opposed the principle of clearly defining corporate objectives in the first place, there were many others who were against making sure they were understood throughout the business because of the hostages this would give to fortune. Managers were found to be dominated by external social values (often class-biased) and extremely hesitant about subscribing to any organizational culture. My own experience as a consultant in over 50 British organizations has shown that embarrassment or vagueness (or both) is often the first reaction when you begin to talk about organizational values and strategies.

Yet there are organizations where this is not the case, where all the 7-Ss have been developed, and where they are in reasonable balance. Perhaps the most significant feature of these organizations is that none of them has looked for a single solution, a magical answer, or a quick fix. They have all realized that employee communication is part of a process and that this process takes time. These organizations include such diverse businesses as Unilever, Glaxo, Marks and Spencer, ICL, Jaguar, and the UK subsidiaries of IBM, 3M, and Johnson and Johnson. Current attempts to introduce large-scale culture change into the British civil service are going to take much longer than ministerial pronouncements and permanent secretary addresses to the troops would seem to anticipate.

How long does it take?

All of the case histories of successful organizations talk in terms of years rather than months being required to build a really fruitful pattern of communications based on knowledge, understanding, and involvement. This is because in many cases the clutter of years has to be cleared. In an excellent case history, Terry Mullins of Johnson and Johnson UK describes how it took 12 years from the time the company adopted a policy of moving towards single status in 1974 to the current comprehensive programme being in place in 1986.[22] During this time there have been many benefits. Productivity increased in real terms by 37 per cent, for example, between 1977 and 1984; 250 job titles have been reduced to 53; anomalies and differences in pay and conditions between groups or locations can now be addressed without prompting counterclaims; perhaps most important of all, the company is now able to adapt rapidly to change and has a body of employees who have shared in the development of the new culture. But to affect everyone at every level in the business took over a decade.

At ICL, even getting culture change among the management has taken five years. A series of articles describes the process, which was characterized by a number of false starts.[23] In this case the incoming management were from a different corporate culture—Texas Instruments—and ICL itself had been the product of a series of mergers in the 1960s and 1970s. Initiatives were launched to brief management on corporate strategy; a value statement, 'The ICL Way', was introduced in 1983, reinforced with company-wide 'Way Ahead' meetings; and these were followed by an 'Excellence' award scheme covering all employees. However, communications activities did not really begin to be fully effective until a major structure change was put in place introducing a series of market-oriented, decentralized, semi-autonomous business centres on top of the traditional functional organization, thus creating a matrix management. Furthermore, a major educational programme for the top 200 managers was introduced early in 1984 as the other key element in getting the necessary change. The training programme focused on industry issues and strategic concepts rather than on particular techniques. The result has been the creation of a common perception of problems and a common language at the top of the organization among management from different functions and different countries. The educational programme has been taken down the line to the next 1600 managers in a carefully structured programme.

A small part in reinforcing the process has been played by the house journal, *ICL News*. In 1984 this was rethought and relaunched, and much of its content now stands comparison with the leading computer trade publications. It tells people what is happening in the industry and what ICL is doing. Over the following two years its circulation, which is demand-led, went from under 22 000 to over 34 000. It was used to ensure that every employee was informed about important new developments. For example, on the day that the new mainframe Series 39 was launched in April 1985, every employee was able to read a 12-page supplement explaining how the product had been developed, what its market position was, and what the marketing and production requirements were.

The Nissan UK case presents a totally different scene: building a new organization on a greenfield site. The way it works out over the next few years will be a real test of all the thinking described in this chapter so far. Nissan's philosophy is simple. Peter Wickens, Director of Personnel, quoted it as follows:

> As a company we aim to build profitably the highest-quality car sold in Europe. We want to achieve the maximum possible customer satisfaction and to ensure the prosperity of the company and its staff. To assist in this, we aim to achieve mutual trust and co-operation between all people within the company and make NMUK a place where long-term job satisfaction can be achieved. . . .[24]

In order to achieve this end, Nissan is concentrating on line management, particularly on supervision. Wickens pointed out that they spent over 100 manager days in selecting their first 22 supervisors, who have the same standing as a professional engineer or buyer, financial controller, or personnel officer. Each supervisor is responsible for selecting the people who will work for him. At the start of every shift, every day, everyone in the company meets to talk together in his or her work-groups. There is no place for a monthly briefing group, which is a procedure many other UK organizations still regard as a dramatic innovation. Wickens makes the point that

> Communication is not about company newspapers, notice boards or the corporate video; it is about face-to-face talking together. Every employee has one hundred per cent responsibility for the quality of work they do. There are workshops where any employee can go to develop an idea for improving tooling or working methods.

A single union agreement has been made with the AEU which provides for complete mobility and flexibility, and at manager and white-collar levels there are no job descriptions and no complex job-evaluation structures. Also, there is single-status working:

> All the time we continue to treat a major section of our workforce as people who are not to be trusted, who have to clock in, who have worse sick-pay, shorter holidays, worse pensions, separate canteens, have to walk from a more distant car park: how can you expect those people to have commitment to the company?

So far it is early days, but there is one indication. Against a national absenteeism rate in manufacturing industry of 4.7 per cent, the rate at Nissan UK is 0.75 per cent.

In Johnson and Johnson's case, a successful organization moved systematically forward along a track it believed was necessary in order to develop a flexible workforce, able to meet the more rapid changes imposed by its increasingly more sophisticated marketplace. This economic or 'survival' reason for change was facilitated by the 'leadership' values in the organization, already well established in that section of their company 'credo' dealing with staff:

We are responsible to our employees, the men and women who work with us around the world. Everyone must be considered as an individual. We must respect their dignity and recognise their merit. They must have a sense of security in their jobs. Compensation must be fair and adequate, and working conditions clean, orderly, and safe. Employees must feel free to make suggestions or complaints. There must be equal opportunity for employment development and advancement for those qualified. We must provide competent management, and their actions must be just and ethical.

In the case of ICL, the survival needs in 1981 had been precisely that. The company was virtually bankrupt and was about to be sold cheap to an overseas competitor. A final rescue attempt was made and Dr Robb Willmot was appointed to do the job. The first key actions were to reduce inventory and employment at all levels and to put in better control systems and better management. Strategic planning was also a priority, but naturally enough this took a little longer to come through into action. When it did, it transformed the business from being a technically-driven, production-oriented maker of a broad range of computers to a customer-driven company based on identifying specific market sectors and providing what the customer needed. That was the imperative behind the ICL change programme, and it is why Johnson and Johnson's case differs so much from ICL's: in the former there was continued progression along an established path so that management was not a prime communications target; whereas in the latter there was the need for a virtually total change of direction, and this required a major management education programme and a statement of a set of corporate values in 'The ICL Way' as fundamentals.

The Nissan case illustrates the advantages of being able to begin at the beginning. Its progress should be watched with attention over the next decade to see if its underlying assumptions have a lasting validity implicit in the model shown in Table 5.3.

Johnson and Johnson's ability to use organizational culture, ICL's need to change it, and Nissan UK's recognition of the importance of getting it right from the very start indicate how central cultural concepts are to the way an organization works. However, culture can be a fairly loose concept and its analysis is sometimes based on little more than an examination of symbols such as how people dress or how the plant and offices are laid out, or whether people use christian names or surnames in meetings. But culture is at the heart of communication.

Culture and communication

Schein[25] suggests that communications failures in organizations often result because of very real differences in the way that people perceive things, because they belong to different cultural units, rather than because of lack of clarity, lack of frequency, or even just the generally normal defensive behaviour between one group and another. He also points out that organizations nearly always consist of a series of overlapping groups, each of which has its own view of the world. In some large organizations this is even positively encouraged, through a structure that manages units by financial controls alone and makes it plain that the way the desired results are achieved is entirely up to the unit. If these cultural differences are not perceived and taken into account, there is little chance of genuine corporate communication being achieved across an organization if this is required. Schein sets out a number of basic assumptions which lie at the heart of any culture:

1. *Relationship between the organization and the environment* For example, does the organization see itself as dominating and being able to change its environment, or does it see itself as needing to harmonize with its environment by finding, for instance, one or more suitable niches to occupy? ICL provides an example of a business moving from the dominant assumption to the harmonizing one. This required a major shift from a technical to a market organization with all its consequences for employee communications and training.

2. *The nature of reality and truth* For example, are experience and wisdom, however defined, taken as the valid basis for judgement, or is physical or intellectual proof necessary before a decision is arrived at? In the comparatively mature and reasonably stable circumstances of Johnson and Johnson, where a culture had been tested by time and had proved successful, it would appear that the case for harmonization was based more on wisdom than on a carefully calculated set of economic benefits.

   Do different sub-cultures work on different time-scales? For example, does 'soon' mean the same thing to the R & D executive as it does to a sales director? Are values absolute or relative, moral or pragmatic?

3. *What humanity is really like* The most important of this set of assumptions has already been explored in this chapter—whether workers are basically lazy and need continual control and are really motivated only by fear and by money, or whether they respond to freedom and challenge and can be motivated by praise and recognition. In practice, of course, individuals vary of themselves and also through circumstance. Nevertheless, or even because of this variety, organizations will tend towards one view or another, and this has important implications for the nature and style of communication. Nissan's reliance on the daily face-to-face meeting where anyone can raise any matter shows an important emphasis on individuals and their role in the organization.

4. *The nature of human activity* These assumptions deal with how things happen in an organization, with management style, and with the way decisions get made. At one end there is the action-oriented approach

which essentially says, if there is a problem, it needs fixing fast, and then focuses on task, efficiency, and discovery. At the other end there is a somewhat fatalistic acceptance of the status quo and a tendency to let things take their course in the belief that everything will work out all right in the end. In between the two is a more controlled approach, which spurns the impulsive, rejects the passive, and seeks achievement through rules, clearly defined roles, and mutual understanding. ICL in its corporate renewal demonstrates clearly the action-oriented approach in full drive—necessarily so, given the challenge.

5. *The nature of human relationships*   These are the assumptions about the proper way for people to relate to each other in order to make the group safe. For example, are co-operation, communication, and group working viewed as most effective, or is competitive individual accountability the watchword, or is the most importance given to membership of the founding family or the people in closest touch with the owning institutions? Depending on the answer, the organization will function quite differently, and this will extend through its systems, structure, and style.

The value to the communicator of consciously examining corporate culture, particularly if attempts are being made to change it, is that obstacles to understanding can be identified, likely resistances anticipated, and potentially damaging contradictions forestalled. Blake and Mouton[26] describe how a structured approach to a merger of two businesses with widely diverging cultures led to what the chief executive officer mainly concerned felt was a successful operation in six months instead of the normal six years. The virtue of the exercise lay mainly in getting the key people on either side to recognize their differences, articulate them, and work on the most fruitful reconciliation of the two.

Culture cannot be changed by communication, because communication is a vehicle through which culture expresses itself. Cultural change follows behavioural change, often quite slowly. Communication can help behavioural change—for example, by making sure that people know what the organization's objectives actually are. In IBM UK, for example, the singing of company songs may or may not take place, the wearing of dark suits, white shirts, and sober ties may or may not be encouraged; what is fundamental, however, is that everyone knows that the business is, *inter alia*, dedicated to being a low-cost producer, and that affects every aspect of IBM UK's activities. Communications are then used to back this up—in training, in the preparation and monitoring of the business plan, in line management communications, and in the mass media, such as the internal video programmes explaining performance. Perhaps this example would be better titled 'culture modification' rather than 'culture change'. The underlying IBM culture, overpoweringly described by Buck Rogers, for ten years vice-president of marketing, remains: 'The individual must be respected. The customer must be given the best possible service. Excellence must be pursued.'[27] Other concepts such as being a low-cost producer have been added, rather as amendments have been added to the US Founding Fathers' original Constitution.

Major cultural change perhaps takes place only at times of organizational crisis, often accompanied by changes in leadership. Strategy and structure are normally the key issues at these times, and it is the role of the communicator to make sure that people know what is happening and why and what is expected of them. The channels they choose and the tone they adopt will carry important messages about style, and therefore decisions in these areas must be made in the full awareness of the effects they will produce. It is no good closing a factory at the end of November, retaining only a tenth of the workforce, and the following week wishing everyone who is still employed a Merry Christmas, but these or similar incongruities happen! Communications can also help by making sure people in the organization know what the new desired behaviour is. It can help by showing examples, promoting new role models for people who are unsure about what is demanded of them. In British Airways over the last few years, massive change has taken place at the top, among middle management, in structure, in systems, and in training. The purpose of this has been to focus attention on 'putting the customer first'. A small but important role in this has been played by BA's house journal; in every issue there are one or two news reports of staff who have gone out of their way to provide that extra effort or service that delivers customer satisfaction. In ICL the 'Excellence' award scheme highlights those people who are nominated by their peers for an extra-special contribution. In the early 1980s the Post Office used the case history approach to improve performance among its supervisory staff using a special bulletin and video. One of the ideas that came forward from this scheme was so successful that it was taken up nationally and has made a significant contribution to improving the delivery times on business mail. That was an accidental but fruitful outcome not of a suggestion scheme, but of a conscious decision to provide role models which exemplify desired culture values in action.

There are obviously a great number of ways in which communications can help organizations and the people in them. Enough has been said in this chapter about the requirement for sufficient congruity between strategy, structure, systems, style, staff, and even skills to exist before shared values can begin to be effective. Given that enough attention is being paid to this, how should communications be managed?

Managing employee communications

The current movement to improve employee communications was triggered by the build-up of pressures that led to the establishment of the Bullock Commission, which reported in 1977. It was given impetus by the Health and Safety at Work Act 1974, the Industry Act 1975, and the Employment Protection Act 1975 and its subsequent Code of Practice on disclosure of information issued by ACAS. Interest was maintained by the consultative document, *The Future of the Company Reports* (1977) and by the White Paper on *Industrial Democracy* (1978). Since then, subsequent industrial relations legislation has tended to encourage employer practice rather than establish employee rights; however, the underlying onward movement continues.

There is little doubt that the 1970s saw the greatest peacetime shift towards employee communications since the beginning of the Industrial Revolution. A 1980 survey indicated that, although in 1968 less than 5 per cent of UK organizations had a formal policy on employee communications, by 1979 this had grown to 34 per cent.[28]

For a large number of organizations during the last decade, employee communications was seen to consist of activities that, if indulged in, were probably going to do some good. This led to a wide range of initiatives. New house newspapers sprang up. The financial report to employees became an overnight success, and managements vied with each other to produce award-winning oversimplications of their company report for shareholders. Bemused groups of employees found themselves sitting in semi-darkened rooms being addressed on video by a strange man claiming to be their chairman or managing director, laboriously reading his lines off a primitive autocue. Responsibility for managing communication was often diffused. In some, the finance director claimed the Employee Report, personnel the video and its accompanying presentations, and marketing the house journal.

Other organizations took the path of carefully managed development. Rowntree Mackintosh provides a good example of the latter. This is a major public limited company with world-wide operations and with some 13 000 employed in the confectionery division, the largest part of the UK operation. The division is strongly unionized, with over 90 per cent membership, and has four main bargaining groups: factory process workers, represented by three manual worker unions; the craft workers; clerical and technical staff, represented by APEX and TASS; and the sales force, represented by a certified independent staff association. In the mid-1970s there was a variety of employee communications in place, but there was no one person responsible, and no overall plan. Prompted by the CBI study, *Priorities for In-company Communications*,[29] the company began a programme of developing its employee communications policy and practice. It commissioned a survey comparing two factories, Fawdon and Norwich, which had two different communications patterns. The survey looked at types of information required and sources of information used. There were large variations between the two in terms of knowledge, satisfaction and sources used. The conclusion was that an employee relations manager should be appointed to have overall responsibility for communications. This has included development of the consultative arrangements originally instituted in 1919; the installation throughout the business of regular discussions down the line through a team briefing process which makes sure that local issues are properly dealt with; a complete overhaul of the company newspaper and the introduction of five local editions on a regular monthly basis; the introduction of an annual report for employees to back up the twice-yearly presentations on the state of the business; a revision to and extension of the profit-sharing scheme; and the introduction of quality circles. In the view of the management, the steady development of an integrated communications policy and plan have built up understanding, trust, and a greater level of involvement within the business.

The fact that in this case the employee relations manager reported to the personnel director is immaterial. In other organizations there are people in similar roles reporting to the chief executive or the public affairs director. The important thing is that one person is given responsibility and resources for employee communications. Until this happens, and that person's responsibilities extend beyond the provision of the newspaper, the video, or the message on the noticeboard, the organization concerned will not be able to do an adequate job in communicating with its employees.

There is probably only one rule for managing employee communications, and that is to treat it as an important management process in its own right. Develop it in terms of strategy, structure, systems, staff, style, and skills, and do this in the light of the current and desired shared value system of the organization. The employee communications manager should be just as involved as any other key functional head at the planning stages of any important organizational change or development, product or service innovation, strategic acquisition, or public policy pronouncement. Sadly, the broader role of employee communications usually comes to mind only when there are questions of closure or redundancy—and sometimes not even then.

Strategies

Most organizations who have developed strategies for employee communications have more than one objective in mind. Employers, like employees, are not completely single-minded. For example, a firm may wish to improve communications partly in order to head off compulsory measures which may be introduced under the Common Market Fifth Directive; partly in order to demonstrate to customers, competitors, and politicians, and also to the firm itself, that its organization is forward-looking and socially responsible; and partly in order to gain fuller commitment and involvement from the employees in order to achieve improved quality, customer service, and productivity. This may sound cynical, but there is nothing wrong with these motives, which often exist alongside deeply held moral beliefs about justice and equality. Organizations are complex and varied, and this must be taken into account.

The relevant communications strategy for a particular organization will depend on its overall strategy. The McGill Strategic Audit typology[30] indicates the main types of organization or organizational situation likely to be encountered. Most of these have two manifestations, the more successful and the less successful. These are:

1. (a) *The entrepreneurial conglomerate*, usually run by a powerful figure committed to expansion and with clear goals and strategies
   (b) *The impulsive organization*, often taking on new challenges without properly thinking them through
2. (a) *The dominant firm*, old established and a leader in its market
   (b) *The stagnant bureaucracy*, an organization that has gone to sleep
3. (a) *The giant attacked*, a large organization having to face a hostile environment
   (b) *The headless giant*, a conservative organization living on the past with little leadership
4.   *The adaptive organization*, alert to its environment, responsive to new demands, and able to build on its strengths.

The employee communications strategy will be different in each of the seven types listed above. It may well be less different in the case of organizations seeking to move from any of the first six towards type 4, the adaptive organization. In this instance the initial emphasis, as the ICL case demonstrated so clearly, must be on management communications and education and training.

In the cases of types 1(b), 2(b), and 3(b), the communications strategy will be doomed by the organizational environment. There may well be employee communications activity, but it will be a case of 'going through the motions' because whatever is said will fall on ears that are cynical and uninvolved in the main. The optimum employee communications strategy in these cases is to do as little as possible, concentrating on 'defensive' communications that try to stop things getting worse.

The communications strategy for a type 1(a) organization will tend towards top-down communication related to the 'words and actions' shown at level 1 in Table 5.3; communication of objectives, 'reason why' type information, and performance feedback. The predominant cultural values will tend to be those concerned with ideas of being able to dominate the environment and being action-oriented, with an emphasis on task and efficiency. A good description of the problems and opportunities facing a communicator in this situation is provided by Handy, who describes the 'power' culture.[31] In this culture, influence is exercised through a small number of key individuals who are trusted by the leader. Decision-making is rapid and comparatively informal. Unless the employee communications process is plugged into this network and has built a capacity for quick and often imaginative reaction, it will find itself regarded as a necessary evil rather than as an integral and important contributor to organizational effectiveness.

For a type 2(a) organization, the communications strategy will concentrate more on the level 2 activities shown in Table 5.3—those concerned with morale, such as consultation and attitude surveys—and the predominant cultural values will be based on a mix of the firm's assumption that it can dominate its environment and its belief in the importance of experiential wisdom. In Handy's terms, this will be a role culture, where a 'steady state' is assumed to be the norm; where there is considerable emphasis on functional responsibility within a series of units such as production, finance, purchasing, sales, marketing, and personnel; and where integration is usually achieved at the executive board level. Risks are usually avoided; change is made through committee structures and established procedures and is slow.

Employee communications in this environment at its best will be worthy and at its worst will be buried by paperwork. Imagination and innovation will stand little or no chance.

A type 3(a) organization, the giant attacked, will be concerned with developing via 'words and actions' shown in level 4 of Table 5.3. It will focus on making explicit shared values probably taken for granted hitherto, and it will provide employees with information about its environment, in particular the threats that are being posed and their likely consequences. Its cultural characteristics will be those obtaining before the attack began. For organizations that successfully resist the attack, the experience may lead to quite major changes towards becoming an adaptive organization. En route, it may well demonstrate an increase of elements of Handy's 'power' culture and also characteristics of his 'task' culture. In the 'task' culture all the emphasis is on getting things done through bringing teams together to solve problems; the ability of the individual to contribute is more important than role or status. Employee communications in this situation is crucial, because the way in which it is handled at a time when the only rule is effectiveness will determine its subsequent role when the organization emerges from attack.

Type 4 adaptive organizations have employee communications strategies covering the full range of 'words and actions' set out in Table 5.3. In particular, they will concentrate on focusing attention on the external world.

They will make people aware of competitive pressures and the organization's required competitive advantages. They will set out to ensure that markets and customers figure large in communications, that information about technology is presented in the context of applications and benefits, and that issues of quality and value and service are highlighted.

STRUCTURES

The first and fundamental need is to locate responsibility for employee communications in one place. In a small organization this may involve just one person at one level. In a large organization, a hierarchy of people related to the structure of the organization is required. In some firms these may be full-time posts, in others it may form part of a job in either a line or staff function. The responsibility is for making sure that employee communications is planned and resourced and that it is monitored, supported, and developed. It is not a responsibility for carrying out the communication: that must always be the primary responsibility of line management. In this task the employee communications manager will work closely with personnel management, public affairs management, and general management.

Some organizations differentiate between communicating with management and communicating with the rest of the employees. This is perfectly acceptable as long as there is one central point where both come together. The differentiation is usually made in large organizations where there is a strong emphasis on management development and where corporate-level communications with employees are handled predominantly through mass media such as newspapers, videos, letters from the chairman, news flashes for notice boards, and so on, and where unit-level communication is handled by unit-level management. In these cases the job for the corporate employee communications manager is to ensure that enough corporate information reaches far enough down the line in the operating units. In practice, this structuring often leads to an unsatisfactory situation where there is a lack of clarity about the role of the manager in the operating unit in so far as employee communications is concerned. This comes about where there is inadequate definition of the boundary between how a manager is being developed as a manager, in which role his duty to communicate is but a part, and his responsibility to be the central and effective focus of the corporate communications process reaching all employees. Insistence on making sure that the manager actively communicates can be resisted by those responsible for organization development because they fear encroachment on individual autonomous personal or unit growth. This type of argument is not allowed where the organization's financial resources are at stake. The same imperative should apply to human resources.

Another area where effectiveness can be lost is in the parallel structure activities of the organization as a whole. It is quite possible to find production spearheading a quality involvement campaign while personnel are carrying out a drive on timekeeping and absenteeism and marketing are launching a new product or service to the public which will make further demands on employees. Conflicting demands on the organization are a fact of life and are inescapable. The smart organization, however, sets out to manage them rather than just let them happen. The Post Office, for example, set up an internal communications committee which met quarterly and reviewed all major internal communications initiatives, their objectives, and their costs, timing, and methods. All the main sectors of the business were represented. The administration for the committee was provided by personnel department. General Motors in the UK runs a similar operation under the aegis of the Public Affairs Committee.

SYSTEMS

The first priority for any employee communications activity is for it to relate to the mainstream of the organization. Employee communications is all about running the organization effectively. This means that the basic systems of the organization itself should at least be reviewed for their *communications* as opposed to their *control* effectiveness. Probably the two most central of these are the planning and review system and the appraisal system.

There are now few organizations that do not have a planning process in place. This will usually consist of a 12-month budget and a longer-term forecast stretching to a time horizon judged suitable for the type of organization it is. Progress against budget will be reviewed, probably on a monthly basis, and the budget itself may be subject to revision, probably quarterly. The preparation of the budget and the forecast usually begins several months prior to the commencement of the next annual period and is the subject of meetings and an exchange of views and information. Experience in a large number of organizations has demonstrated that often no attention whatsoever is paid to the provision of information about corporate assumptions, goals, objectives, strategies, or values during these processes, other than narrow financial targets. This is more than a wasted opportunity: it is detrimental to the effective performance of the organization in both the short and the longer term. Similarly, in the performance review process that probably takes place monthly, too often communication is focused on imaginative rationalizations about why things turned out the way they did instead of going back to basics and examining what should have happened and what lessons could be learned if it did or did not. These meetings are an important potential channel for a two-way flow of new corporate information. They are rarely perceived as such. And the idea of lateral transmission of lessons learned is even rarer: a great pity, because the adaptive organization needs as much information from its environment as it can get.

The appraisal system is equally important, because that too is based, or should be based, on the specification of objectives and a review of performance against those objectives at the level of the individual. The most recent IPM survey suggests a resurgence of interest in appraisal and attributes this probably to a need for greater efficiency and productivity because of the marked increase in schemes including performance objectives—up to 81 per cent in 1985 from 57 per cent in 1977.[32] The survey also, interestingly, shows a strong upsurge in schemes including first-line supervision (from 60 to 78 per cent), clerical staff (from 45 to 66 per cent), and manual workers (from 2 to 24 per cent). It is vital for the organization that its corporate goals are clearly understood and successfully translated into individual objectives during this process. Again, experience in a wide range of organizations suggests that this is the exception rather than the rule.

Other mainstream systems that should be scrutinized from a point of view of their corporate communications effectiveness are recruitment, induction, and training. Management training is obviously of particular importance.

As far as the systems and procedures required for the employee communications process itself are concerned, these follow normal organizational patterns. Thus, there should be a statement of objectives, a plan for carrying out those objectives, an allocation of resources to the plan, and a means of measuring performance against plan. Such systems are extremely rare in the employee communications arena, even among those organizations that have developed an employee communications strategy and structure.

STYLE

The way an organization communicates, or fails to communicate, with its employees is probably the most important communication of all. Communication that is irregular and associated with bad news tells just as clear a story as Nissan's daily discussions between a work-group and their manager. Some organizations pay an incredible amount of attention to minor points of style, such as insisting that the house newspaper should be printed on cheap-looking paper so that the employees will not think that money is being wasted on it, while simultaneously dooming it to irregular appearance depending on the availability and willingness of top executives to clear the copy. The watchwords for style in any employee communications are simplicity (but not condescension), regularity, honesty, and relevance. Given these, the quality of the paper or the expensiveness of the video production fade into insignificance.

Where style is most important is of course in the most vital communication channel of all: line management. Research conducted by myself and others in over 20 organizations shows that management style correlates very closely with levels of commitment, trust, involvement, and job satisfaction among employees. It is, as is so often the case in the social sciences, difficult absolutely to prove a causal relationship. However, the evidence begins to look at least as convincing as that which associates the heavy smoking of cigarettes with the likelihood of getting lung cancer. Typically, we find, within a single level of employees in a single part of an organization, that people managed by someone who tells them what their objectives are, how these fit into broader corporate goals, asks their help in achieving them, and gives them feedback on how they are getting on are at least *twice* as committed to the organization and *four* times more satisfied with their job than those who are managed by people who keep their distance.

Style in employee communications is ultimately resolved as the sum of the individual styles of the managers in the organization. Whoever is responsible for employee communications cannot escape that inevitability. Hence the need for their involvement with management development and training.

STAFF

Although the qualities of the people needed to do a good job in the employee communications function will obviously vary according to the type of organization, there are certain basic requirements. Some of these are common to all people successful in staff as opposed to line functions—the ability to persuade rather than command, to prepare and work to a budgeted plan, to work in teams, to have the confidence both of top management and of those below, to be trusted, professional, and expert. There are others, however, that are more role-specific.

Staff in the employee communications function should have a broad understanding of the economy and their organization's place in it. They should know the type of organization it is and the implications of this for what should be communicated and how. They should be able to express themselves with clarity both verbally and visually. They should be able to empathize with their audience. They should understand how their organization works, and be able not only to detect what the key business systems are but to understand how they could make helpful organizational communication inputs into these systems. They should equally have an understanding of external communications, especially media relations, because a great deal of information received by employees arrives through these sources. They must obviously have an understanding and a feel for industrial relations. This is asking a lot, but equally, a lot is necessary if the job is to be done effectively.

There is no reason why staff in employee communications work should not be rewarded according to the success they have in reaching their objectives, except for the fact that few organizations have such objectives. Their development and training should be twofold: internally as part of the management development process, and externally in specific areas of professional skill.

SKILLS

The management and personal skills required in employee communications are outlined in the preceding section. Over and above these are specific technical skills necessary for the employee communications function and for the people working within it. These divide into three main areas:

1. *Providing the resource for those communications originated centrally* (for example, producing slides, newsletters, videos, newspapers, an electronic news service, intelligible booklets on the pension scheme, the share scheme, and so on). This resource can be built into the function if the volume demands, or it can be bought out, depending on the volume and frequency. It should also be available as a centre of knowledge to other people in the organization who have the need to produce their own materials. In a sense, the skills needed here will be analogous to those required by the advertising and marketing function, but they are differentiated because of the different audience needs. Advertising and marketing are oriented primarily towards individual needs, whereas the employee communications audience requires an orientation towards the way *groups* think and feel. In my experience, this difference provides major credibility problems when it is not recognized. The closest parallel with advertising and marketing skills comes when the employee communications function is involved with a campaign to achieve a specific goal. This is very often an outcome of the parallel organization at work. For example, a major effort may be launched to improve product quality or customer service, or a sudden co-ordinated effort may be required to enlist employee support in resisting an unwelcome take-over bid. The role of employee communications in these circumstances is to consider available channels, to decide which is most suitable for what purposes, and even to create new channels if necessary, and to plan, co-ordinate, and execute the flow of information accordingly, sometimes at high pressure and in a short period of time.

2. *Understanding and being able to improve the quality of face-to-face communication within the organization* This encompasses a knowledge of group behaviour, of leadership skills, of how to handle meetings and how to listen, of counselling, of the two-way nature of communication, of making presentations and involving people, of the processes of group behaviour, of consultation, of the nature of task groups, and of quality circles. The employee communications function should be aware of all

these skill areas and should be able to provide assistance to the organization either by itself or in association with the firm's training function or external experts. It should be able also to diagnose weaknesses in these areas and take initiatives to correct them.

3. *Being able to provide a measurement of the success or otherwise of employee communication activity* This can cover a range of approaches. For example, straightforward behavioural measures can be used. If a share scheme is being offered, then the take-up rate of the offer compared with take-up rates of similar offers in other organizations can be used as a measure. Another measure is the use of the survey. Surveys can be used to measure knowledge, understanding, and attitudes, and they can also be used to find out what people's experience is. Furthermore, these four components can be linked to examine the reasons behind the results obtained. It has been found, for example, that an understanding of a presentation of company results and of their relationship to an individual's own job is positively linked to the length of the presentation and the amount of subsequent discussion.

If the employee communications function is not seen as one of the natural places to turn for these skills, if it is not continually keeping itself up to date with developments in these fields, then it is doing less than the job demanded of it.

SHARED VALUES

Shared values are the essence of employee communications. To reiterate the opening sentences of this chapter, 'Employee communication is all about running the organization effectively. It is about making sure people know what needs to be done, understand why it's necessary, feel committed to achieving it, and have a chance to use their own knowledge and skills to do it better if possible.'

The employee communications function has an important role to play in this process. To do it well, however, it must be seen as a true function in its own right and must be managed accordingly.

Notes

1. T. J. Peters and R. H. Waterman, Jr, *In Search of Excellence* (Harper and Row, New York, 1982).
2. V. Stewart and A. Stewart, *Tomorrow's Men Today* (IPM/IMS, London, 1976).
3. K. Legge and E. Mumford, *Designing Organisations for Satisfaction and Efficiency* (Gower Press, Farnborough, Hants., 1978).
4. A. J. Pearson, *Setting Corporate Objectives as a Basis For Action* (National Development and Management Foundation of South Africa, Johannesburg, 1980).

5. A. H. Maslow, *Motivation and Personality*, 2nd edn (Harper and Row, New York, 1970).
6. R. H. Waterman, Jr, T. J. Peters, and J. R. Phillips, 'Structure is not Organisation', *Business Horizons*, School of Business at Indiana University (June 1980).
7. Peters and Waterman, *In Search of Excellence*.
8. T. J. Peters and N. Austin *A Passion for Excellence—The Leadership Difference* (Collins, London, 1985).
9. R. M. Kanter, *The Change Masters—Corporate Entrepreneurs at Work* (Unwin Paperbacks, London, 1985).
10. E. Mayo, *The Social Problems of an Industrial Civilisation* (Routledge, London, 1949).
11. D. McGregor, *The Human Side of Enterprise* (McGraw-Hill, Maidenhead, 1960).
12. Maslow, *Motivation and Personality*.
13. F. Herzberg, *Work and the Nature of Man* (Staples Press, London, 1968).
14. M. Arnott, Opening address at CBI Conference on Employee Communication, January 1986 (Charles Barker, London, 1986).
15. K. Gill, *Industrial Society*, 62 (May–June 1986).
16. *Survey of Industrial Relations and Employee Communications* (EPIC, London, 1985).
17. *Employee Communications—A Study of Section 1 of the Employment Act 1982 in Operation* (Institute of Directors, London, 1985).
18. J. Northcott, *Micro Electronics in Industry* (Policy Studies Institute, London, 1986).
19. R. Miyajina, 'Comparative Study of Managerial Values between the British and the Japanese' (UMIST, Manchester, to be published).
20. C. Barnett, *The Audit of War* (Macmillan, London, 1986).
21. P. de Woot, *Le Management stratégique des groupes industriels* (Economica, Paris, 1984).
22. T. Mullins, 'Harmonisation, the Benefits and the Lessons', *Personnel Management* (March 1986).
23. C. Lorenz, 'Corporate Renewal', *Financial Times* (12, 14, and 16 May 1986).
24. P. Wickens, CBI conference on the Character of the Company, June 1986.
25. E. H. Schein, *Organisational Culture and Leadership* (Jossey Bass, London, 1985).
26. R. R. Blake and J. S. Mouton, *Solving Costly Organisational Conflicts: Achieving Intergroup Trust, Co-operation and Teamwork* (Jossey Bass, London, 1984).
27. B. Rogers, *The IBM Way* (Harper and Row, London, 1986).
28. M. Arnott, C. Minton, and M. Wilders, *Employee Communications in the 1980's* (Charles Barker, London, 1980).
29. M. Brandon and M. Arnott, *Priorities for In-company Communication* (CBI, London, 1976).
30. D. Miller, P. Friesen, and Kets de Vries, *The Strategic Audit*, Working Paper no. 7644 (McGill University, 1976).
31. C. Handy, *Understanding Organisations* (Penguin, Harmondsworth, 1976).
32. P. Long, *Performance Appraisal Revisited* (IPM, London, 1986).

6.

LOCAL COMMUNITY PUBLIC RELATIONS

John W. Hackett

A volume on infectious diseases will set out the symptoms, diagnosis, prognosis, and treatment of a disease and any likely complications. Unfortunately, there is no such simple method of dealing with community public relations because every opportunity or activity is based on an infinitely variable set of parameters (some of which may well affect the blood pressure, but that is purely a side-effect). No two organizations are the same; their objectives, structure, products, and/or services vary, as does their status within their environment.

Objectives

For this reason, it is not practical to lay down ground rules for handling specific situations. With luck, you will never be called upon to deal with the problems of contaminated effluent or carcinogenic compounds. (I have had to deal with both, although not simultaneously.) How then does one learn to handle community relations programmes effectively, and how do we learn from the experiences of the past? First, we must be clear what we mean by corporate, and more specifically community, public relations. Every organization finds its equilibrium within the environment in which it resides, in the same way that an individual co-exists within a family unit. For a variety of reasons, the relationship may be positive, friendly, and creative, or it may deteriorate into mere acceptance on sufferance or—at worst—total rejection.

There are undoubtedly advantages to be gained from an awareness of the sensitivity of local response to a company. The organization is not a lifeless commodity, but a living entity; employees have to be found, nurtured, and from time to time replaced. During recruitment, internal PR programmes come into effect through literature, interviews, and induction courses; but once the recruit is a fully fledged member of the team, communication has really only just begun, and the long period of assurance and reassurance can be set in train. This should include the provision of advance information about corporate projects such as charitable involvement, so that staff are the first to know what is going on—rather than the last. Then they can and will show pride in their collective involvement, rather than pique at not being told.

Every enterprise is inevitably brought into direct contact with all facets of life: national and local government, public services, the press, the church, philanthropic institutions, the financial community, and many, many others. Then there are the accidental as distinct from the formal contacts, which can prove to be extremely useful. The interface with these groups is what community relations seeks to establish and maintain.

A few years ago my own company was embarking on an important venture in Western Australia, and, having met the Australian High Commissioner formally, I was invited to a reception at Australia House in London to meet the Lord Mayor of London. This fortuitous meeting led to the Lord Mayor visiting Hereford (where the company is based) and the establishment of valuable links, both commercial and social, between my company, the City of London, and the Western Australian Government. It was an opportunity not sought, but recognized and immediately used to advantage.

This leads to the conclusion that a detailed awareness of one's own organization—its objectives, its strategy, and its marketplace—is the best possible starting point for planning and exploiting community PR opportunities, for without such knowledge creative ideas may well be missed. Not a day goes by without the chance of strengthening the links between an organization and its local community.

Elsewhere in this book press relations is analysed in detail, but here I would like to stress the key role that provincial newspapers play in all community relations, making a close personal liaison with the editors, journalists, and photographers as well as the advertising staff of local papers of major importance. Not every company news release will find its way into the national press, yet a story, for example, about new plant and machinery affecting employment levels, is of considerable interest in the area from which the majority of the workforce is recruited. It goes without saying that detailed knowledge of the trade press and specialist media is also extremely important. Nor can the value of personal contact be overemphasized; if as a company PRO you have recently walked round your factory with the local news editor, his response to your next news release or telephone call will be altogether different than if it has been a year since you last met.

Community public relations is all about communicating. The success of any enterprise can be achieved only if every employee understands and supports the objectives that he and the enterprise are striving to reach. It follows that, the more widely those objectives are known and understood, the greater the degree of commitment there will be from all those involved, both within and without. If it can be demonstrated that such lines of communication do indeed exist, then one of the first principles of social responsibility has been established.

A company is, in many respects, like a warship. Its size is variable, but its purpose and sense of direction are, or should be, clearly defined. It is manned by a crew with a wide range of skills, and it needs to be self-sufficient and successful within its chosen area of operation. But 'no man is an island'; our warship has to be provisioned, and it needs a home base where the ship's company are welcome and feel at home. The community that supports an enterprise is in a similar position. It supplies many of the provisions— material, social, and spiritual—and it is a haven in stormy weather. This leads to a mutual pride in achievement which is a two-way process, constantly needing attention; this attention can be achieved through the implementation of a community PR strategy that is both flexible and sensitive.

Opinion formers

The words 'opinion formers' are somewhat ambiguous in that they seem to imbue those to whom they are applied with some special authority. In fact, the opinions such people hold will be as good—or as bad—as the information they are given, and their ability to comprehend its value. We all have opinions: objective, subjective, prejudiced, cynical, or even misconceived. The relationship we have with any particular group will vary enormously; with some it will entail almost daily contact, with others, infrequent association; but it will always be dynamic, because no business ever stands still.

In listing some key opinion formers, it must be left to each individual enterprise to establish what its relationship with some or all of them should be, and at what level. The church, for example, can help in the celebration of corporate anniversaries as well as in remembering past servants of the company, and in assisting individuals in times of personal celebration or crisis. Some typical groups that may be considered in drawing up any local community PR plan include:

- Church: all denominations
- Government: national, including EEC; local councils and councillors; county, city and parish councils
- Media: national, local, and trade press; radio/TV; COI and overseas
- Education: universities and colleges of further education; schools; special schools (blind, disabled, etc.)
- Medical: hospitals; homes; research institutes
- Chamber of commerce: representing retail outlets, banks, building societies, etc.
- The law: including courts, lawyers, JPs, probation service and prisons, police

- The arts: museums, music, festivals, fetes, societies
- Sport: sporting events and provision of facilities

Some other areas to be considered include tourism; the armed forces; special local traditions, characters, and celebrities; and finally, the provision of a speakers' panel comprising people with both knowledge of the company and the ability to speak effectively, keeping opinion formers informed through Rotary, Round Table, and similar local groups.

Top management

It is usually easier for senior management to become involved in the planning of community-related functions than, for example, for those on the shop-floor; but, although there are some functions at which the chairman or chief executive should be the ambassador, at others it may be more appropriate to see the accountant or shop steward. If these responsibilities are shared, then the generation of ideas for corporate involvement will come from a far wider cross-section of the company, and thus will more accurately represent the corporate philosophy.

Local events

It should not be difficult to suggest a number of worthwhile events which will underline or bring about the positive, friendly, and creative relationships with the community at large referred to earlier. There are, for example, always opportunities to support the arts, either through direct sponsorship or through involvement in festivals, fetes, and exhibitions of all kinds. Employees will be members of many of the local societies, and when they see practical help coming from their own organization they will take a special pride and interest in their involvement.

Some years ago I was invited to be one of the industrial representatives on the Board of Governors of the Hereford College of Art and Design. As a result, I was able to instigate an annual lecture, known as the Bulmer Lecture, to be given by a respected personality within the sphere of art and design education. From modest beginnings some five years ago, this lecture has now become one of the highlights of the academic calendar, and attracts speakers of the highest calibre. As a result, the company name is linked in this way with the arts and specifically with the local college, demonstrating a willingness to become involved in something of intrinsic value not directly connected with the business but of value and interest to the community.

Such participation, as long as it is effectively communicated, cannot help but have a positive effect on employees, on the local community, and on future recruits, because it demonstrates not only that the company is successful but that it has a heart. Naturally, in times of restraint one does not go out to squander hard-earned profits on peripheral causes—the protection of jobs is the top priority—but each company must have a measure of in-built philanthropy which is stimulated out of a wish to be a good and responsible citizen, and not for the possible publicity value that could result.

It is the intangible in public relations that is both intriguing and frustrating. As has been said, no two opportunities are the same or have similar solutions, which is why so many articles and books on PR lack substance; it would be quite impossible to enumerate everything. But having, through training and experience, learned the basic skills of communicating, then the opportunities will be recognized and the fun can begin. The value of an event, be it a royal visit or a darts match, can be assessed and planned. Every detail must be thought through, tested, and rehearsed until nothing has been overlooked. The day dawns and you get caught up in the momentum of it all. Later come the post mortems—and the bills.

In a recent review of a book on public relations, the reviewer wrote something far more profound than anything in the book itself, and it could be the motto of all of us engaged in local community public relations: 'The real power of public relations is not that it creates better images for organizations, but that it creates better organizations.'

As mentioned, the objectives of any enterprise must be fully understood by those involved in its activities if there is to be effective communication, and thereby a full understanding by those inside and outside the organization. Assuming that the organization is a profit-earner, and through its products or services has an interface with the public, statements regarding profitability, and, where appropriate, earnings per share, are of enormous interest to far more people than just shareholders.

One aspect of community relations that must never be overlooked is the relationship of the workforce with the employer. Relationships, as we know, are not static things but need to be worked on; and, as current practice and legislation demand, improvements can always be made to working conditions and terms of employment. It is as much a public relations function as a personnel one to promote the best possible human relations, and to create a situation in which people can enjoy their work.

If a company believes in the principles stated above, it will also believe in delegation, providing maximum freedom of action to employees within their limits of responsibility, and thus will ensure that the community at large, as well as individuals, are fully informed at all times of changes of policy, or the way the enterprise is developing.

One can easily become complacent when a good reputation has been earned, and when the outside view of the company is satisfactory. In this attitude there is a degree of complacency that PR executives should never allow themselves the luxury of feeling. There are three questions that should be asked:

1. What do I think of my company?
2. What do other people think of my company?
3. What do I think other people think of my company?

The last two questions may appear similar, but they are vastly different. We quickly form opinions about the people and the organizations we work for, and over a period of years these opinions will change as we become familiar, or over-familiar, with the way development progresses, or in some cases recedes. With the passage of time, a great deal of stimulation comes from changing circumstances which have to be met head-on, and the opportunities thus presented can be converted into action and improved communication. It is however too easy, after a number of successful events, to believe that solutions come automatically and that there are no new challenges. The business world is as dynamic as a youth's first love affair. *No* two PR problems have the same solution, which is one reason why in management terms public relations is such a fascinating discipline. This is also a reason why new blood and new ideas in any enterprise are so important in keeping it fresh and well fertilized. This has been well recognized by leading PR practitioners in the United States for a number of years, and it is gratifying that in the UK recent developments are leading to educational opportunities and qualifications that will take the profession into the next century.

A great deal has been written about the 'management of change', and this might well be the motto of any community relations programme. The various ingredients that make up any concerted PR programme are outlined elsewhere in this book, but the true community relations programme is probably the most elusive of all. Not a single day goes by without opportunities for enhancing a company's reputation within its particular community. In a long and erudite report recently published on a corporate community strategy by a company with a household name, under the heading of 'Local Community', the entire entry read: 'There is a very considerable involvement in community affairs. The local press is kept fully informed about all appropriate matters.' That company had not even begun to take its place in the community, and it would be salutary to contemplate any crisis management that might be required by them, should even a small disaster occur. Without being personally involved, I can recall a tragedy of major proportions some years ago at Bantry Bay in south-west Ireland, involving the oil terminal. The handling of that particular crisis by the public relations staff involved was an object lesson in how disaster can, in communication terms, be turned to advantage merely by sympathetic communication to those involved in the community of what had happened, why, and what action, both short-term and in the future, was contemplated.

'It will never happen to us!' Too often that has been the epitaph for failed PR practitioners who have not looked for a safe place to land in the event of sudden engine failure.

It may take very many years to build a good reputation for a business: sadly, such a reputation can be destroyed almost overnight by uncaring and unsympathetic attitudes towards people. Personal relationships are always important, but they include the community at every level.

Whether we like it or not, every group, be it a family or a major public company, has a reputation that has been gained, and once gained must be protected. There are numerous ways of doing this, and it is hardly the job of public relations to create a company philosophy in the first place, but what PR can and must do is to be aware, through internal and corporate programmes, of attitudes as well as opportunities, and to respond in the most positive way. With Abraham Lincoln, we must know that, 'With public sentiment nothing can fail, without it nothing can succeed.'

7.

PARLIAMENTARY AND EEC RELATIONS

Douglas Smith

Success in government affairs—commonly called 'lobbying'—has three principal ingredients: good advance intelligence, skilful timing, and a mature, realistic presentation of one's case. I could well argue that these qualities lie behind every successful business activity. It is therefore remarkable how frequently such a commonsense approach is neglected by those who, whatever their personal feelings about them, simply cannot afford to ignore politicians and the political world in which we live.

Constantly I meet businessmen who believe that occasional meetings with MPs or peers—even having some of them grace their board of directors—are adequate to keep themselves both informed and fully protected against any legislative moves that might arise. Others rely upon their trade associations or unions as an efficient early warning system or 'fire service', should such be needed. In some cases their trust is well reposed. The National Farmers' Union, for example, does not miss many tricks; we all know how well food interests have been defended both in Britain and in the EEC over the decades. But other industries are not as efficiently served; indeed, by relying upon trade groups, they have neglected to be efficient themselves. High penalties have been paid for such sloth.

The principal reason for failure is an inability to recognize that political change is a long and slow process but one that can, none the less, creep up on you. A famous statesman likened politics to a tortoise; it hardly appears to move, but seems to travel hundreds of yards if you take your eyes away for a few minutes.

Equally, it is not easy for people outside the world of government to realize how the system works. Indeed, some innocent souls have spent a lifetime in Parliament itself—and picked up their knighthood at the end—without appreciating half of the interrelating factors involved. This is because there is, of course, no set pattern in the body politic, any more than there is for the human body or the law. There are, however, good rules to follow, and one does not need to be a constitutional expert to appreciate them.

Long-range intelligence

First, there is the need for advance intelligence. By this we do not mean simply the monitoring of parliamentary activity, significant though it can be: one has to look a great deal further back than 'the week in Westminster'.

In democracies, change is wrought through political parties. Their policies are formed most frequently when in opposition; in government, politicians tend to be rushed off their feet with difficulties of the day—implementation rather than formation. So it is a wise person who, realizing that no party can rule forever, keeps an eye on what opposition groups are about and makes friends there as well as in the party of government.

Some wild ideas quickly gain ground among opposition parties. Inevitably, they are looking for policies that contrast with those of government; indeed, they rightly commence their thinking from a different standpoint. Academics and theorists abound in this area. Often there are fanatics as well, in Winston Churchill's definition of the fanatic as a person who 'never changes his mind and never changes the subject'. Once a policy is hammered out in some arcane and distant discussion, it can gradually become part of the party manifesto, applauded by further groups of enthusiasts at conferences and embodied in the Queen's Speech should that party gain power, without once being firmly exposed to reality. The hazard is then far more difficult to resist.

Clearly, great issues of policy—the 'nationalization' versus 'privatization' argument, for instance—will not be easily influenced by any one interest group, however powerful. Yet more detailed application of such policies can be amended (or even killed) by judicious action in the earliest stages.

An example is the privatization of the bus services in England and Wales. Fundamental Conservative thinking here was well set in the late 1970s with the proposal to push back previous policies of nationalization. Yet it was the National Bus Company that was chosen for dismemberment and private sale, rather than the more costly British Rail, not only because it was a simpler process, but also because one particular academic gained the ear of one particular opposition spokesman at key moments in the manifesto-making process. It is perhaps amusing to speculate how a proposal to charge rates for farm properties, haystacks, and the like would fare in Conservative circles. The argument would run that these properties are protected by police and fire services like all others, and such services are supported out of our rates: so why should they not be equally, or at least partially, open to rate levy? One suspects that this notion would not even reach the floor of a party conference before being firmly dismissed as illogical and certain to raise food prices. Farmers' profits would not be mentioned at any stage.

The importance of 'intelligence' as against simple 'monitoring' should be plain. It pays to have sources back at the roots of policy formation, in

Whitehall and the EEC as much as in British political parties, which are able to scent danger at the earliest stage, when it is far easier to defeat. Equally, there are opportunities for positive moves to be made influencing policy and effecting change: again, these need to be planned early and promoted discreetly.

Such in-depth monitoring poses difficulties for busy executives and all but the largest organizations. If a company belongs to an efficient trade association or union, then one of these should be carrying out the task—not simply monitoring the daily flow of paper from Westminster, but also studying Select Committee proceedings as appropriate, or policy-forming reports to government and opposition. Such groups—or specialist units within the major companies—will also have their own teams of experts developing research and support policy with skills equal to (or even surpassing) those within government itself.

Monitoring help

The average chief executive cannot, however, hope to have these resources at his disposal. Staff and material costs are high, and are hardly justifiable in covering an area where action could well be required only occasionally. Yet management might very well not wish to rely solely on trade association information, which will, of course, be equally open to the firm's competitors. Fortunately, an alternative exists: a specialist public affairs consultancy can be employed to provide both daily monitoring and high-level intelligence services. By acting for a range of clients, such consultancies or monitoring groups can meet information needs at modest cost. As with a press cuttings agency, the fee depends upon range of subjects covered. But a similar same-day, or next-day, service can be provided, with urgent news passed on directly by phone. The consultancy might well make use of POLIS, an information-retrieval system set up in 1978 by the Commons Library and the Central Computer Agency. External users can buy into this system to check on references to them in Parliament, and companies sensibly do so.

An efficient monitoring agency could also provide political information summaries as part of the service. These could be most helpful to the busy executive. They would include appropriate articles from influential media as well as a digest of political developments, broken down into subjects. At key moments in the political year—Budget time, for example—more detailed reports might be available. In short, there are several routes available to gain an adequate background, enabling you to know not only when to move but equally, what current issues are about when you do. Placing an individual problem or opportunity into political perspective is often as important as identifying it in the first place.

The major error of many, even large, concerns is their failure to have a purposeful strategy in the public area, to set out company objectives and then test them coldly against present and likely future political scenes. If a realistic plan of action can be forged and contacts built in advance, then success is frequent. As an illustration of the nature of such advance contacts, all-party groups are important. They exist on nearly every major subject in Parliament, some far more active than others; if there is not one covering the desired area of activity, it can be formed. A small group of MPs and peers with greater knowledge of an industry or topic and, more important, a real interest can be invaluable, first as a sounding board for any campaign, then as allies in the fighting of it. Such support can be equally valuable in simply gathering information or 'sounding out' government reaction. There are some 50 000 written or oral parliamentary questions asked by MPs every year. Many are party-political in aim, but others are a small part of various lobbying campaigns.

Information alone will not, however, influence decisions, nor will simple internal agreement on a corporate strategy: timing and persuasion—the two other principal ingredients of lobbying success—are also necessary.

Time spent in reconnaissance

Let us assume that we are now armed with accurate information and our arguments are clear. We must then ask, Are they achievable, and, if so, on either a short or a longer term? There really is no point in assailing civil servants or politicians if the moment is not right; better by far, in such circumstances, to plant seeds for future germination, or move towards a far more limited initial objective.

It pays to be quite ruthless in assessing the chances of success or the degree to which it might be gained. There will always be voices recommending action at once, with all cannons firing and troops advancing on a broad front. Political reactions might be more genteel than the machine gun in repelling such an approach, but repelled it will be none the less.

Before attacking, your skilled general will, in any event, have engaged in reconnaissance. It should not be entirely factual. Friends made well ahead of any campaign are able better to assist you. For example, if you have bothered to meet and brief some involved civil servants on your background—and there is always an excuse so to do—then useful advice on detail could well be provided in times of need. Assuming that you have the good sense not to pressurize from the first but simply to open up friendly lines of contact, their response later might be crucial. The same applies to Members of Parliament. These are concerned mainly (apart of course from wider matters of government or specialist committees upon which they serve) with their constituencies and, in most cases, also with their careers. Accordingly, they will be most attracted to people who can assist them in both, and do so with maximum economy of effort for all concerned.

The approach taken by a large American computer specialist over recent years is a model example to consider. The firm was aiming to expand in Britain, but was equally keen to win business from government as from private concerns. Yet its policy was deliberately long-term and down-key. Members of the firm met and briefed all MPs where they had offices or factories, without once asking favours. Indeed, by skilful publicity of local visits from their MPs, they built a useful bank of goodwill. Evidence was offered and freely provided to inquiries being conducted in Parliament on matters of mutual concern. This brought close contact with civil servants as well as MPs and peers who had a specialist rather than simply constituency interest. An all-party group had events sponsored, again most modestly. In short, the American concern was increasingly perceived as British, and built up a core of understanding, with sympathetic friends both in Westminster and Whitehall. So when it faced a real crisis, the 'fire engines' were ready and waiting to assist.

This brief example of competence prompts other advice for those dealing with parliamentarians. Indeed, speaking with MPs and peers is likely to be a task for chief executives rather than any advisers. A poor impression is created if politicians do not have the opportunity to hear arguments at first hand, however much they appreciate the role of any advisers in organizing the occasion or framing a brief.

Too frequently, one hears it said that back-bench MPs and peers are mere cyphers, and that time spent with them is wasted. This is not so. Of course, it is civil servants who handle matters of detail and also, with Ministers, issues of policy. I have already stressed how connections with them should be cultivated. But if only a few MPs and the properly informed peer pursue an issue, it cannot be neglected; nor need one rest with any departmental brush-off. It is all a matter of judgement and balance. To pursue any case solely by way of parliamentary protest is to risk offending those who are fundamentally important; on the other hand, if you place yourself entirely in civil service hands, without pressure potential elsewhere, you are running needless risk.

Light socket rescue

Another example proves our point. Several years back there was a major revision of electrical safety regulations. The new code was, of course, drafted by civil servants, one of whom was consumed by the belief that our usual light sockets, if within easy reach (like standard lamps), presented a real hazard to safety. He recommended that such lamps should be fitted with an Edison screw rather than the common 'bayonet' socket.

The industry learned of these proposals far too late. Their intelligence was poor, and they had not been fully consulted. Certain manufacturers were therefore faced with the expense of major retooling of equipment to meet the proposed standard, and this was linked to a likely fall in sales because of increased complexity in fitting.

A consultancy was called in to advise and act. The consultants identified a dozen MPs who had constituency interests—those places where the manufacturers concerned were based. A suitable time was chosen for a meeting with these members in the Commons. It was explained how damaging the proposals would be to the industry but that they were needless in any event. Home accident records had quickly been combed to demonstrate that very few accidents occurred by fingers, even probing juvenile ones, being thrust into live lamp sockets. A succinct, written brief set out all these arguments. It also gave an indication of immediate action, since a Committee was looking at the proposed regulations only the following week. Members were convinced. A number promised to attend the Committee to put their constituents' case.

It was here that the consultants were wily. They knew the minister who was leading the Committee to be a reasonable and intelligent man. They guessed that he did not appreciate the full extent of any disturbance that might be created. And they wanted to alert him to the proposed objections, because ministers who have traps sprung on them can well turn obstinate, regardless of the force of arguments employed. The minister's parliamentary private secretary—a fellow MP who acts as his eyes and ears in Parliament—was briefed and conveyed the message. When the Committee met and objections were raised, they were sympathetically received; the proposed clause was taken back for review and subsequently dropped.

Of course, the manufacturers saw that all credit was given locally to their respective MPs, who had responded with such energy and good sense. The minister was also pleased at having avoided making an obvious error, and at being recognized by colleagues as a man who was capable of flexible action. Only the civil servant lost—but there is no truth in the rumour that he is now running a transport cafe on the approaches to the Dartford Tunnel.

Clear lessons emerge from this modest example of democracy in action. MPs were carefully selected and skilfully briefed—a short statement of the case, backed by figures and indicating what action they might then take. All the parties were involved; this was not a political issue. One person was selected to put the manufacturers' case (although others were present), and one person again constructed the brief. It was therefore a concise presentation. And when victory was achieved, due recognition was paid to those who had helped, which created warm feelings all round.

The cost of this lobbying exercise, incidentally, was reckoned in hundreds of pounds; it saved the industry quite literally millions.

I could match such a story with others less successful. The tale is told of a captain of industry who, feeling threatened, similarly called together a group of MPs. He hectored them for half-an-hour not only in detail on his particular problem but also on faults in government policy as a whole. There was no written brief to back his words. And he wore his wartime medals clanking on his chest as he spoke. Whether he is now a transport cafe proprietor is not known, but again the lessons emerge. Do not be over-elaborate. MPs are quick to grasp points but cannot be experts on all subjects. They are, however, good at asking questions and skilled at tactics, if given proper time to act. Do not enter into broader political argument, however strongly you may feel. Keep with the subject. Respect MPs' busy time schedule—and recognize their efforts, win or lose.

Their Lordships' House

I referred earlier to the briefing of peers. Frequently the Upper House is forgotten entirely in lobbying approaches, which is unfortunate and ill-advised. There are more than 1100 peers in the Upper House (compared with 650 MPs), of whom about one-third are life peers. Active membership is, however, far lower—around 700, of whom 300–400 are regular attenders.

Their Lordships differ fundamentally from members of the Lower House. They are, of course, older, but often far more experienced. Many have been leaders of industry, commerce, the unions, and the civil service. There are senior scientists, medical men, and soldiers. Party politics has its place, but debates on sweeping issues are less significant; reasoned argument on points of detail is more common, and much sensible amendment of the intestines of legislation results therefrom. Government whips hold less sway here, nor does government always overturn changes made to Bills in the Lords. Accordingly, it pays to brief peers who have an interest in your field. Their knowledge and support can prove equally helpful. They are often stimulating and extremely well informed company, and should not be treated lightly. Lords' committees are also more receptive to evidence offered than similar groups in the Lower House. And, because of the people involved, their reports can carry weight in government or policy-forming circles.

Their Lordships are best approached by letter and subsequent meeting in the Upper House. Since they do not have constituents to concern them, peers are often more free for visits to premises or for lunch. With MPs, meetings in the constituency itself are usually more sensible on local issues.

Meeting the minister

There is one further area where direct chief executive involvement is likely in any public affairs activity. This is when meeting a minister directly. Such an occasion will almost certainly have been preceded by contact at a lower level with the civil servants most concerned. But if progress is not being made here and a policy decision is required, then an appeal to the minister concerned is sensible. Few civil servants will resent such a move, provided it is courteously approached.

Unless the company in question is large, in which event contact can be made direct, quite the best route to any minister is again through one's constituency MP—or several of them, if they can properly be mustered. It is better if they are of the same political persuasion as the minister, or otherwise reasonable people not likely to embroil one in doctrinal disputes. But there are few ministers who will resist a meeting, arranged through their Private Office, with a group that has sensible points to raise and members to support them.

Again, groundwork is vital on such occasions. Too often delegations sail in, are most courteously treated by the minister and his attendant staff, and are then ushered out with polite words of reassurance and future action. At the end they have only a cup of civil service tea to show for their pains. If resistance is anticipated, then a parliamentary question or two in advance is sensible, not simply to establish some facts ahead of the meeting itself but also to give due warning that you are serious and are prepared to press your point. Once more, a briefing note should be brought with you and placed before the minister at the start of your discussion. It will be short on opinion but hard on fact. This will be the basis of your meeting. Do not be deflected from it. Ideally, use a single spokesman, supported by colleagues. Never, never disagree in front of the minister. At the conclusion, courteously ask when and how you will hear the minister's decision. Too serious a delay should not be accepted, and reasons should be on hand as to why a prompt response is necessary.

I must stress that, however well any concern is organized, changes in government Bills and certainly in policy are not achieved quickly or easily. On major issues, governments are rarely deflected, but on matters of detail and practice there is usually room for change. The skill lies in identifying and exploiting this marginal ground, using all the machinery described plus other techniques too numerous to list. Discretion is equally necessary in the selection of your allies. Some MPs can do you more harm than good on certain issues. They are not always the people you might imagine—so be sensible and diplomatic in taking advance 'soundings'.

To return to the basic point, it is preferable by far to ensure that ill-conceived legislation does not reach Parliament in the first place, which takes us back to fundamental intelligence work and civil service grassroots contact. 'Prepare, prevent' is a sound motto for every lobbyist. It applies even more when your aim is the procurement of business, rather than any campaign as such. Here, there are rules to follow and pitfalls to avoid which can be successfully approached only by planning. This applies as much in the EEC, which we now examine, as in Britain.

EEC approaches

Lobbying in the European Community is becoming increasingly important to all commercial concerns, and yet far too little attention is still paid to it. There remains a tendency in Britain to devalue the role and importance of the EEC. Many MPs at Westminster, and sadly not a few civil servants in Whitehall, are keen to do this, principally in defence of their own position and power. It is foolishly naive. Both constitutionally and politically, the EEC already plays a strong part in governing Britain. Wide-ranging decisions are taken in the Community which now pass directly into UK law or have to be introduced into it by the government. The areas covered are considerable—from company law to VAT—and fast-growing. They cannot be ignored. Yet monthly, one hears reports of lavish receptions called at Strasbourg that clash with a Budget vote; glossy brochures arriving long after the key debate; a costly presentation neglecting some important EEC languages. British firms in particular need to guard against cosy lobbying analogies with Whitehall and Westminster. Indeed, it is American firms, with their experiences of the complex Washington system, who generally present their cases best in Brussels.

We must start with some basic facts. First, power within the Community is diffused. The right to initiate legislation lies with the Commission of the European Communities in Brussels, which also has executive power and the right to enforce policies already agreed. It can therefore take legal action against, and fine, companies breaking EEC rules.

The Commission has 17 Commissioners, serving four-year terms, and controlling 10 000 staff recruited from member states. Here is the Community's largest legislative source, managing the Community budget (mostly agricultural) but also holding other powers. For example, anti-dumping action, competition policy, the classification of goods, and the free movement of goods are Commission responsibilities, all of which are exercised more and more frequently.

Then there is the European Parliament, elected directly in five-year terms, and currently consisting of 518 members, of whom 81 are from the United Kingdom. The Parliament is there to advise, but is steadily acquiring greater ability both to block and to amend legislation and even to initiate it. It has also, of course, traditional powers to vote the Budget and sack the Commissioners.

In Brussels the Economic and Social Committee sits as a third force, representing employers, unions, and other 'various interests' (who include the consumer). There are 189 committee members, and although they are essentially consultative, their specialist view of legislation can be influential. The Committee meets monthly for two days, a number of sections providing reports for discussion led by 'rapporteurs'.

The Council of Ministers is perhaps best known to the British. Theoretically, it has the last word on legislation, and also takes decisions on matters like farm price reviews. But the Commission is not the Council's civil service; that must be clear. In Council meetings ministers aim to win decisions in their own government's favour, but there is a spirit of compromise abroad. All 12 member states are represented on the Council; the UK has 10 votes, as do France, Germany, and Italy. There are 76 members in all.

More important perhaps than the individual ministers themselves are the national permanent representatives (COREPER), who meet in Brussels and organize the many Council working parties. Although there is only one Council, in practice it meets in many forms according to items under discussion. UKREP is Britain's office with COREPER; it comprises some 40 officials drawn from various Whitehall departments.

The European Court of Justice, sitting in Luxembourg, is to many the most powerful institution of all. It is the supreme constitutional authority of the EEC. The Court—never to be confused with the European Court of Human Rights in Strasbourg—hears Commission cases against firms or governments, as well as appeals against Commission decisions and fines. It also interprets Community law on behalf of national courts. And its rulings are final.

Those seeking finance should not ignore the European Investment Bank, which has invested £2½ billion in the United Kingdom, in the form of interest-free loans, and administers a variety of EEC borrowing and lending operations.

Finally, there are the various national authorities implementing Community laws—governments, regional and local authorities, agricultural intervention boards, bodies like the Manpower Services Commission (for example, in the case of the EEC Social Fund), and so on.

The relationship between all these bodies is currently in a state of flux. Indeed, one can anticipate far more uncertainty and shifts in power within the EEC than will occur in the more settled scene at Westminster. A simple example will suffice. As a result of the Single European Act, the Commission is acquiring new powers of delegated legislation, and draft laws will be subject to a second reading in the European Parliament after the Council of Ministers has voted. Such changes are, of course, significant. They mean that the closest watch must be kept on the EEC in years to come.

A second vital principle to grasp in dealing with the Community is that the EEC law is a new legal order, with characteristics of its own. The English legal tradition places great emphasis on the literal meaning of statutes. As A. P. Herbert once remarked, 'If Parliament does not mean what it says, it should say so.' But Community law is different. Each of the nine official languages is of equal validity, and the intention of the legislators is important.

Community legislation takes three main forms:

1. *Recommendations* These have no direct legal effect but are intended to guide national legislation.
2. *Regulations* These are directly binding once published in the Community *Official Journal*. So are decisions on such matters as fines.
3. *Directives* These are binding as to 'the results to be achieved' but have to be enacted by national procedures within a time limit. Legal rights can be created even if a particular country fails to meet the deadline.

Consultation and compromise

A final main element in this complex political scene is the large number of Community documents produced. These are of varying status and require the most discriminating monitoring.

To follow the trail of proposed Community law through all the relevant documents can be a tricky task. Any proposal usually starts life in the Commission as a 'situation paper'. At this stage the Commission will consult interested parties, but with a marked preference for lobbies organized at a Community rather than a purely national level. Hence the plethora of lobbying groups by trade associations in Brussels (which include the Peloponnesian Association of Applied Dried Fig and Pistachio Nut Processors and Wholesalers).

The Commission will then publish its draft proposal, which goes to Parliament and Council. Parliament refers it to a specialist standing committee, who appoint one of its number as a 'rapporteur'. Other interested committees may appoint 'draftsmen of opinions'. These appointments are made on a political basis (there are currently eight political groups), but the task of the rapporteur is to represent the views of the committee as a whole. The committee will report to Parliament, who will vote on both the draft Commission proposal with any amendments and the Committee report. Meanwhile, the Council of Ministers will have considered the proposal in working groups and COREPER. Attempts will be made to reconcile the Parliament's and Council's views, the Commission acting as 'honest broker' and 'guardian of the treaties'.

Once adopted, the law is published in the *Official Journal*. If it is a directive, however, it must now be enacted in the 12 member states, where its track can best be followed through the Commission's ASMODEE data base.

It will be seen from the above very necessary description of processes how the emphasis is on consultation and compromise. This contrasts, often very sharply, with procedures in the UK Parliament.

Threat to duty-free

The way in which the British Airports Authority (BAA) approached the threat made to a substantial part of its income in the early 1980s provides a good illustration of the various forces at work within the EEC.

  The BAA exists primarily to run airports, but a large part of its annual profit in fact arises from commercial activity, notably its duty-free airport shops. It was, therefore, properly alarmed to learn that the whole principle of duty-free allowances for EEC travellers was at risk as a result of a judgment in the European Court of Justice. This arose when a German supermarket chain challenged the legality of sale of tax-free dairy products aboard craft that sailed on day trips deliberately outside territorial waters—the so-called 'Butterboats'. Procedural law required that the case be referred to the European Court, as duty-free allowances are governed by EEC law, and it duly declared in July 1981 that the 'Butterboats' were in contravention of EEC regulations.

  It was here that the BAA became concerned. It knew the Commission had introduced legislation in 1980 to abolish duty-free allowances. To several senior officials, such sales to people travelling within the EEC were a straight contradiction of the idea of a common market. The Commission proposal was rejected at the time by member states well aware of the popularity of duty-free goods. But if this principle were now revived in the light of the Court's 'Butterboat' verdict, it could well rule unfavourably for BAA. A further difficulty lay in the refusal of Germany to accept the 'Butterboats' ruling. Elections were due there, and it was considered unwise to remove cheap butter from the poor while retaining cheap duty-free goods for more wealthy air travellers.

  The lobbying task was, therefore, twofold. First, the aim was to make it widely known that duty-free allowances were at risk. The Commission was making reassuring statements on this which were known to be deceptive. Second, there was a need to press for legislation to remove any existing ambiguity over duty-free allowances and, in effect, to protect them forever.

  Publicity was quickly achieved. This was a strong news story, and there were important interests other than BAA prepared to weigh in. A Brussels press conference for European media was followed by national briefings, all aimed at alerting EEC member governments to the potential loss of income and unpopularity.

  The Commissioner concerned was approached and proved sympathetic. Members of the European Parliament were also fully briefed, the emphasis here being on the certain anger among the electorate when MEPs stood in the forthcoming elections if European travellers had lost a privilege that non-EEC travellers retained. And in Britain the government was persuaded to intervene in the Court in the Commission's case against Germany. Member states can make such an intervention where they have a direct interest. Other countries also intervened in this way, but Germany presented a special problem. Here it was necessary to provide the government with arguments discouraging the existing stance on cheap butter. A survey was therefore commissioned to show exactly which social groups used airport duty-free facilities. They proved to be far more broadly based than many had imagined, and so the less wealthy would be hit by proposed legislation as well.

All these moves served to highlight arguments against restrictive legislation across the Community. Questions were asked in the European Parliament; letters poured into the Commission from a range of interests; the media had a field day. Despite this, resistance did not collapse overnight. We were repeatedly told that proposed moves were in the direction of fiscal harmonization, and the duty-free allowance was an obstacle to this happy Euro-objective. But in early 1983, a year after saying that legislation to support duty-free allowances was impossible, the Commission approved a draft directive that could provide a foundation for exactly this. The pressure had, in effect, caused a major rethink, followed by tactical withdrawal.

Although a lengthy case history, the duty-free issue does illustrate how campaigns within the Community need to be conducted at a number of levels and that we must be aware precisely of the powers of all bodies concerned. This applies to all lobbying, of course, but within the EEC the formula is especially complex, and accordingly calls for wider knowledge of institutions as well as greater skill in timing. In this case, all the various bodies were approached at some stage.

Fight and publicize

Two particular lessons also emerged. First, do not be daunted by statements from officials that 'of course there will be a change'. Whatever the theory, in practice one can always fight and delay. Witness the Japanese success in resisting decades of action against the mass sale of their goods abroad, while the land of the Rising Sun remains protected against similar foreign competition.

Second, never neglect the media. I shall return to this theme, but over the proposed abolition of duty-free allowances—a topic affecting millions—the clamour aroused in press and on radio was a very significant factor in changing minds.

Finally, a warning: such dangers do not go away. Once again, there is talk of 'harmonization' on duty-free allowances.

Broadly, the lessons of EEC activity are similar to those applying in Britain. They are, in brief:

1. Maintain a strict watch on impending legislation. The Commission publishes annual programmes, and each incoming president of the Council (it changes every six months, revolving around the member states in turn) makes a statement of intent. There are also long-term programmes, notably Lord Cockfield's White Paper on *Completing the Internal Market* by 1992. Early warning means greater influence and freedom to move.

2. Make use of European members of Parliament, who can obtain any Community documents; put questions to Council on the Commission and get answers to them; amend legislation; be a focus for contacts; and influence not just one but 12 governments. It is not, of course, necessarily the case that UK members will be the best contacts for particular UK campaigns, but at least they will direct you to parliamentary colleagues who can better assist. If the cause is acceptable, the country matters less than you might imagine.

3. Keep in close touch with UKREP (the UK part of COREPER). It is far better to lobby the UK government early rather than rely on a British 'veto' at the end. It might well not be forthcoming or effective.

4. Use Community law. If you think you are being hit by unfair competition, then complain to the Commission. Clearly, such steps call for specialist advice.

5. Even if you are not in an assisted area, there are still ways of winning EEC finance. This applies to the fields of high technology, training, and education in particular.

As with UK lobbying, it pays to build bridges in advance. There are officials and politicians within the Community who are delighted to talk with genuine business groups or particular interests—indeed, most bureaucrats positively welcome such approaches, which sadly is not as common in Whitehall.

Lobbying the town hall

Local authorities are almost entirely neglected by many commercial concerns, thus demonstrating a strange set of priorities. Of course, British local government is a waning force. Recent years have seen a significant, and saddening, diminution of their authority, to the benefit of a Whitehall which scarcely has a record for more efficient administration. Yet local government accounts for more than a quarter of all public expenditure in the UK, and employs well over 2 million people. It also is responsible for decisions closely affecting business.

Statute law controls British local government very tightly. It works to Acts of Parliament, with few general powers to move as it chooses, in contrast to the practice in most other EEC countries or North America. Yet there are still wide areas of action, and flexibility of decision can be shown to those who approach town halls correctly.

A first need is to establish which particular department of a local authority is concerned with your requirement. Powers differ widely between the various units but there is always an officer in authority, and invariably he or she will be helpful to an early approach. The word 'early' is again important. Often, companies will proceed to a detailed stage of planning and preparation—for example, the site of a new plant—without even making contact with the council whose approval at several levels is ultimately essential. There is then considerable annoyance at the changes the council subsequently insists on making. Thus, a letter to the head of the department in question (a telephone call having told one who it will be) should outline the nature of any request ahead of any meeting to discuss it.

The levers of real power in any council usually rest with a few individuals. In some authorities they are senior officers—the chief executive is concerned in most matters of a commercial nature at some stage, as well as the treasurer and director of planning. In others, elected councillors hold the whip hand, usually 'chairs' of major committees selected from the ruling party. The movement towards, in effect, full-time, semi-paid councillors has accelerated in recent years. Usually decisions are made between a few leading councillors and the senior officers, but, with more than 400 councils to consider, there can be no strict pattern to follow. Again, therefore, we fall back on reconnaissance. Your first contacts should guide you, but a little background work, not neglecting the local press, is well advised.

The majority of local authorities are keen to assist business development in their areas. Commerce yields rate revenue for the civic coffers (indeed, see how high local rates are before you move into any community) as well as jobs for the population. Invariably, a council will have some form of development plan by which it is guided. A sensible company will study this and frame any request to meet its objectives. As negotiations proceed, the key people can quickly be identified. If councillors, they will appreciate as much as MPs and peers being treated with the respect properly due to those giving their time and effort, often on a voluntary basis. And they are keen publicly to be associated with any success just as much as your national politician. Officers are equally concerned to produce positive results. The more senior the officer, the more likely you will be to meet with willingness to give support rather than nitpicking objection. This is a generalization, clearly, because some low-level officers in town halls are magnificent; but others are not.

Frequently local newspapers, and also to a growing extent local radio, can be most helpful. If they fall in behind your campaign, it can be a great stimulus to both councillors and officers. A band-wagon can begin to roll, carrying any proposal along and speeding the various processes. Councillors from the area most concerned will wish to be involved if the project is, for instance, a new plant or extension to existing works. They may well be humble back-benchers, but their advice and voices could assist if delays emerge. Rest assured also that they will not shield their faces from the local photographer or fail to speak to any available microphone.

Using the media

Mention of local press brings us logically to the whole area of media support in government affairs activity. This is frequently neglected by lobbyists, who often enjoy legal backgrounds and therefore concentrate upon constitutional aspects of the task. What they sometimes forget is that politicians and civil servants are influenced by the media as much as the rest of us. They read—admittedly not always in detail or in depth—the daily press, some serious weeklies, and the Sundays in particular. And of course they watch television, or listen to the radio as they shave. So journalists—press, radio or TV—should be friends of the lobbyist as much as any civil servant or politician.

Again, the point is illustrated by details of a recent campaign. This was conducted on behalf of Airbus Industries, the European aviation consortium, which needed to get national funds committed in order to move ahead with a development programme matching American competition in the coming decades. There were obvious political allies for the campaign—those with component factories in their constituencies where the job factor loomed large. There was also one serious opponent: a Prime Minister who, supported by her Treasury, was deeply sceptical about whether investment in aircraft manufacture would ever yield a sensible return. In this doubt she was supported by some heavyweight aviation correspondents whose knowledge of past events in the industry was considerable and whose enthusiasm for Airbus support did not have the grassroots motivation of our politicians.

To convert the serious media to the Airbus cause was, therefore, a primary objective. The usual public relations methods were employed—one-to-one senior briefings; visits to Airbus headquarters (fortunately, well placed in gastronomically attractive, sunny France); factual surveys to demonstrate a healthy commercial trend. Over a period of months, key journalists began to amend their hostile line. The political allies, much encouraged, worked on the Prime Minister. Eventually she was won over as well.

Media are, in fact, an immense ally in the lobbying process. At Westminster there are scores of journalists and broadcasters, often casting around for stories. Such stories must have a political thrust, but then that is nearly always the case with public affairs activity. And they must involve politicians in person, which is usually the case anyway. The degree of political attention it is possible to attract to any campaign if there is radio, press, and especially television interest will be surprising even to the cynical. Of course, the aim is to gain favourable comment, and no politician will speak against personal or party convictions. Equally, the promise of a camera grinding away on Abingdon Gardens, against a backdrop of the Great Palace, will bring MPs rapidly out of Committee or Chamber; and, once they have declared themselves publicly for a cause, their help can properly be sought in other ways. The ability to gain publicity for politicians is, as I have previously stressed, one of the best cards in any campaign pack.

This lesson—the promotion of others before oneself—is a key to the effective lobbyist craft. Many concerns are capable of massive self-deception in their campaigns, and can be encouraged in it by less worthy practitioners. Mentions in the Chamber; early day motions; adjournment debates; successful drinks parties in Westminster—all leave one with a warm feeling of achievement without, in the event, gaining real ground. Politicians and civil servants—who after all can be confronted daily with requests from a dozen interests—are adept at the sympathetic answer that has no substance.

Given a sensible corporate plan for pushing any particular interest, the next steps are good timing and persuasive argument. But the greatest attributes of them all are patience and modesty. Let others wear the garland of laurels. It matters not at all, provided your point is proved and the campaign won.

Further reading

Butler, Arthur, and Smith, Douglas, *Lobbying in the British Parliament* (Public Relations Consultants Association Guidance Paper, 1986).

Davies, Malcolm, *Politics of Pressure: The Art of Lobbying* (BBC, London, 1985).

Patterson, Ben, *Lobbying in Europe* (Public Relations Consultants Association Guidance Paper, 1983).

Rodgers, William (ed.), *Government and Industry: A Business Guide to Westminster, Whitehall and Brussels* (Kluwer Publishing, Brentford, Middx, 1986).

Seeley, Ivor H., *Local Government Explained* (Macmillan, London, 1978).

8.

BUILDING AN INTERNATIONAL REPUTATION

John V. Cook

Reputation and its objectives

A company's reputation develops, or is developed, through the passing on of personal experiences, rumours, editorials, memories of exhibition stands, and so on—a great variety of possible influences, all of which build up a series of perceptions in the memory, some good, some bad, some almost intangible.

When thinking of schooldays, one tends to remember the good times; but in business, it is the memory of bad things that lingers on, while good things are expected anyway, and the memory of them tends to be frustratingly short. In simple terms, therefore, it is a long, hard, and often expensive job to develop a positive international reputation—and all too easy to lose it. A corporate reputation will clearly take much longer to establish for a multi-product industrial conglomerate than for a single-product consumer company, but, since bad news travels fast, both types of organization should take great pains to ensure that the good reputation remains unsullied.

But what is so important about a reputation? Why should companies go to a great deal of trouble and expense to create it—and anyway, who needs to be impressed ? There are three facets of the situation:

1. *No reputation* In a zero situation, perhaps for a newly established company, the first priority is for potential customers to learn that it and its products or services exist. Or perhaps a company well known in its own country wishes to take over a company in a country in which it is unknown: its prime target is to create an awareness of the organization's existence and background in the new country. Neither of these companies can proceed very far unless it can establish, quickly or otherwise, a reputation with, respectively, its customers or the stockholders of the target company. Without a reputation, without an image, without perceptions, neither company can expect to progress, since those it wishes to influence will not react favourably towards a company they have not read or heard positively about.

2. *A good, positive reputation* A good reputation, on the other hand,

provides a personality behind the company or product, and this will help the buyer's decision-making process beyond price and specification.

3. *A bad, negative reputation* Although it is said that no publicity is bad publicity, a bad reputation puts a company in a below-zero situation, since, as said earlier, a bad reputation travels faster and lasts longer than a good one. It takes a vast amount of positive activity (and usually money) to erase the bad memory, let alone to rebuild a good reputation—and even then, the bad comes back to haunt from time to time.

Having established the importance of a positive reputation in support of a company's direct activities, those readers of an economic mind should turn to priorities and targets, so as to define as precisely as possible whom they wish to influence; because progress is measurable only where there is a basis for measurement.

The building of a corporate reputation can be planned and controlled just like any other business activity, and should be based on clear targets, such as:

● Job functions, e.g. housewives, shop owners, MPs, financial managers
● Industry or user groups
● Geographical regions
● Time objectives

With a clear picture in mind of the group, big or small, simple or complex, in whose minds the reputation is to be established, the active planning process can commence. The next stage is to identify the framework for the reputation or identity to be created. A company that is well known for its work in a particular field, its success in a topical area of technology, or its ability to improve its customers' productivity has a much clearer and more memorable identity than one whose name is well known but diffused.

Benchmark studies can be helpful in determining the perceptions of the company among its target audience at the beginning of the campaign, and subsequent studies should be undertaken to check progress. These can be carried out on a local basis by interviewing samples of customers, or by mailing out questionnaires on a random geographical basis. Such studies can provide a picture of the present areas of reputation with their strengths and weaknesses, from which can be developed the structure for the future identity. As precisely as possible, management should determine:

● How do we wish to be known?
● What do we want our customers/the world to think about us?
● How would a typical target person describe us?

Building a reputation in the home country of an organization is a matter of time, discipline, good products and services—and good communications. In the United Kingdom, for a British-owned company, all the necessary facilities are available for establishing good corporate relations. For a UK company operating overseas, the facilities may be better or worse according to the country of operation, but in general the problem is tougher.

Local organization or central?

The handling of international corporate relations depends on the international organization stemming from the parent company. In each country outside the home market, there are two basic ways of handling commercial business: through a wholly or partially owned company or office, or through a distributor–agent–representative.

Through the company-owned local operation, full control of corporate relations can be handled as an extension of the 'parent', relying 100 per cent on the local reputation of the company, its products or services, and its personnel, and supported by local media publicity. Through local distributors, agents, and representatives, direct control is not possible, particularly since the image of the parent company and its products tends to be filtered through the primary reputation or otherwise of the local representative. In principle, local representation is chosen on the basis of the agent's ability to sell on its own reputation. However, with a product or service that already has an established international name and reputation, local distributors with ability but no reputation can absorb and reflect this reputation and build on it.

THE MEDIA

Since reputation develops by communication, it follows that the media for this communication must be by word of mouth; by general, vertical, or horizontal press (vertical = specific industrial or consumer interest press; horizontal = publications representing a job function or interest spanning several industries or consumer areas); by radio or television; by seminars, conferences, and other sponsored functions.

These facilities exist to a greater or lesser degree in all countries, which means that local corporate relations have access to them. But they also exist on an international basis, as there are many printed media that circulate internationally to various interest groups, such as investors, finance officers, CEOs, sportsmen, etc. Radio and TV programmes are often syndicated and thus circulate around the world, while seminars, conferences, and exhibitions often draw visitors from overseas who tend to be more seriously interested than local participants.

Much corporate relations work can be carried out from the central office utilizing international media facilities of all types, but it should be emphasized that for many businesses this may be insufficient to influence the majority of the potential international audience. Here again, it is important to define clearly the demographic targets for influence with the corporate message. The more precise and clear the definition, the more accurately the media can be selected, since most international media—and local media in many countries—provide good data on the job functions, status, and geographical distribution of their circulations.

The availability of good international corporate media, however, may be insufficient to cover the total corporate targets; or there may be a weakness in one or more of the data categories, most likely in the geographical distribution. This is where it is useful to disseminate the message through local sources, which are particularly valuable when the same message appears in all languages throughout the world at the same time for maximum impact. From the organizational point of view, therefore, the centralized international corporate relations campaign is strongest when co-ordinated with local distribution of the same message but in the local language.

However, the local reputation is just as important as the international reputation; and, although care must be taken to integrate the local image with the international, it is better if the local (centrally owned) company establishes a strong reputation of its own—even to the extent of being viewed as an entirely local company.

The logistics of PR practice

There is no perfect PR organization that meets all needs. The starting point, however, should invariably be to establish the policy, the targets, the message and the timetable, and then to look at the problems of world-wide execution.

There are two basic ways of solving the organizational problem:

1. To establish a central public relations department with experienced, professional people
2. To appoint a public relations consultant with proven experience of international corporate relations

The ideal is a combination of the two, but it depends very much on the method already established to handle home market PR.

A typical operation would consist of a small central department, with specialist units responsible for compiling and distributing information on financial and investment matters, product and market matters, and internal communications. Each unit, for home market purposes, would draw on information from overseas in order to give to the home media a balanced picture of world operations.

From this pool of information it is an easy step to organize the redistribution of home and international activities outwards, back to the overseas companies and representatives and also to the international media. Much of this work can also be handled by a PR consultant, but, however organized, it is vital that it be carried out as far as possible on a person-to-person basis with the media.

On the local level, it is important that all overseas companies and representatives are aware of the overall PR policy and objectives so that a co-ordinated picture of the company and its international activities is presented. Their responsibility is to disseminate to their national media such items from the central distribution as can be translated into topical and newsworthy material. For local political or other strategic reasons, it may be necessary to play down the overseas news in favour of material with a strong local flavour, but the overall policy should be followed as closely as possible.

In addition to promoting the international scene in its national media, the local company/representative should look at its own reputation to ensure that its methods, products, and service both meet group standards and follow group policy. According to the size and sophistication of the country, it is also important that a person or persons should be responsible for represent-ing the company on a day-to-day basis with the media, to keep them informed of, or to create interest in, the company's activities.

Apart from the routine supply and distribution of company information, the central and local PR departments can occasionally work together very successfully on specific PR projects, such as major exhibitions, conferences, or international press visits. Taking the latter as an example, let us assume that a major activity—say, the installation of equipment or the opening of a plant—is to take place somewhere in the world. Central PR discusses with local PR whether this can be an event of interest to the world's press or to a subdivision thereof, e.g. a group of international technical press or the press of adjacent countries. Facilities and a programme are set up and invitations sent out both locally and internationally. Much detailed organization is required.

Here is an opportunity, locally as well as centrally, for professional assistance by an experienced consultant. With a programme of sufficient interest and topicality, with a high level of speakers, visual presentation material, ample documentation to take away, and good and efficient hospi-tality, much positive media coverage can be achieved. Such a project is expensive; but, if the hypothetical cost of taking a similar amount of advertising space world-wide is calculated, compared with the resulting editorial space and/or radio or TV time, it can prove good value for money, as well as promoting a co-ordinated and impactful message extremely accurately.

A few PR consultancies have branches in major cities around the world, and these have the ability to handle a co-ordinated international corporate campaign partially through their own organization and partially in conjunc-tion with their clients' overseas offices. A similar means of handling by consultants can be through a loosely linked group of independent local PR consultancies who operate as an associated international group. The associate in the country of the client's local office usually acts as the fulcrum of the PR operation.

Variations in PR professionalism

In all professions, standards and individuals vary, and public relations is no exception. Whether 'public relations' in the United Kingdom or 'publicity' in the United States, there are large, medium, and small consultancies, with varying levels of experience and expertise, staffed by practitioners with varying levels of experience and training. The professionals in-house—the PR managers, corporate relations executives, etc.—can also be of varying standards, although in the above two countries there are diploma courses of study, supervised by trade associations, which help to improve the theoretical level at least. In many other countries, degree or diploma courses can be found which include public relations in wider-ranging communications or marketing subjects, but which can hardly serve as the basis for a career in public relations. Here, practical experience is the main criterion, and care must be taken in hiring the organization or the individual.

On the other hand, in some of the least likely countries, PR practitioners can be found with US or UK training, with a wide range of skills and experience, and working most successfully for local multinationals or for PR consultancies.

An example of the variations around the world can be found in my previous company, which has its own sales companies in 50 countries and distributors in a further 85. The facilities and standards vary dramatically from country to country. In the parent company (in Sweden), there are three highly trained professionals, each with long and varied experience, responsible for various aspects of press relations, and at least one PR person in each of the main product divisions, all with responsibilities for part of the overall corporate relations programme.

In the 50 sales companies, responsibility for corporate relations varies from communications manager and/or press officer in the bigger companies, working on their own or with a local consultant, to the managing director or his secretary (among their many other functions) in the smaller companies, sometimes with the assistance of a local PR consultant.

Co-ordination of policy and activities is handled from headquarters, as is also the responsibility for training and standards. Regular training sessions, and less frequent conferences for education and the exchange of experiences, are carried out under headquarters control, as are the selection, appointment, and briefing of communications personnel and consultants.

The distributors in the 85 other countries are independent companies and, therefore, less under direct control of their principals. However, many have their own very professional communications departments which work to promote not just the products but also, in conjunction with Swedish headquarters, the corporate philosophy of the company.

Special problems

DIFFERENT CULTURES

Sometimes one needs to modify the corporate message in order to take into account certain national or regional attitudes and characteristics or standards of sophistication. Although most corporate relations activities fit into the basic rules of human relations and psychology, it is important to realize that what is accepted in one country may be received adversely in another and not understood at all in a third. In many Western countries, superlatives and excesses of speech and the written word are understood and accepted for what they are, whereas in other countries they are taken literally (and legally).

In many Third World countries (and not only there), there is a suspicion of international and multinational companies, and some diplomacy may be required in adapting locally an international corporate theme. Care must therefore be taken in preparing material for international media.

LANGUAGE

You have only to read hotel brochures and menus on your travels abroad to recognize that language 'howlers' can dramatically reduce the accuracy and credibility of the written or spoken word.

Although English is widely read and understood around the world, and international publications in that language abound, there are many international and regional publications in other key languages, such as Spanish, French, German, and Arabic, apart from the native language press of the individual countries. How can a carefully written message with subtle nuances be guaranteed to appear in the world's press without losing its fine points? Of course, you could always distribute the message in English and expect it to be translated accurately by the local media, but the risk of inaccuracy is great, although it may be necessary to accept this for some countries or languages. However, the risk can be minimized by ensuring that the English is simple and unambiguous; in fact, this should always be the objective for texts for translation.

There is a further risk, which may be greater than that of inaccuracy. Because of the extra work involved in translation, and because the editorial offices usually have much more copy than they need and thus are very selective, the material is less likely to be used if it is not in the language of the publication.

Which languages should you have the copy translated into, and how do you make sure that you get the best translation? The simplest and least controversial solution is as follows. First, the best translation is obviously not a literal one, but one that is rewritten in the language and style of the country while retaining the necessary nuances of meaning. This can be achieved through in-house translators, any one of whom may be sufficiently up to date linguistically and technically to produce a good translation. But their reliability needs to be proven. Ideally, the next stage is to send the translation, together with the English original, to a local branch office for checking. It should be borne in mind, however, that no two people will translate a text in precisely the same way, and, for one's own satisfaction, it may be wise to check any revisions with the original translator.

Furthermore, you should choose carefully which country should check the translation, as not every French, Spanish, or German-speaking country writes or speaks precisely the same French, Spanish, or German. Quite basic differences exist even between the English of the United States and that of the United Kingdom. In general, written texts ideally should be checked in the principal country for each language, e.g. France for French, Spain for Spanish, West Germany for German, etc.

ECONOMICS

The economics of building a reputation is difficult to calculate. Letting a reputation develop or build itself may appear to cost nothing—all that is necessary is for salesmen to go out and sell, while new business will develop from satisfied customers talking to friends in their line of activity. But if a company wants the sales curve to turn upwards, or if it wishes to reduce its selling costs (and increase its profits) by saving its salesmen from making cold calls, from having to 'sell' the company as well as its products every time, or if it wishes to keep its competitors at bay, then some form of communication with the market becomes necessary.

This is the moment when direct action must be taken to develop the firm's reputation according to the objectives and targets discussed at the beginning of this chapter. How much to spend very much depends on the size of the problem, and on the size of the target audience and its geographical distribution. It depends on the way the PR administration is organized, and also on the period during which the campaign is to operate. On the other hand, costs can be balanced with benefits, such as saving salesmen's time by following up qualified enquiries rather than cold calling; increasing the flow of orders by enhancing the firm's reputation; and maintaining a higher price as the result of having established a reputation for quality.

POLITICS

Developing an international corporate reputation involves both subjective and objective politics. A 'foreign' company or operation may be affected by local or national political attitudes, while at the same time, or alternatively, local or national politics can be used to further its reputation. In the former case, political pressures may be imposed for local ownership or manufacturing facilities, for example.

There are also the pressures that come from operating in markets of political regimes that are unpopular in the home market or elsewhere. How these pressures are handled depends on the individual policies of the organization, but very careful diplomacy must be used if the reputation is to survive unimpaired. On a local basis, it is valuable to have a 'friend at court' who can advise and act as an intermediary; and a well established corporate reputation can give strength in negotiations.

Possibly even greater diplomacy is required in handling international pressures or those from the home market, and the ability to handle them may depend very much on the quality and experience of top management in dealing with the media and the administration. If there is a risk of such issues developing, it is wise to prepare and rehearse attitudes, policies, and the answers to awkward questions.

On the other hand, the corporate reputation can benefit greatly from careful contacts with local and national politicians, not from the point of favouring one party against another, but more by creating a positive awareness with all parties. It is unwise to appear to support one party against another, as local and national administrations can change unexpectedly. Local board members, sponsorship of local events, and good local public relations, however, can all have a positive effect on the local and national political scene.

MEDIA

The media vary in their mix and sophistication from country to country. Television does not yet cover all countries and communities; furthermore, in some areas radio has a stronger influence than the press, whereas in others the provincial press is more dominant than the national. In organizing a world-wide or regional corporate relations programme, these local variations must be taken into account.

It should also be borne in mind that the media may have political allegiances as well as financial demands, and the latter may inhibit news coverage, particularly in the press, if adequate advertising space has not also been booked. This may seem contrary to the usual media ethics where advertising expenditure is not allowed to influence editorial content but it certainly happens and is a factor to consider.

Press media with international circulations are published in many parts of the world and in a number of languages, and although London and New York tend to be the main publishing centres, most publishers have representation in the main business capitals of the world. Personal contact is vital on a regular basis here; regular information and social sessions are recommended for the foreign press in the company's home country, and good contacts with the local organizations should be maintained.

National and international exhibitions, symposia, and local or international sponsorship are good opportunities to enhance corporate reputations. They all require thorough organization and good co-operation locally.

CORPORATE ADVERTISING

The influence of the media may be weak in certain areas, or the speed of development of the reputation may be too slow. Corporate advertising may be used to emphasize or strengthen certain perceptions which may be key aspects of the desired reputation, or to strengthen awareness in key geographical areas, and this should be designed and co-ordinated (possibly even financed) by the headquarters communications function. It should always be remembered, however, that building a reputation is a progressive activity, dealing with the mind and memory in a highly competitive environment, and corporate advertising has a long-term rather than short-term effect. Carefully conceived and planned, it is an extremely effective support to the corporate relations programme. But corporate advertising is also expensive and should not be treated lightly. Never consider it a tap to be turned on and off as the economic climate changes from year to year.

Summary

An international reputation is a fragile thing, but its value is immense. It has to be created and built up over a period of time. However, provided the objectives and strategies are clear and the execution carefully and professionally handled, it is possible to develop (and progressively check on) a reputation that is positive, with clear, specific perceptions, within a prescribed time scale. It is fragile in that misfortune or bad planning can spoil the reputation, but a professional approach can limit the effects of adverse situations and even turn them to advantage.

Organizing the development of an international reputation depends on the head office facilities and those in the local firm, but they should have a clear understanding of all the local and international variations and problems of language, media, political and communication standards in order to exploit the strategies prepared to achieve the planned objectives and time programme.

And having reached the planned objective within the time scale, it is vital to *maintain* the reputation, because a good reputation can be the subject of envy for competitors, for the media, and for politicians. It needs protecting.

Finally, do not overlook the support that can be given by skilfully created and placed corporate advertising, to echo the main strategies or themes of the overall campaign and to help keep the memory fresh after the main activities have been completed.

9.

CORPORATE ADVERTISING

Angus Maitland

Corporate advertising is perhaps the most controversial element in the mix of communications techniques available to a company. Its controversial nature arises from its high cost, the intangible nature of its results and, equally importantly, from a mixture of fear and misunderstanding among the most senior company executives. It does not deliver the direct and measurable impact on market share that a marketing campaign might be expected to achieve and this makes it difficult to justify. All this is reflected in the low and spasmodic expenditure on corporate advertising in the United Kingdom.

Why fear? Corporate advertising is not simply a sub-sector of advertising. It is the face and voice of a corporation. It is a highly public communications technique, and its sponsor cannot hide behind the editor's name as can be done in the results of a corporate press relations campaign. Its use demonstrates a clear and unequivocal commitment to the message contained in the advertisement, and in a rapidly changing corporate environment, such commitment takes courage.

Why misunderstanding? One can only speculate that the misunderstanding stems partly from poor management training and partly from the business culture of the United Kingdom. UK executives in general seem to be afraid of the media and perhaps in consequence affect a degree of contempt for it. This can be contrasted with much greater use of corporate advertising in the United States. There are signs that this is changing. A most visible indication has been the recent desperate attempts of companies fighting off take-over bids to make up, in a matter of weeks, for years of non-existent image projection. It is disappointing that it seems to have taken the ultimate corporate threat to focus the mind of UK management on corporate advertising.

The rationale

What can corporate advertising achieve, and in what circumstances should it be used? Both questions are far from a resolution, but a combination of research and experience has provided the basis for much greater understanding.

Perhaps the best known study on the effectiveness of corporate advertising was commissioned by *Time Magazine* from the US research consultancy, Yankelovich Shelly and White Inc.[1] Through a delightfully simple technique of pairing corporate and non-corporate advertisers, the study was able to demonstrate, using 700 personal interviews with 'upscale business executives', that corporate advertisers enjoyed a higher awareness, a greater familiarity and a better image than non-corporate advertisers. For reasons of cost and less kindly, commercial motivation, studies such as this have been the province of major media with an interest in developing corporate advertising business. A second Yankelovich study investigated questions such as the difference between the effect of corporate and product advertising on corporate image.[2] Different approaches to the question of effectiveness have been taken; for instance, the 1984 Erdos and Morgan Inc. study for Barrons analysed the findings from a mail sample of over 3000 respondents from a variety of publics on their views of the effectiveness of corporate advertising.[3] None, however, has quite matched the elegant simplicity of the Yankelovich design.

An examination of the history of corporate advertising in the United Kingdom might suggest that corporations' experience of it has been mixed. Few have pursued the technique with regularity. ICI advertised with some consistency in the 1960s and 1970s, and theirs was the first serious campaign on TV. It was intended to increase consumers' familiarity with the company and make the public aware of the ways in which ICI research and products benefited the nation. ICI was able to demonstrate a steady upward movement across a range of attitudinal measurements, and the investment the company has made in corporate advertising has been credited with the relatively high reputation the company has enjoyed, both externally and among its own workforce.

There is evidence to suggest that corporate advertising needs a fairly lengthy time period to run if it is to be successful. Shell called a halt to all advertising, except that for lubricants, after the oil crisis of 1973/74. Soon the company's advertising agency, Ogilvy and Mather, began to notice small but significant downward movements in the attitudinal measurements in their tracking studies conducted among the general public.[4] Within a year the following picture emerged on three important measures:

'You can depend on their products'   − 2%
'They have done a lot to make life easier' − 2%
'Their products give real value for money'− 1%

Although Shell had some reservations about corporate advertising at that stage, a short but heavy corporate campaign was mounted in the autumn of 1975. The results, measuring 1976 over 1975, showed a dramatic increase on nearly all the favourable measures. By then Esso, BP and Texaco were running corporate advertising campaigns, but they were outperformed by

Shell—despite the fact that its campaign lasted only two months. It seems that Shell was able to tap the goodwill built up in investment in corporate advertising over decades.

The long-term nature of corporate advertising, and the need to consider its effectiveness in the context of other communications techniques, are well illustrated by the best known corporate advertising campaign in the United Kingdom, the £16 million British Telecom 'Power Behind the Button' campaign. This is an example of the creative synergy that can be derived from a close working relationship between agency and client, in this case Dorland and British Telecom's Director of Corporate Relations. Theory would suggest that the enormous success of the BT flotation, in terms of the sheer size of the issue and the number of private shareholders who subscribed, would be preceded by significant attitudinal shifts. This assumption has been encouraged by the media and is encapsulated in Newman's book on the subject in the phrase, 'the corporate campaign was the bedrock for shifting image and perceptions as well as attracting interest in British Telecom the company.'[5]

Evidence that this is somewhat oversimplified is contained in the book itself. The corporate advertising campaign was launched in November 1983 and ended in August 1984. It was followed by a £10.5 million offer advertising campaign from August 1984 to November 1984. Table 9.1 shows the percentage point changes in six attitudinal tracking measurements between November 1983, August 1984, and November 1984. Rather than a wholesale shift in image, the evidence suggests that the central objective of the corporate advertising campaign—the emphasis on BT technology—was achieved dramatically when the campaign ended; the measure 'use up-to-date technology' had increased by 15 percentage points. However, by the time flotation occurred over two months later, it had decayed by 7 percentage points. Other attitudinal measurements of a non-technological nature moved

Table 9.1

	Nov. '83 %	Aug. '84 %	Nov. '84 %
'Spend a lot on research & development'	28	41	33
'Provide a good service to their customers'	58	56	53
'Very profitable'	57	61	57
'Use up-to-date technology'	46	61	54
'Charge too much for their services'	51	49	51
'I like their advertising'	16	30	24

Source: British Telecom/MORI

imperceptibly or declined; and still others, not shown in Newman's book, such as 'respond quickly to the needs of businesses' and 'give good value for money', also declined. What the retold BT saga often forgets, perhaps inevitably because it is not good copy, is the years of effort and investment that BT laid down long before the year preceding privatization, through an intelligent and creative corporate communications programme which gave the company a robust rating across a comprehensive range of attitudinal measurements. *That* was the bedrock on which the successful privatization was built. As Newman herself says in her book, 'British Telecom's image strengths in the Autumn of 1983 were considerable'.

A number of important conclusions can be derived from the above about corporate advertising.

1. It is an expensive technique, but it works.
2. It can build image strengths, but they will decline if it is not sustained. However, having advertised, rebuilding can be achieved rapidly.
3. It may not achieve image objectives that are outside the content of the message.
4. There can be no significant gap between the corporate message and the customer's perception of service and product.

Corporate advertising objectives

The BT experience also demonstrates that corporate advertising is only one technique among many which can be successful in image building. The argument for planned corporate communications is clear and widely accepted: all companies have an image—what Kotler calls 'the simplified impressions persons hold of an otherwise complex entity'[6]—and the rationale for corporate communications is that this process can assist in matching image and reality.

If it is accepted that there exists a real corporate need, then the next decision layer concerns the selection of techniques. The process is highly complex and poorly understood. It helps to separate the longer-term objectives of corporate communications. Oversimplifying, these are:

● To ensure that a company's activities are properly understood.
● To derive the behavioural benefits that greater knowledge and understanding can give.
● To shape the behaviour of staff, customers, consumers and others to the benefit of the company.

The ability of communications to shape behaviour has been demonstrated consistently in the study of psychology; and, since the early work of Hovland and others on communication and persuasion, the communications industry has a vast amount of data at its disposal covering a wide spectrum of issues, from the tendency towards consistency in attitude change to the specifics of credibility of source.[7]

Technique selection depends on the nature of a company's publics and the existence of short-term problems that need to be addressed. For instance, the attitudinal changes that led to a re-rating of the shares of the BOC Group on the London Stock Exchange in the autumn of 1982 were achieved mainly by personal contact with chemical sector analysts—a total audience of no more than 50, and a result that increased the market capitalization of the company by millions of pounds. (Descriptions of the BOC Group's City communications programme and its results are available from several sources.[8]) Contrast this with the Shell campaign above, aimed at an audience of millions.

The whole area of corporate communications demands rigorous planning. Companies must be clear as to the objectives they are pursuing and realistic as to what can be achieved. Planning implies a number of logical stages in the process. These are:

1. *Understanding the publics*   Clearly, those noted above vary in number, sophistication, understanding, and perception. Desk and field research are necessary to understand audience profile, knowledge, and attitudes.
2. *Defining objectives*   Companies must decide on priorities, and these can be encapsulated in a statement of objectives.
3. *Selecting techniques*   The size and sophistication of the audience will help determine the techniques used to communicate.
4. *Developing the programme*   This includes programme planning, budgeting, agency selection, and campaign research and development.

Unless the process of communication is developed on the basis of audience understanding and coherent objectives, the results can be damaging, as demonstrated by BAA's (formerly the British Airports Authority) experience.[9]

In 1983 the new Director of Public Affairs of the BAA was faced with an unusual problem. The market research agency carrying out tracking studies for the BAA concluded that the more it communicated, the more it decreased its research ratings, and that these would improve if it did nothing! However, doing nothing was not an acceptable option at that time, with decisions on major controversial issues such as the development of Stansted Airport being imminent. It was essential to establish the reputation of the BAA in order to ensure credibility for its arguments.

A research-based analysis was initiated. The key target market of politicians and opinion-formers was identified and carefully analysed to establish strengths and weaknesses. A detailed communications strategy was prepared, including advertising, videos, letters, and press releases; also a new industry magazine, 'Airport', was launched for free distribution at major airports. The previous advertising campaign was carefully researched and was found to be ineffective and possibly counter-productive.

A new advertising agency was hired to develop a new campaign, communicating in a positive way the facts about BAA. The first advertisement was a simple quiz designed to involve the target audience and to communicate seven key facts, notably that the business was a successful world leader in its field and did not cost the taxpayer a penny. Further advertisements have followed, with a similar approach.

After two years the result was dramatic. Favourability had actually doubled, and the decision to develop Stansted was approved by Parliament. Even more important was the influence on the local community: a major research programme demonstrated that people living in areas near the airport swung from 3:1 in favour of airport development (January 1985) to 5:1 in favour (January 1986).

Having touched on a number of United Kingdom case studies, and before examining the process in detail, it is useful to bear in mind the terms of reference which corporate advertising can cover. The Publishers' Information Bureau in the USA described these well, along the following lines:[10]

1. To educate, inform, or impress the public with regard to a company's policies, objectives and standards.
2. To build favourable opinion about a company by stressing its management ability, skills, technology and so on; and to offset negative attitudes.
3. To build up the investment qualities of a company.
4. To sell the company as a good employer.

As Garbett points out, the huge scope of these terms of reference has undoubtedly contributed to the difficulty in naming the functions.

Understanding the audience

It has been suggested that in advertising it is audience responses that matter;[11] a simple and unarguable proposition, but one that is all too often ignored.

Drucker identifies marketing as 'the whole business seen from the point of view of its final result, that is, from the customer's point of view'.[12] When Drucker wrote this over 30 years ago, he noted that in Europe 'there is still almost no understanding that marketing is the specific business function'. Corporate advertising must also be viewed from the audience's standpoint. And, like marketing in the 1950s, there is still no widespread appreciation in European industry of the need for response-oriented corporate advertising developed on the basis of desired audience responses.

It might be argued that it is difficult to establish audience response until corporate advertising has run for some time—perhaps two years—and that by any measure it is an expensive way to experiment. But this ignores the remarkable progress that has been made in behavioural research over the last 40 years. Indeed, the existence of a sophisticated behavioural research industry is often widely ignored by business, even when major budgets are being deployed.

A European research study conducted in 1982[13] concluded that around 80 per cent of international bank advertising was largely ineffective. The study, among the chief executives and the chief financial officers of Europe's largest companies, assessed spontaneous and prompted awareness of international bank advertising programmes, and spontaneous and prompted responses to the advertisements when these were used as stimuli. The fact that this section of advertising is one of the largest international categories can only underline the lack of communications professionalism in some of our largest financial institutions. A follow-up study showed that few international banks had used advertising research.[14]

Typically, benchmark and concept testing advertising absorbs around 5 per cent of a corporate communications budget. A small proportion of an investment which is professionally deployed can save the other 95 per cent being wasted. It does, however, involve skill and effort to conduct such research: perhaps that is why, more often than not, it is ignored.

The value which can be derived from primary attitude research is heavily influenced by the investment which is made in preparatory research. Much work can be done in understanding audiences before the formal research process is initiated.[15] This is particularly important in preparation for sampling. For instance, while consumer populations tend towards normal distribution and are therefore suited to random sampling techniques, more specialized corporate audiences, such as Westminster, Whitehall, and the City, need to be studied and understood in detail before they are sampled; and this understanding must be present when the findings of a survey are analysed.

The role of corporate advertising research

There are two areas that research needs to cover, and these form the crucial links in the advertising planning process. The first, concept testing, is concerned with ensuring—as far as this is possible—that the planned advertising campaign is eliciting the desired responses from the target audiences. The second, benchmark and tracking research, is designed to provide data on knowledge and attitudes, and involves a continuing process of monitoring.

Following a careful study of the target audiences, a communications programme should start with a benchmark study, designed to quantify knowledge, opinions, and attitudes, prior to any investment being made. The decision to employ corporate advertising is unlikely to be taken before such research is complete. A benchmark study fulfils two functions:

1. It sets a baseline for awareness and attitudes, against which the progress of the campaign can be monitored.
2. It identifies areas of lack of understanding and misperception among audiences, thus providing the hard data for the corporate advertising brief.

While this approach is conventional and widely used, there is some evidence that, by itself, it may be insufficient. Without entering into the quantitative versus qualitative research debate, it can be stated that the need to understand often complex behavioural responses may not be met satisfactorily by the 'cafeteria' technique, which involves respondents being confronted with a range of statements dreamed up by the research sponsor and the research company.[15] This technique is aimed at defining the image of a company through its association, by the respondent, with some or all of the statements. There is little doubt that this can lead to oversimplification of highly complex behavioural issues, and great care is needed in interpretation. Parallel qualitative work using focus groups is a wise precaution and can usually add significant insight.

Analysis of research findings against the background of communications objectives provides the material for the creative brief and the guidance necessary for developing effective advertising strategy. There is no 'correct' way to create good advertising. However, the use of proposition and concept testing as a key element in the developmental process can help to ensure that corporate advertising is reaching its audiences in a relevant and effective way. Research techniques are, to some extent, determined by the nature of the audience; where small groups can be recruited and researched, the focus group technique, using concept boards, will probably be most appropriate. The objective of this research is to determine the most effective way in which advertising can produce the responses sought by the advertiser from the audience.

It is at the concept-testing stage that research interpretation is most important. By its nature, qualitative research depends much more than quantitative research on the interpretation of the message; and, if corporate image questions are being studied rather than brand preferences, then the quality of interpretation becomes crucial. The advertiser should keep two simple behavioural 'laws' in mind: first, research executives tend towards a positive conclusion (it is extremely difficult to report to a client that no conclusion can be drawn from the research), and second, creative executives tend towards absolute belief in their own ideas. The choice of supplier in both areas is a decision fundamental to successful corporate advertising. While there is no substitute for conducting primary research into the experiences of other advertisers, initial guidance can be given by organizations such as the Advertising Agency Register[16] and the Market Research Society.[17]

Developing a corporate advertising programme

Assuming that a potential corporate advertiser has been through the benchmark research stage and has clear and coherent communications objectives, then it is time to think about budgeting, briefing, and agency selection.

Budgeting is the quantitative expression of a plan and it is, of course, concerned with the future. It is based on management's definition of corporate objectives and is a process where greater accountability is necessary.[18] Budgeting for corporate advertising may seem a long way from corporate objectives, but corporate advertising must be a direct reflection of these objectives. Too often, advertising budgets are arrived at by a process that can only be described as serendipity. Some form of task-related method is by far the most satisfactory, and here the existence of quantitative baseline measurements is clearly helpful.

Judgement is required in estimating the amount of exposure to advertising that is likely to yield attitudinal change; a host of case studies exists, such as those of TI, and Dunlop, and that of BT, referred to earlier. The media research and planning function, described below, will then recommend the most cost-efficient means of achieving this level of exposure.

Armed with a brief and a budget, the next task is to select an agency. This in itself is a complex and demanding process. Sufficient information can be gathered quickly in order to draw up an appropriate list, and the typical procedure is then as follows:

1. Receive a 'credentials' presentation from each agency to establish its record, resource, client base, and so on.
2. Draw up a short list.
3. Brief the short-listed companies.
4. Receive a written and verbal presentation.

The huge investment in time required to brief an agency fully should be a sufficient incentive to any company to undertake selection with great care.

Earlier in this chapter the internal audience was considered. Corporate advertising is, or should be, a profound corporate statement and, as such, it should be a management priority to communicate its purpose to employees. Management should keep employees informed throughout the advertising cycle; and indeed, if employees are a key audience, they need to be included in the research process.

Different companies are organized in different ways to handle a corporate advertising campaign, but this should never disguise the need for sensible integration of communications techniques. It is crucial that management and relevant executives are aware of all communications activities, and there must be some form of central control. If this is not the case, elements of a company's communications and marketing programme can work against each other, often to the serious detriment of the company's image. While to some extent a company's marketing programme must be driven by market needs, all those concerned must be aware of marketing communications programmes, at the very least. Most advertising agencies now employ planners, and application of the planning cycle to a company's overall communication programme is a worthwhile discipline.

While there is tacit acceptance in all parts of the advertising industry of the central importance of creativity, there is a growing awareness of the need for better direction of the creative function: the quest for creativity that works. While the sensitive measurements of brand market share can quickly kill creative consumer advertising or make it the hero of the hour, a greater element of faith is required in the creative process in corporate advertising. Brand preferences change quickly, but deeply entrenched attitudes change very much more slowly. Corporate advertising's job is to change attitudes. The role of creativity is threefold:

1. To ensure that the attention of the listeners, viewers or readers is caught.
2. To ensure that the audience's interest is sustained.
3. To ensure that the message informs and persuades effectively.

This is not a small task and needs some patience, skill and a great deal of hard work. A subjective creative medium is being used to translate corporate policy into a digestible popular message, and the fact that readers or viewers who do not know the company must recognize some kind of benefit puts enormous pressure on the creative function.

The end result of the research and creative process is good advertising and, while value can be added to it by judicious media selection to ensure the right kind of editorial environment, it must be able to stand up on its own. According to Ogilvy[20] it can achieve this in three ways:

- By being 'plain spoken, candid, adult, intelligent and specific'.
- By penetrating 'the filter of indifference with which most people regard corporations'.
- 'It should be the quiet graphics and speak the language of editors—not ad men.'

Good advertising gives the creative communicator scope to merchandise it in many ways, and so add value to the technique. Many of the most compelling merchandising campaigns have been born in an atmosphere of some desperation in bid-related advertising, for instance, Imperial Group's 'Famous brands growing famously' which failed in the end, and APV's 'Nobody knows our business better' which, in its success, created a watershed in mergers and acquisitions development in the United Kingdom.

Reaching the audience

Media research data present the corporate advertiser with a huge challenge. Most of the data have been gathered and paid for by those with the greater direct commercial interest in the findings that are shown by the data. It must not be concluded that such data are misleading, but caution and judgement are urged in their use—a sensible process with any information.

There are several important secondary sources available to the media planner covering UK and European corporate audiences.[20] These include:

1. *The European Business Readership Survey*, published every 2 years and based on an unweighted sample of over 10 000 senior executives in European companies with more than 250 employees.
2. *The BMRC Businessman Survey*, again published every 2 years and based on an unweighted sample of over 2000 businessmen and women with managerial responsibilities in UK companies.
3. *The Pan-European Survey*, published every 3 years, with an unweighted sample of over 7000. In this case the universe is professional and executive men in Europe.
4. *Institutional Financial Managers in Europe*, published every 3 years, with an unweighted sample of over 1100 senior financial managers in European companies with turnover in excess of US$150 million.
5. *European Finance and Investment Specialists*, published every 3 years, with an unweighted sample of over 1200 investment and money managers in Europe.
6. *Chief Executives in Europe*, published infrequently, with a sample of over 1200 chief executive officers in European companies with a turnover in excess of US$150 million.

Each of the above surveys includes information on readership habits by country or region, company size and type, and respondent responsibility. These criteria can be taken in isolation or cross-referenced using computerized techniques which take into account readership duplication between titles to determine actual coverage of specific target audiences.

There are a number of other secondary sources that are inhibited by lack of access to computer analysis, but are useful in examining readership of small groups.[22]

It is unlikely that the screening criteria for such surveys will be sufficiently rigorous or comprehensive to match exactly the audience for a corporate advertising campaign. For instance, where corporate advertising is being used primarily as a marketing weapon, audience definition may be highly specific. A good example is the Standard Chartered Bank International corporate advertising campaign that has been running since 1983 and is now in its fourth year. The Bank had defined its target audience as principal decision-makers for a range of specific international banking services in corporations of a certain size with a minimum proportion of turnover generated from export business. This kind of audience profile is not available from secondary sources and, in the case of Standard Chartered Bank, much useful data were gathered during the primary advertising research studies. For instance, the *BMRC Businessman Survey 1984* shows that 38.7 per cent of respondents with main responsibility for finance and accounting read the *Financial Times* and 26.3 per cent read the *Daily Telegraph*.[23] However, Standard Chartered Bank's own research survey conducted among a carefully defined customer audience showed that, in fact, 94 per cent of this audience in the United Kingdom read the *Financial Times* and 38 per cent read the *Daily Telegraph*. These studies also showed the need to use qualitative and quantitative techniques and to link creative approach with media rationale.[24]

Of course it is dangerous to equate readership of a medium with readership of the advertising contained in it. Some attempts have been made to fill this gap with reading and noting studies, particularly by individual publishers. For instance, *International Management* runs an 'ad-evaluation' programme designed to assess the impact of each advertisement on a representative panel of readers. However, it is increasingly the responsibility of the advertising organization to ensure that its advertising is having the desired effect on the target audience, through well established market and attitude research techniques.

Media departments are becoming increasingly sophisticated, and their responsibilities to ensure maximum cost effectiveness are also growing. Generally the media planner will work from the same brief as the creative department—now increasingly developed by account planners—and he or she will be responsible for recommending the optimum level of coverage within the agreed budget. The likely coverage delivered by various media mixes can be evaluated using the sources referred to above. The average frequency of seeing an advertisement can also be calculated using these sources. Timing is also an important media consideration and the 'drip' versus 'burst' debate is likely to continue into the foreseeable future. Great effort also goes into advertisement positioning, based on theories concerning reader behaviour and the value or otherwise of juxtaposing an advertisement with relevant articles.

Positioning is a prime consideration in the media buying function. The buyer's job is to place advertisements at the best possible rate in the most powerful and visible positions, and to balance rate against position.

Television versus press

Most of the above discussion has used press media for reference as, certainly in the United Kingdom, the press has been the most frequently used medium for corporate advertising. However, the high-budget corporate programmes, designed to influence public opinion, have of course used television.

The choice of advertising medium depends on the message, the audience and, to some extent, budget, although task-oriented budgeting is becoming more usual. Press campaigns have been used traditionally to reach senior decision-makers and will probably continue to be used for corporate campaigns aimed at such elite groups, who tend to be 'light' television viewers (i.e. those who do not watch a great deal). One advantage of press advertising over television is that more detailed information can be presented. And, although the press does not have the impact of television, the use of colour in magazines and newspapers has added a further dimension to press advertising.

Television undoubtedly has an increasingly important role to play in corporate advertising. It is by nature a mass medium and is extremely effective in rapidly building awareness, as demonstrated in earlier references to TV campaigns in this chapter. In addition to those mentioned, BP has also used television to great effect, as demonstrated by the results of its research.[25]

The use of Channel 4 programmes, in addition to other ITV programmes such as 'News at Ten', makes it possible to target more precisely the advertising aimed at 'light' viewers, for example those in AB groups. This is a relatively cost-effective and sophisticated method of TV buying, and many advertisers still seek mass audiences, although the demand for such upmarket airtime is now increasing.

A marketing dimension

It has long been realized that corporate advertising can result in real marketing benefits. British Telecom's 1984 corporate campaign has been credited with a significant call stimulation impact, and Guinness's bid advertising with a short-term increase in the consumption of its stout product called Guinness.

This relationship between familiarity, favourability, and increased purchase is not surprising in behavioural terms, but it is often ignored in the planning and development of a corporate campaign. It is particularly relevant in the industrial market where buyers are less susceptible to sales promotion.[25]

Monitoring the programme

Earlier in this chapter the role of benchmark and tracking research was discussed. Monitoring a corporate advertising programme is not simply a case of replicating the benchmark study and examining changes across a range of factual and attitudinal dimensions.

Corporate advertising is not the only formal way in which a company communicates with its audience and indeed every action is a form of communication. Also, of course, the best planned advertising campaigns can be destroyed by exogenous factors.

Clearly, therefore, it is important to ensure that the monitoring factor has much wider terms of reference than those implied in the tracking research procedure. It must be able to evaluate the impact of a variety of factors on a company's image and reputation, and to comment intelligently on the relationship between the behaviour of a company and its communications. When these become out of tune, the seeds of long-term damage, which can often be quite serious, are planted. The monitoring function must be the guardian of corporate advertising in the sense that the latter must carry the truth and not attractive fiction.

The future

As our world grows in complexity—while becoming much more accessible to people through improvements in the ease of travel and the efficiency of communication—the need for corporate communications in general, and corporate advertising in particular, must grow.

With change becoming even more rapid, and corporate and financial institutions becoming bigger and more international, progress can be assured only by widespread understanding and appreciation of companies' activities, objectives and general behaviour in a wide social, political, economic and ethical sense.

Communications techniques and technology must continue to improve to meet this need. To achieve this, more talented people must be attracted into the field of corporate advertising, particularly in the creative and planning disciplines, and a greater sense of reality must develop within those major corporations whose activities increasingly affect our everyday lives. Also more creative use must be made of the media options that are at present being improved and added to by technology.

There is now an enormous range of advertising opportunities to reach both mass and specialist audiences in cost-effective ways. The benefits of corporate advertising are clear. All that is needed is the vision to use it to its maximum effect.

Notes

1. Yankelovich Shelly and White Inc., *A Study of Corporate Advertising Effectiveness* (Time Inc., 1977).
2. Yankelovich Shelly and White Inc., *Corporate Advertising/Phase II, an expanded study of corporate advertising effectiveness conducted for Time Magazine* (Time Inc., 1979).
3. Erdos and Morgan Inc., *The Image of Corporate Advertising. An Assessment of Corporate Advertising by its Target Audiences* (Dow Jones & Co., 1984).
4. *Source*: Shell, 1986.
5. Karin Newman, *The Selling of British Telecom* (Holt, Rinehart & Winston, New York, 1986).
6. Philip Kotler, *Marketing Management*, 3rd edn (Prentice-Hall International Inc, Englewood Cliffs, NJ, 1976).
7. C. I. Hovland, I. L. Jarvis and H. H. Kelley, *Communication and Persuasion* (Yale University Press, New Haven, CT, 1953).
8. A. J. Maitland, To see ourselves as others see us. *The BOC Group Management Magazine*, 1983.
9. *Source*: BAA (formerly British Airports Authority), 1986.
10. E. Garbett, *Corporate Advertising, the What, the Why and the How* (McGraw-Hill, Maidenhead, Berks, 1981).
11. S. King, Public response: the key to corporate advertising, *Advertising Writer*, 1978-9.
12. Peter Drucker, *The Practice of Management* (Harper Bros., Wilmington, NC, 1954).
13. A. J. Maitland, The marketing problems facing international banks and the role and effectiveness of international bank advertising, paper presented to Conference on Financial Communications in a World Recession, McFarlane Conferences Limited, London, April 1983.
14. The follow up research study was published in the same paper (Note 13).
15. Ronald McTavish and Angus Maitland, 'Industrial Marketing', Chapter 6 in *Macmillan Studies in Marketing Management* (Macmillan, London, 1980).
16. Robert M. Worcester, Evaluating the corporate image campaign, Oyez/IBC Conference, Amsterdam, 1981.
17. The Advertising Agency Register, 62 Shaftesbury Avenue, London W1.
18. The Market Research Society, 15 Belgrave Square, London SW1.
19. A. J. Maitland, Greater accountability in marketing budgets, *The Accountant*, February 1982, Volume 186.
20. From an address on corporate advertising by David Ogilvy, in Garbett's book (see Note 10).
21. These readership studies are conducted and published by Research Services Limited, London.
22. For instance, MORI's readership surveys of MPs (1984), financial journalists (1982), and 'Captains of Industry' (1985).
23. Conducted and published by Research Services Limited, London.
24. A. J. Maitland, R. Michelmore, International bank advertising—vive la différence, *Media International*, June 1984, describe the Standard Chartered Bank approach more comprehensively.
25. The results can be seen in *Viewpoint*, the marketing journal of the Independent Television Companies, Issue No.21.
26. For a detailed analysis of the industrial marketing 'difference', refer to Chapter 1 of the book in Note 14.

10.

SPONSORSHIP

Patrick Nally

Let us begin with a story . . .

The chairman said to his fellow directors, 'Before we move into lunch there is just one other matter I would like to raise. As you may know, my wife takes a great interest in local affairs. She has told me there is a great need for a proper youth club in this area, but it is difficult to find the money needed. I feel this company should make funds available for this worthwhile project. It would be good for our name to be linked with this social activity, and no doubt, the children of many of our workers would be able to use such facilities. I trust I can have your agreement to the allocation of £X000 to this—well, I suppose you would call it—corporate sponsorship?'

Not a fairy tale. It is something that still happens, albeit less frequently, in the board rooms the world over, and even now, the chairman of many a major organization cannot understand why his wife should not play the leading role at company-supported functions.

Our illustrative chairman said, 'I suppose you would call it sponsorship.' He was mistaken, unaware that what he was allowing himself to indulge in, with his wife's persuasion, was *patronage*. That is a very good thing if you can afford to do it, as a personal gesture, but it has nothing to do with sponsorship. Planned sponsorship is part of the very businesslike communications programme of an organization, from which, unlike patronage, an equally businesslike return is expected.

It might be useful, as well as noteworthy, to look at the definition of 'sponsorship'. This varies according to the age of the dictionary. Back in 1930, a 'sponsor' was listed as a godfather or godmother; and 'sponsorship' as providing a surety for another person. By the late 1950s there was little difference, except that in addition to 'surety' there was 'vouchment' and 'responsibility' for another's obligations. Moving into the 1970s, new words came in such as 'contribution', 'pledge', or 'security'; more interesting, these words are all related to a return. There is even one definition referring to finance for a radio or TV programme in exchange for the right to advertise before or after it.

This last concept was, in fact, initiated by an American editor in whose country it operates, but it is almost repeated in the latest supplement to the

Oxford English Dictionary in the form of recognizable financial support or promotion of a radio or TV programme. This is still frowned upon in the UK. The other latest *OED* explanation is that very basic idea, the support of a fund, usually for charity, by pledging against a certain unit completed.

Thus, we are still left with the need to establish the definition of sponsorship as it currently operates, and will do so even more in the future, in relation to industrial, business, and commercial activity.

Sponsorship, despite the difficulty in providing a consistent definition, has evolved into a truly effective medium of communication—effective, that is, in involving the aims and activity of an organization with its major publics, including its 'market', by association with areas sympathetic to both the public and the organization. The areas and interests in which it is most applied—sport, music, the arts—have an emotive impact. Their various facets can affect selective groups or publics, yet they are international and can transcend language, race, and environmental or political differences.

Communication, as we all know, over recent years has become global and instant. New techniques demand new approaches. But that is the technical side. Communication has also changed its definition over the years. It now infers an exchange, not a one-way operation. In selling and marketing (and of course sponsorship is used here), the return is comparatively easy to estimate; in general public relations also there are aspects for quick assessment; but others move into the broader scale, long-term programmes. Corporate relations? Well, doesn't everything contribute to the corporate face and reputation?

Mutual co-operation

Sponsorship can be used purely to achieve good corporate relations, but its use in any other area can add to or subtract from the corporate message. It can burnish or dent the corporate image if it is used without adequate planning.

Perhaps the most important element, and one needing very serious consideration and forward planning, is the conclusion of sponsorship. As already stated, the main areas where it is applied have great emotive effect; whether in sport, music, or the arts, the real lives of people are involved. If you are going to use sponsorship as a corporate tool of communication, you have to take on the responsibility of this human, emotional involvement and to plan and organize for the time when you will wish to withdraw. If you just 'pull the plug out', it will be disaster not only for the people involved but also for your own organization—a ricochet effect.

With the new role of sponsorship, there have been changes on the other side of the communication contract. The arts, music, and sport have had to adapt to being active co-operators, not just passive receivers. The whole scene is now very much one of mutual co-operation for mutual progress. Both sides have to appreciate the possible benefits, and many institutions and organizations have to learn to define their own rights and policy in this new environment.

So in this situation, sponsorship has to be expertly organized and orchestrated, with the choice of subject and the balance of investment and potential achievement carefully judged. For instance, whether in sport, music, or another area, there has to be a careful investigation and advance planning of the rights of such items as display, which may be controlled by myriad contracts or unspecified lax arrangements.

Moreover, successful sponsorship is not just a matter of getting your name exposed widely and frequently, although even this, provided it is within the right context, can supply some of the effective communication required— especially for corporate relations. Any investment in sponsorship really needs, and deserves, wider thinking, to capitalize on every aspect of an organization's operation.

Not surprisingly, therefore, sponsorship has become a subject for discussion and decision at the highest levels—between corporate executives on the one hand and those representing major interests or the national/international bodies on the other.

That the current definition of sponsorship is established, even if it is not in the dictionary, is best illustrated by case studies showing its corporate use. In the examples that follow, the detail is quite as important as the whole concept.

Comparable achievement

The Davis Cup for tennis is one of the oldest major sports awards, founded in 1900. The international computer and communications company, NEC Corporation of Japan, started as Nippon Electric in 1899. How and why did the two get involved?

It started, on one side, with the International Tennis Federation (ITF), the governing body responsible for the international control and co-ordination of tennis, with the Davis Cup being the sport's 'Olympic'—the event for nations. The ITF retained a consultancy to assist with much needed investment in and stimulation for this event in the wake of 'professional' tennis, plus the need to secure finance to promote the game world-wide.

NEC, on the other side, wanted to project its name internationally in both the marketing and the corporate sense. Having considered this prestigious competition as its appropriate ambassador to the world, the Corporation agreed to become its first international sponsor, simultaneous with a radical change in the Davis Cup structure.

The event had immense potential in terms of international tennis, involving more than 60 countries with year-round exposure. But the format was confusing. It required 16 months of play to complete each year's competition, leaving the public muddled and uninspired. Yet, as an international event organized at national level, it was perfect for NEC's corporate needs in that the national organization could be exploited internally.

To encourage and support the backing of NEC, a complete overhaul began in 1981. There was a daunting situation of existing contracts plus national and local agreements. Almost every Davis Cup team and individual tie had its own sponsorship arrangements. The Davis Cup had been considered impossible to sponsor as an overall international relationship with one company.

The ITF, with its consultancy, restructured the competition. The 16 strongest nations would compete for the trophy in a simple, knockout tournament. Other teams would gain promotion to the top group via zonal competitions, with both the world groups and the zonal events being significant local occasions.

Thus the World Group was born, bringing Davis Cup tennis into a classic 16-nation format. The competition could take place in four well defined rounds and could be completed in one year, with each round having pre-set weeks reserved in the international tennis calendar for top player participation. The advantages were that nations could plan well in advance, and TV could be 'packaged' to show a selection of ties from each round so that coverage would appeal to wide audiences, including those countries not directly involved. Most important, the competition would be recognized and appreciated by the general public. As part of this reorganization, all commercial rights were gradually brought into the central control of the ITF.

The changes were also important to NEC in that it could achieve consistent exposure at more than 60 Davis Cup ties every year. A new standard formula, plus attention to display related to TV filming techniques, ensured maximum recognition of the organization's involvement. Even more, it assured a significant corporate community platform on a global basis.

Within NEC's international rights, other complementary international sponsors in specialized roles were introduced to help the overall finance and promotion, all working together for mutual advantage. Clothing and equipment, soft drinks, timing, and transport have a consistent identity throughout the competition and the world, thus adding to the total organized impact.

The complete reformation took some years, but the results have been significant. The event is adequately funded. Television and press coverage and spectators have increased because the event now enjoys a higher standard of presentation than at any time in its history. This is achieved by detailed co-ordination of all the 60 tennis federations responsible for staging Davis Cup ties, plus experienced supervision at all the World Group ties and zonal finals. This degree of care and presentation is very important, and it involves NEC and the subsidiary sponsors in the co-ordination of print, publicity, entertainment facilities, press centres, and public relations operations.

A major part of the new Davis Cup operation has been a planned and deliberate expansion of TV coverage to reach audiences everywhere. For instance, the final was shown in 7 countries before the new scheme, in 30 countries in 1982, and in 40 countries in 1985. Total competition coverage has grown from 443 hours in 28 countries in 1982 to 726 hours in 58 countries in 1985. In addition, NEC's name and logo have been exposed in a huge volume of print, including posters, programmes, and tickets, running to more than 2 million items annually.

The Davis Cup has become a truly world-recognized and -appreciated part of the tennis scene, and NEC, having been the initiator and supporter of this transformation, has become known and respected by the sort of public that ought to know its status.

Precise identity

The phrase 'long-term perspective' can be used to describe Canon's comparatively long-term use of sponsorship as a medium of communication. Way back in 1976, the company name was frequently confused with that of another firm already well known in the domestic equipment area. Apart from this corporate problem, Canon was trying to establish its own name and quality in other fields, especially in professional photography, where recognition would provide valuable ammunition for marketing to the general consumer. As the company developed and its product range expanded, a wider corporate understanding was needed. For all of these objectives, Canon has used sponsorship.

Initially, the concept of working with sport was born of the strong attraction surrounding events in this sphere to professional photographers. So moves were taken to make Canon the official camera and to provide essential services to photographers at major events, starting with the Montreal Olympics in 1976. This is a programme that has expanded ever since.

It did not take long to observe that sport also offered a neat and apposite opportunity to communicate the company's desired overall reputation for innovation, precision, and technical skill. Thus, sponsorship thinking expanded to include all aspects of Canon's operation—copiers, calculators, and business machines *ad infinitum.*

The public contacted were both specialized and various, owing to involvement in national, European, and world major events. The year 1977 saw co-operation with the World Ski Cup, European Swimming Championships, World Ice Hockey Championship, and Formula I motor racing. In 1978

Canon was involved with the Soccer World Cup. In 1979 the company took on a four-year investment in a top-level international football programme, Intersoccer 4. Via this it acquired, apart from vast general publicity, exclusive use of Canon cameras and equipment at major international events.

At all of these events, as in all good sponsorship, it is not just a matter of getting the Canon name plastered around. Canon equipment and technical services provide a real, tangible, and useful contribution, with high professional standards which are both appreciated and noted. They also educate the public about the company.

The impact of the investment in sponsorship was not allowed to go unnoticed by staff and distributors. Programmes, including seminars, manuals, and videos, alerted public relations and marketing people as well as distributors to the potential of the Canon connection with popular sport. At the same time, a valuable bond was forged between the different product divisions. All were joined in a combined activity which not only attracted their personal interest but gave everyone new ideas and enthusiasm for their company role.

So the concept moved on, with the organization convinced of the value of its corporate investment programme on both an internal and an international basis. Now Canon is into athletics—the 1982 European Athletic Championships and the inaugural 1983 World Championships. Here, with proper organization, TV coverage of 1537 hours, in 137 countries, to an audience of 1377 million was achieved.

The involvement has continued over a range of sport, linking in the messages of the management board. Not everything is obvious. Canon quietly supports the activities of international sports organizations and their meetings, thus maintaining a presence within, as well as a knowledge of, the world scene.

Canon is able and willing to acknowledge sports sponsorship as a major element in the company's communication strategy, both externally and internally. It has changed the profile of the company, and 10 years later, the name is known throughout the world for many products, without being confused with cookers.

Tomorrow's public

If you are 100 years old and your name is the best known and most often seen even in many of the most remote corners of the world, what do you have to say? As far as the Coca-Cola Company is concerned, it is that you are not out of touch, not complacent, and have a lively, universal interest in the future.

To communicate its messages, the organization chose a language already international and capable of being truly universal—football. The first step into football sponsorship was taken in 1976 with the signing of an important contract with FIFA, the governing body of world soccer. This agreement, which was the first example of global sponsorship, linked FIFA and the Coca-Cola Company in a series of programmes designed to achieve different objectives within different areas—plus a major concentration on youth.

The FIFA/Coca-Cola World Development Programme, now operating under the title Coca-Cola Football Academies, was initiated with the concept of using the expertise of advanced soccer nations in Europe and South America to upgrade coaching skills in developing football countries. The basis of the concept was that the most effective way to advance the level of football was to upgrade administrative and coaching capabilities. This would have a snowball effect.

The project has been a major community relations exercise, and one taken extremely seriously by the football world. The Coca-Cola Company has moved into an important area of development and education. A FIFA World Youth Championship for the Coca-Cola Cup was established in 1977 and is second in world soccer events to the World Cup. It has now been staged five times, most recently in the USSR. A championship for players of 19 years and under, it still brings in players already playing professionally for their countries. The standard of football is excellent, and the event is of great interest to both the media and football fans around the world. In 1985 102 nations entered the championship, which was held in the Soviet Union with 32 matches televised in 50 countries; 500 journalists were accredited to the event —200 from overseas and 300 from the Soviet bloc.

That the Development Programme has helped to close the 'gap' between developed and developing countries is shown by Nigeria who, having won a recent under-16 world tournament in China, took third place in the World Youth Championship. The Programme has led to good relationships with China as well as the USSR and other countries with whom it is usually difficult to communicate.

Capital is made on the investment in the Championship via sales activities in all the individual participant countries, using the resultant knowledge of and goodwill for the Coca-Cola Company.

Another part of the very comprehensive overall programme is a Soccer Skills project, planned to provide to bottlers the potential for involvement and activity with youth. It is adapted to suit different conditions in different countries and operates under various titles. For instance, in the United States it was named 'Kick Me' and was thoroughly and professionally mounted, progressing to national finals. Bottlers had the chance to hold open days, in which to promote and generate publicity. The first international final was staged in Argentina alongside the 1978 World Cup.

A third part of the whole scheme is 'Go for Goal', developed to provide practical teaching materials for the World Development/Football Academies project. It took a year of co-operation with a top youth coach to complete this package, which consists of five 15-minute coaching films, five slide presentations, 10 classroom wall charts, 64 individual coaching cards, a booklet and a referee's book translated into 12 languages and distributed in more than 40 countries. Endorsed by leading football associations, the material, identified with Coca-Cola, has been used in thousands of schools, by millions of schoolchildren.

The Coca-Cola Company's great commitment to youth, and its long relationship with FIFA, has given it a dominant presence within world football and in the World Cup. For Coca-Cola, football has opened doors, created goodwill, and kept the company face to face with a global public. It has provided an effective medium of communication with developing countries and with millions of young people throughout the world. It would be difficult to find a more effective means of illustrating the character and role of a centenarian organization for tomorrow's publics.

Fair play

As a change from thinking on the international, global level, we can look at an example illustrating operation within a national orbit. A classic corporate case could be the description applied to the results of a plunge into sponsorship by an insurance company.

There is possibly nothing more 'classic' in sport than cricket, even to many countries designated as 'Third World', and despite a slightly quaint image in those areas that as yet do not participate. It cannot be disputed that in many countries cricket is a very serious matter, attracting a great deal of solid interest, nor that England is a leading illustration of this fact. 'That's not cricket' is still a truly idiomatic phrase. The symptom is displayed by just the sort of people with whom an insurance company would like to establish communication.

There was a time in 1977 when the long-standing establishment of cricket was under attack. A concept of turning it into a commercially organized form of entertainment was showing signs of success, undermining the faith of top players and creating alarming problems for English test cricket. This was when the plunge was taken. Cornhill Insurance decided to save English test cricket. The company gathered together its promotional and communications resources and lumped the major part of them into sponsoring the cause.

Although this was a rapid decision, it was followed by classical, meticulous, and long-term attention to organization and the achievement of results—not only for the cricket, but also for Cornhill. As another classical touch, the company took on independent research to monitor an awareness of its name and function as a measure of the effect of the investment.

To get the company name associated with such an establishment institution as test matches was going to be difficult, and Cornhill took specialist consultants on board. The contract was with the Test & County Cricket Board (TCCB), but, although this meant that the Board recognized the new name 'Cornhill Test' as official, it did not, and could not, guarantee general acceptance and use. A great deal of sensible and honest contact with the appropriate media was put into action. The company made it clear that its intentions towards cricket were sincere and that it was keen to assist the media with statistics and other services. At the same time, it was not afraid to be equally straightforward about its wish for the Cornhill name to benefit.

The adoption of the new title developed faster than expected, albeit still gradually. At the same time, the company name and special logo, used cleverly but within the rules of the TCCB, established a different communication line, via the grounds, with related TV coverage and on all printed material.

In 1978, when the sponsorship started, the 'unprompted' awareness level was only 2 per cent, very low indeed against other insurance companies. Not many people knew of Cornhill in relation to insurance. By 1980 the figure had improved to 17 per cent, and this held for 1981; 1982 showed a further increase to 21 per cent, putting Cornhill ahead of almost every other company in the field, and this percentage is sustained in the latest poll to date.

Another aspect that has been surveyed with satisfactory results is recognition of the company's support for cricket. Among men interviewed, as many as 50 per cent have mentioned Cornhill as being connected with the game, a figure way above that for any of the other companies that qualify.

The moral cannot be lost that it is a good thing that Cornhill has placed its name, in association with insurance, firmly in the public mind, but even better that it got it linked with that solid, classical, fair-play image of cricket.

Rejuvenation

It is a long jump from classical cricket to rock music, but the move can be both a useful and correct exercise.

You may not totally accept the McLuhanism, 'the medium is the message', but there is no doubt that wise corporate thinking will include careful consideration of the type and method of message to be used. This applies to sponsorship quite as much as to any other form of communication. So it came about that four organizations became involved in a tour of Europe by that super-star group, the Rolling Stones. Super-star, that is, to certain publics. To an organization whose purpose and activity is concerned with those particular publics, it is important to become known to them and to bear a familiar, sympathetic image.

It is not easy to communicate with the average young person or teenager. Families know that as much as large companies. Conventional marketing and promotional tactics are missed, ignored, or, if noticed, treated with detached disdain. Suppose, therefore, you could get over the message that your organization is truly interested in the same things as they are? The challenge was grasped by companies in the fields of audio tapes, jeans, and motorcycles. One of these was the Italian motorbike manufacturer Piaggio, who took on the sponsorship of that part of the rock tour taking place in Italy. At that moment Piaggio had the image of an aging, *passé* company.

The story of this operation is both unusual and bitter-sweet, and could probably be taken as either a warning or an example in matters of sponsorship.

This was not like a sporting event where part of the linkage of the sponsor's name could be with the event itself, thus getting TV, radio, and print exposure. There was no way top rock stars would let their names be attached to that of a company, unless it was in an endorsement contract of suitably megasize proportions. There had to be other ways of making Piaggio's connection evident both to the audiences and to all those other fans interested in and excited by the tour.

Aspects perhaps not adequately anticipated, and certainly not given the attention they deserved, were the history of rock and pop concerts in Italy and the impact the Rolling Stones visitation would have on local politics and general news. For five years Italy had been frozen out of the rock tour circuits. Rioting and general bad behaviour had made the country unacceptable to the popular music fraternity. Such behaviour had convinced some political elements that rock groups were an undesirable and dangerous influence, to be kept away from Italian youth. So the very decision by the Rolling Stones to include Italy in their tour was a breakthrough which, while causing great joy and excitement in some quarters—plus media interest— also produced bitter political debate and upheaval, which in turn attracted media coverage.

Add to this scene the fact that it was this aging, *passé* Piaggio organization that was producing such a revolution, and you have an electric shock impact which caused the whole Italian nation to regard Piaggio in a new light, immediately.

As far as the basic, or routine, operation of using the sponsorship to make contact with its public was concerned, the Piaggio organization was highly efficient. Great use was made of the contracted facility to use the well-known Tongue and Lips logo by incorporating it with the Piaggio logo into an official event symbol. This was exploited in every possible way on print material, in a wide range of merchandise, and in promotional effects and campaigns.

All of this achieved excellent recognition of the Piaggio name and involvement. An experienced observer, one of the consultant team advising the company, said of a massive concert in Turin—which was competing with

Italy playing in a World Cup soccer final on TV—'one had to be there to experience the frenzy, the excitement, the pure magic . . . all associated with the Piaggio name.'

That was the sweet part. The bitter element, especially when viewed on the corporate level, was the lack of realization and exploitation of the true status of the Rolling Stones and, even more, of the politically live impact of their 'invasion', which extended the communications possibilities so much. One could say that sponsorship moved in too late for total involvement, or that, with its particular and unusual environment, the project proved too big for the company concerned, or that, with a little more flexible, on-the-spot, rapid thinking, a successful operation could have been converted into an even bigger, broader corporate exercise.

Without any regrets for what was achieved—after all, the main objective of making Piaggio a youthful, dynamic entity was attained in one step—there must be a little taste of what might have been—or could be.

Conservative elegance

No such aftermath from the sparkling, clear-cut jewel of sponsorship communication presented by watch-makers Ebel for their seventy-fifth anniversary. For such an organization, it was essential to echo and maintain its already established reputation for distinctive design, perfect precision—in other words, for desirable, sophisticated luxury.

Ebel already knew its public very well and was aware that nothing should be done to harm its relationship; however, given care, there was no reason why such an event as a seventy-fifth anniversary should not reinforce and expand the company's sphere of influence and appreciation.

The ideal concept was found. Ebel linked in with a modern, musical legend, a world-famous conductor and composer, and a charismatic, controversial personality to boot—Leonard Bernstein. This was the medium which could link the groups Ebel wished to reach—a musical, theatrical interest appealing to, yes, the affluent, but also the young and old, the classic and the modern.

An arrangement was concluded that Ebel would sponsor six concerts in world capitals, each capable of providing its individual aura of elegance, style, and culture. In Vienna, London, Rome, New York, Munich, and Paris, the 'glitterati' sought to attend, while Ebel retained exclusive tickets for special customers and guests. A most unusual and felicitous bonus in the arrangement was the fact that the Ebel title was associated with the Bernstein name throughout: these were the Ebel Bernstein concerts.

In London the performance was a Royal Gala, attended by the Queen and Prince Philip and televised by the BBC. In each venue, hospitality via a formal dinner attended by Bernstein and his soloists was provided for customers and business associates of Ebel. Obviously, all the concerts attracted enormous media interest, especially in the 'quality' area.

It has to be emphasized that this was a unique operation, created and tailored to suit the specific corporate needs of the organization. But then, even on the most modest scale, that is what any sponsorship should be.

Little and large

The case examples quoted above probably give the impression that sponsorship is for large companies with large budgets and large ideas. But this is only because they happen to be interesting stories which illustrate how sponsorship works, or should work.

The same principles can apply to other situations. The most important precepts are those already indicated, which also pertain to all other areas of organized relationships. You need to know what you want to communicate; you need to seek the appropriate medium; and you need to ensure that there is going to be two-way action. Needless to say, to extract maximum mutual benefit there has to be detailed, effective, imaginative—i.e. professional— implementation. The responsibility for this falls very much on the side of the sponsor.

Successful sponsorship could be likened to a happy marriage, which is achieved only by the right match and a lot of hard work.

(*N.B.* Figures have not been quoted here because, apart from the fact some organizations would object (although company reports and reference books can be consulted), it is the familiar theory of the length of a piece of string. At the beginning of this chapter it was emphasized that the balance of investment and potential achievement had to be carefully judged, just as with any other investment aspect.)

Another bonus

The above examples do not relate immediately to social responsibility, i.e., to making a contribution to the social balance sheet. It is well recognized that, within the current trends of society and the enormous increase in total communication, organizations are faced with new responsibilities to achieve moral credit, both within and without. This role has to be part of overall corporate responsibility and thus involves all general public relations and communication.

The exposition of social responsibility sometimes referred to as sponsorship, such as seconding staff to associations, charities, and development or conservation projects, or providing other facilities and help to such causes, does not constitute sponsorship in the definition discussed here. However, if you look back at some of the examples just summarized, you will see that they did, like other aspects of corporate relations, contribute to the social balance sheet.

Information and further reading

ORGANIZATIONS

Association for Business Sponsorship of the Arts, 2 Chester Street, London SW1. Supported by companies concerned with expansion of sponsorship of the arts.
The Sports Council
Sports Sponsorship Advisory Service, 16 Upper Woburn Place, London WC1H 0QP. Basic information on where sponsorship is needed.
Institute of Sports Sponsorship, Francis House, Francis Street, London SW1P 1DE. Top-level link of interested organizations.
The Sponsorship Association, 32 Sekforde Street, Clerkenwell Green, London EC1R OHH. Broadly based professional body of those concerned with sponsorship.

PUBLICATIONS

Hollis Directories Ltd, *Public Relations Annual*, Contact House, Lower Sunbury Rd, Sunbury-on-Thames, Middx TW16 5HG. Section on who sponsors what plus sponsorship consultants.
Sponsorship News, PO Box 66, Wokingham, Berks RG11 4RQ. General information monthly.
Mintel Publications, *Mintel Sponsorship Survey*, 7 Arundel Street, London WC2 3DR. High-level academic survey including finances.
Financial Times Library.
Time Magazine Library.

11.

MEDIA RELATIONS

Roger Haywood

Creating goodwill and understanding through effective news coverage

When organizations consider the many publics upon whom they depend for success, they often overlook one of the most important: the media. Sometimes this omission is not accidental. The argument runs that the media are a *channel* of communication, enabling the organization to reach the desired audiences. However, at the same time the media constitute one of the most important audiences, and they should receive a treatment that is as considered and professional as for any other group.

If your organization treats the media simply as 'messengers', then it is unlikely to develop the most effective programme of media communications. News and comment on the organization may be superficial and spasmodic. Those stories that do appear may also be tackled on a one-by-on basis, rather than as further chapters in an unfolding story; this deeper coverage is more likely to result when the journalists concerned are kept fully briefed and understand the policies of the organization.

(There is an incidental but important factor that supports this more imaginative approach towards the media; journalists are not commenting on the organization *only* when they are writing stories or broadcasting—they are projecting a perspective every time they discuss the actions and policies of the organization with the many key opinion-leaders with whom they regularly mix. Surely it helps to keep such influential figures well-informed and imbued with positive attitudes?)

Even talking about 'the media' can be a danger for some less experienced levels of management. This convenient word covers an enormous range of publications, from national daily newspapers through to publications operating at a regional, local, or even parish level; trade, technical, and professional journals from the popular to the esoteric; special-interest publications ranging from women's magazines with circulations in the millions to little handbooks designed for small groups of buffs. And, of course, there are the broadcast media with an equally wide spread of local, national, and even international programmes. It is for these reasons that the expression 'press relations' should be avoided and 'media relations' used instead. (Similarly, few company statements are likely to be 'press' releases; most will be news releases.)

Above all, remember that, whatever the variation in style of publication, the people creating them are journalists, individuals with professional skills; and it is towards these people that the most effective media relations campaign must be directed.

Understanding how the media work

The news media are run by journalists. Certainly, all important decisions about what news appears in print or is broadcast are taken by journalists. Even at the highest levels of management, the journalistic viewpoint tends to be the most important.

The summary of this journalistic viewpoint is, What will interest my readers, listeners, or viewers? If you understand and remember this simple fact, you will have mastered the most important step in understanding how the media work. Every time you write a news release, draft an article, supervise an editorial photo session, set up a media interview, or discuss an angle with a journalist, remember to put yourself in his or her shoes. What will interest their *audience*? What will be acceptable to their editor, who is (or should be) the most perceptive focus of the readers' interests?

Journalists need material that is relevant, topical, accurate, fast, comprehensive, substantiated, concise, unbiased, and, ideally, exclusive—or, at the very least, with a special angle. Furthermore, they require this material in vast quantities and in a non-stop regular flow.

Some of the realities of effective media relations can be learned only through experience at the sharp end—working with journalists. Most of the guidance points in this chapter are drawn from personal experience (covered in more detail in *All about PR*—see 'Further reading' list at end of chapter). Aspiring PR practitioners should also study the concise notes on news releases, press conferences, organizing special events, and so on that are published by the Institute of Public Relations as practice papers and by the Public Relations Consultants Association as guidance papers.

Learning to appreciate what is news

The PR adviser must be critically objective in the preparation and issue of news material.

It only takes an observation of how the media work to recognize that central to any effective media relations campaign must be a hard core of news. Many journalists believe that a news sense is a very rare quality. In truth, it is based largely on common sense. Bad news is *not* the only news; but it is only the *exceptional* story, good *or* bad, that will make news.

And it is perfectly legitimate to *create* news. If it is new, has never been done before, is interesting and relevant ... it is news. The first woman chairman of a public company is news. The first export order for an unexpected household product (such as hair curlers) to China is news. A 16-year-old apprentice being invited to open a new high-technology laboratory is news. The winner of a travel scholarship who has never been abroad is news. The invitation of careers teachers to the launch of a new product is news. Effective PR practitioners should use this 'new is news' factor to create improved coverage.

Obviously, what is news in an engineering publication may not be news in the parish magazine, and what is news for a local radio station may not be right for national television news.

Earning the respect of journalists for your organization

PR practitioners who are efficient and businesslike will demonstrate to any journalist that they reflect the quality of their organization. Practitioners who are friendly, available, constructive, helpful, and co-operative will probably be pleasant people to deal with—and therefore might come higher up on the list of contacts that every journalist keeps for comment. Why should journalists work with people they don't like and who will not help them, when there is someone who will provide equally good copy but is more understanding?

Journalists rate candour as a key quality in an executive responsible for public relations, and prefer to deal with PR people whom they know personally.

The principle is simple. Effective PR practitioners start by building their own reputation with journalists, and from this will spring the good work undertaken on behalf of their organization.

A recent survey of some Washington correspondents confirmed that there was virtually unanimous support for the fact that a news conference should be held to handle a major news announcement only where questions were essential. Some two-thirds of the respondents felt that news conferences were abused as a communications technique yet virtually all claimed to read press releases.

Combining activity to create a campaign

Different elements may often be combined to create a balanced media relations campaign. Indeed, sustaining effective media relations entails not just the occasional (or even regular) flow of news, but the development of a relationship between the organization and the media that is honest, direct, and two-way. A particular objective (for example, better customer awareness) may be tackled by creating a campaign of media relations activity; when such campaigns are undertaken continuously and in parallel to meet broad objectives, the activity comes under the category of a media relations *programme*. (In other words, a *campaign* has a beginning, a middle, and an end to meet an identified objective, while a *programme* is the continuous sum of such components.)

NEWS RELEASES

News releases should be issued only to those journals that have a direct interest in the material. Do not scatter stories to all. Always provide a contact name and telephone number. Be certain that the telephone is properly manned, if necessary 24 hours a day, 365 days a year.

It takes many years of training and experience to be able to present information in the concise and direct style necessary for news releases to be used by editors. A basic writing ability is essential; but, with care and practice, an average writer can develop into a good news writer. Certain guidelines that may be helpful:

1. Always ask who, what, why, where, and when, and be sure that these questions are answered in every news story. Train yourself to eliminate just as vigorously as you add. If material does not answer one of these questions, what is it doing in your story?
2. Develop your writing skill. Draft, redraft, edit, polish, and perfect the copy. Read publications and understand what makes news and how it is put together. Analyse the writing skills of good journalists: understand the good; criticize the bad.
3. Write stories to suit the publication. If, for practical reasons, your story has to go to a wider range of media, always draft it in the style to suit the most popular of these. Better still, produce different stories for different types of news outlet.
4. Always keep the copy tight, concise, and factual. Never fudge an issue or create a misleading impression. Substantiate any claims. Separate fact from belief by putting the latter into quotes. ('Research chief, Dr John Smith, confirmed the vehicle exceeded 200 mph. "We believe it's the fastest in the world", said . . .', etc.)
5. Write the story from the point of view of the journalist. Although it is a statement from your organization, it should be presented so that it can be used directly in the publication with the minimum of editing. Comment, observation, or speculation should be included in a story only in quotes or footnotes.
6. Get the main news point into the first paragraph and preferably the first sentence. Organize the paragraphs so that the most newsworthy are at

the top. This will allow the journalist to edit from the bottom; the paragraphs you can most easily afford to lose, therefore, should be the ones towards the end of the story.

7. Keep sentences short, use positive and not negative statements, use active verbs, avoid inverted clauses, and cut out any subjective material or superlatives. Keep separate points in separate sentences. Break each collection of points into separate paragraphs.

8. Put the copy into modern journalistic style. Eliminate any old-fashioned phrases, formal or pompous language, jargon peculiar to the industry, and clichés or colloquialisms that are not accepted as standard current English (or the appropriate language).

9. When you have written your story, check through to make sure that it meets all these criteria. In particular, be certain that the news is at the *beginning*. Often, draft news releases can afford to have paragraph one taken out!

10. Go through your copy again: tighten, edit, improve, check all spellings and punctuation. Get someone else to read it before it goes for release, asking them to criticize and query. Avoid becoming sensitive about your own copy; learn to be self-critical. Push yourself to the highest standard possible.

INTERVIEWS

Within your organization there are some fascinating and authoritative people. Present them to selected media for interview. Prepare briefing notes; arrange a convenient time and place for the interview; provide travel arrangements, and lunch or other facilities that would be hospitable, but no more. Before the meeting takes place, brief the person interviewed and, separately, the journalist. Train your interview subject in media techniques. Help your interviewee with any tricky questions that may be asked. By all means, attend the interview to effect the introduction, pour the coffee, or whatever; but do not take part unless the interview is going off the rails. In the worst case, remember that you *can* stop an interview, but you cannot ask a journalist to forget what has already been said. Trust journalists and get them to trust you. Say as little off the record as possible; however, never lie or hide the truth. If the timing of a question or discussion is not convenient, then explain why you cannot help, and offer to give an early story as soon as it is possible.

EDITOR MEETINGS

Make sure that you regularly meet the editors of key publications for your industry. They should know you well enough to be able to talk to you at any time they wish. Make sure that your meetings with them cover some items of substance and are not merely social occasions. Pick up a strong news story for each such meeting, then follow it up periodically. Arrange for key editors to meet relevant senior personnel within your organization as necessary (see 'Interviews' above).

ARTICLES

Many publications carry authoritative articles. Make sure you are monitoring all publications relevant to your industry. Recognize opportunities for articles. If you see a news story that is contrary to your company's views, suggest an article as a follow-up. If you see a trend in the industry of which others may not be aware, suggest an article to cover it. If one of your management colleagues introduces a new technique in his area, suggest an article to describe it.

Always agree with the editor on the deadline, length, and style. And always meet the deadline. Clarify with the editor whether this article is to be published as a by-lined piece from the company or as if it had been prepared by an independent journalist.

Edit drafts or background notes into acceptable journalistic style. Never allow yourself to be overruled by any manager who has less PR experience. Take responsibility for final approval of all copy issued by your organization. Explain early to all managers preparing drafts that you will be editing their copy. If any executive is unreliable in delivering on time, suggest that the main thoughts are put onto tape; alternatively, ask to interview the executive.

FEATURES

Many publications carry regular features covering particular subjects that will be of interest to readers. For example, home magazines may regularly look at bathrooms; industry journalists may regularly look at marketing or exports. These often provide opportunities for contributions—perhaps by-lined by an executive of your company. Suggest a facility visit to your organization for the publication's editor. Alternatively, arrange an interview with a senior executive or provide company background notes.

To identify opportunities, ask relevant publications for their editorial features lists. Calendar those features that come up regularly at the same time each year. Write regularly to the features editor with new ideas. Make sure you do this well in advance.

LETTERS

Publications like to receive authoritative letters on topics of interest to their readership. Be sure your company writes where relevant. Agree on a corporate policy. Encourage regional personnel to write letters to the appropriate media. Help them in their initial drafts. Ensure that any response to a published item is very fast; some letters can actually be sent by telex or telephone, or be hand-delivered. Look for opportunities to open a debate, as well as contributing to an existing discussion.

PRESS OFFICE

You must have a press or information office to deal with media enquiries. There should be enough telephone lines to deal with the expected level of calls, including emergency situations. Be sure that there is a proper procedure for dealing with telephone press enquiries. Press officers must know to whom to turn for information. Every call must be answered immediately. If the information is not available, then the call must be returned within the time promised. Journalists respect PR people who meet deadlines. Do not offer to call back if you know the information will not be available. Say so; explain why. Do not be tempted to present information that you cannot give. Do not allow your colleagues to hold back information that is already openly available. Avoid unnecessary secrecy.

Be sure that the press office has up-to-date photographs of all the senior management, together with short, current biographical details. Only use effective photographs, and hold a range of situations—formal photographs, action shots, and so on. Build up a complete library of news photos in black and white, in colour negative, and colour transparency. Include, for example, all manufacturing processes, products, export activities, factory locations, the fieldwork of your society/charity, and other relevant items.

Make sure that all current statistical and financial information relating to the organization is readily available. Build up a library of company information and standard articles that can be sent in the post, immediately on request. It is helpful if the press office is equipped with telex and facsimile transmission. A subscription to one of the commercial news distribution services and a London messenger service is also invaluable.

Read every newspaper and trade publication relevant to the industry. Senior executives must be advised of any relevant references. Follow up any news opportunities that result from this media monitoring. Make sure that there is a telephone number available 24 hours a day, 365 days a year. Also ensure that all PR personnel have the telephone number of every key publication and the home numbers of senior executives.

Making media conferences effective

An ill-planned or unnecessary media conference can spoil your potential for future events. If you waste journalists' time, do not present the right information, or are not well organized, you may well receive poor coverage from your event. Even worse, you will find it difficult to get journalists to report future activities or attend other events.

Different rules apply to press receptions and to media conferences. A press reception is usually arranged to provide an opportunity for executives and media to meet, perhaps to provide background, often as a social or semi-social gathering at an event that the media are already attending—say, an electronics manufacturer's reception at a business fair. A media conference, on the other hand, is a news event, where new information is to be presented and *discussed* by the media.

Be very objective when considering a possible media or news conference. The first question to be asked is whether the conference is really necessary. If the information could be better handled by issuing a news story, arranging an interview, or placing an article, then it is probably not necessary to hold a news conference. Remember that a weak press conference may attract the media—but only once.

Some companies feel that they should hold an event because it is about time they met the press or because they want to introduce a senior executive, or even because there are sufficient funds in the budget to allow such an event. Unless there is hard news, resist this temptation; perhaps instead you could hold a suitable reception when the opportunity arises—say, at your next national exhibition.

There are a number of factors that would make a media conference advisable:

1. *The strength of the news* It is essential that there is a strong, urgent news angle. A review of company progress or an update on the market is unlikely to be strong enough. Ask yourself if the journalists you propose inviting will be as enthusiastic about attending when they know the story.
2. *The need to discuss angles* If the implications of the news require discussion, then a media conference might provide the ideal opportunity. If the news needs to be interpreted in different ways by different publications or by the broadcast media, it can be sensible to call the journalists together to give them the opportunity to ask questions.
3. *The human relations side* Some new developments have a human relations aspect, and this can be difficult to put over in a printed news story. If you have a good news story *and* a magnificent boffin or a powerful new marketing director, then a media conference might be welcomed by your industry journalists wishing to establish contact with these executives.
4. *The complexity of the story* On occasions, the sheer complexity of the

news makes it difficult to put over in the printed form, in which case journalists will appreciate the question-and-answer nature of a conference. This might apply in high-technology sectors, or with a new campaign launched by an environmental group, or a major change in a company's overseas investment programme.

5. *The courtesy factor* Some announcements are of such importance to specific industry sectors that the relevant specialized journalists would expect to hear these at first hand. If there are only a few publications concerned, this might be better done as a personal briefing with the editors concerned, possibly over a working lunch.

LOCATION

Judge whether the interest centring on your organization's location, say, is stronger than the convenience and possibly better attendance of an event in the capital or regional capital. If it is a completely new process, test facility, or production development, an historic building renovation or a conservation project, then a site visit may be appropriate. If it is a product launch, a production expansion, or an appeal announcement, it may be better held in the city.

Journalists on national newspapers or consumer publications are most unlikely to spend a day visiting a remote facility unless it is of the utmost significance. One persuasive method of getting heavyweight journalists from behind their desks is to give them the opportunity to meet the top people they cannot normally reach.

Equally, the pressures on the limited time of trade journalists must be considered. They may justify an excursion if the story is strong enough, or if they will see processes or meet people important in their industry.

VENUE

In-plant, on-site, or hotel? Again, the decision depends on what is to be seen. Often a press conference will be timed to run over lunch; therefore, catering facilities will be important, which will probably give a conference venue or hotel the edge.

Often, a convenient hotel room is all that is required. But sometimes an imaginative and relevant alternative can be located. Effective media conferences have been held in universities, hospitals, training ships, historic castles, and even in aircraft.

An essential point is to check carefully any possible venue, personally. Make sure that the standards are acceptable. Novelty will not excuse poor facilities, inconvenient location, or bad catering.

Do not run an event longer than necessary. Complete the business briskly. Journalists under pressure will be able to get their story quickly and leave; those who want to probe further will be able to stay on. Many successful press conferences are held late morning or late afternoon; this enables them to run on to refreshments, buffet, or even lunch or dinner, as appropriate.

Try to allow a few minutes for latecomers at the start of your conference, for example by arranging the start to run over coffee or drinks.

HOSPITALITY

Treat attending journalists as important business guests—in other words, as appropriate to the occasion. If the event is to run over lunchtime, a buffet is normally preferable to a formal sit-down lunch (although a formal lunch might be best for a handful of senior financial journalists meeting the chairman). Hospitality should be good, though not lavish. There's an old editor's saying that still holds true—'What counts is news, not booze.'

PROGRAMME

Try to plan to complete the business *before* the less formal hospitality part. Lunch before the business should be avoided, even when travel times may mean a delayed lunch.

A typical programme for a city centre event might be:

11.30   Arrival, sign in, press packs, and coffee
11.45   Introduction by a senior director
11.55   Product demonstration or facility visit
12.15   Questions and answers
12.30   Drinks and lunch

Any travel, assembly, and meeting times would be longer for, say, a media conference on site.

RECEPTION

One of the PR team should receive your guests, check them in (against the list of acceptances), hand out any press information, and introduce them to the senior director hosting the event. The PR reception official needs to have the necessary cloakroom facilities, plus telephone, typewriter, train times, and other information journalists might require.

Badges are more acceptable these days, though some journalists still object. Certainly your own staff should carry their names and positions in large, clear lettering on their badges. Avoid guest badges that can tear delicate materials or adhesive ones that will mark suede and leather.

INVITATIONS

Draw up a press list and send your invitations out between three and six weeks in advance. The date must be checked to ensure that it does not clash with any competing or major public event.

Printed invitations are sometimes useful to set a theme, but they are not essential. A personal letter with a reply-paid card is probably best. Be sure you give enough detail to enable journalists to judge whether they wish to attend. Draw up the acceptance list and ring round nearer the date to check any non-respondents. Confirm any substitutes or replacements.

CONTENT

Try to put life, style, activity, and pace into the event. Avoid unnecessary gimmicks. Always demonstrate a product or system where you can. Keep it smooth-flowing and professional. Use film, video, tape, slides, charts, and models as relevant and necessary. Ensure that you use only articulate and well-informed speakers. Keep the number presenting to a minimum. Make the presentation positive and direct but *not* a sales pitch. Avoid panels of worthies. Train and rehearse your speakers. Brief all other participants, particularly on handling the media and dealing with questions. Agree on answers in all difficult areas.

PRESS PACKS

Printed information relevant to the story should be collated into a suitable media pack. A specially printed folder may be relevant if your organization will be holding many such events. A standard folder is acceptable provided it is attractive: it is the contents that count.

The folder will contain the news story and main news picture. Other items might include copies of speeches, background industry statistics, personality pictures and biographies, and an organization profile. Do not overload with unnecessary material. Include no standard items; all copy should be prepared particularly for this event. Certainly think carefully before including publicity items such as sales leaflets.

FOLLOW-UP

On the day of the event, mail the information pack to those journalists who were interested but did not attend. Note any special requests from attendees and process these—requests for pictures or facility visits, for example. Issue appropriate thanks. Collate all costs and check against original budget. Hold a debriefing session with the responsible executives to analyse good and bad points. Record these to influence future projects.

Media conferences can achieve very dramatic results. From my own experience, a media conference enabled one office equipment manufacturer to sell the whole of his first year's production, a small provincial company to significantly cut staff turnover, a manufacturer to improve relations with factory neighbours, and a construction company to secure better financial backing from the City.

To make a press conference work, however, you must help your organization to define exactly what it is you intend it to achieve and to ensure that these are realistic aims. Your immediate market at a press conference is the journalists who attend; their primary responsibility is to their readers, listeners, or viewers.

If what your organization has is of relevance and of interest to the public served by the media, you will have an effective conference. If not ... you should not have called one!

Using the special needs of the broadcasters

The ability of radio and television to reach an audience can be appreciated from the cost of their advertising! Advertisers spend this sort of money because of the audience delivered, the attention achieved and, most important, the results obtained. Yet both radio and television are available media for good editorial ideas; too few of these come through PR channels.

PROGRAMME REQUIREMENTS

Local radio stations are always looking for local news. National radio programmes like 'You and Yours' and 'The Food Programme' regularly use commercial news items. Television programmes such as 'Nationwide', 'That's Life', and 'Tomorrow's World' also use commercial news items, presented in the right way.

Local and national radio and TV can reach millions. Programme makers are all in the ideas business. The sheer volume of radio and television currently being broadcast in the United Kingdom means that there is a massive demand for good material. The same is true across much of Europe, the United States, Canada, and in many other industrialized countries of the world, where an estimated 90 per cent of public information is now received through broadcasting.

In Britain, the annual, *Who's Who in Broadcasting*, will help identify the people who put together such programmes. A news release may be acceptable to put a factual news story in front of the news editor, but a personal approach is nearly always best.

Radio and television are immediate media. Stories will not last. Timing is critical. New stories need to be presented quickly to editors. Facilities for interview, location recording, studio guests, and so on must be provided immediately they are required. Deadlines are tight and, with electronic news gathering, are getting tighter. Live material from remote locations can now be slotted directly into news bulletins. Some associations and unions are establishing their own studios so they can offer TV stations an instant spokesman on key news topics. Some of these links are by satellite so they can transmit across the nation and, eventually, across the world.

But timing is important in another sense. The presentation has to be crisp, immaculate, and professional. Radio and television audiences have the ability to switch off or change channels instantly. As a result, broadcasters are constantly working to keep a high level of immediate interest in their output.

Effective PR advisers will be creating broadcast news opportunities. But they need to know how to handle a radio or television journalist when approached to provide information or facilities. Check what programme it is for. Will it be live or taped? Will the contribution be edited? Who else will be appearing? Who will conduct the interview or discussion? What topics or questions will be covered? Will there be an opportunity to see/hear the final programme before transmission? Will there be a live debate to counter any misunderstandings or damaging assertions from other participants?

TRAINING

There are many excellent training courses available to help you or your colleagues present your organization's case in the best possible way. Make sure that all senior executives who may be required to broadcast are trained in the techniques. Decide whether you, as PR adviser, are going to act as spokesperson or as behind-the-scenes negotiator.

RADIO INTERVIEWS

These tend to be less aggressive than those on television. This does not necessarily make them easier, however. Listeners tend to have other things to concentrate on—driving the car or digging the garden. The power of the spokesperson's personality has to come over positively. Gestures (or a pretty face) will not help. The speaker has to project his or her interest into the words and voice. This is a skill that *can* be developed.

Ironically, although the speaker cannot be seen on radio, the studio situation can be surprisingly confusing. Often there is only a short informal build-up to radio interviews. The interview subject can be sitting down one moment and then seconds later going out live.

Always take advantage of any rehearsal opportunity. Run through the points, checking tricky questions. But remember that the interviewer reserves the right to ask *anything* he or she likes. This might include subjects that have not have been discussed in the briefing session. If the interview is taped, the interviewee can refuse to answer; the silence will have to be edited out.

TELEVISION INTERVIEWS

On television, attention is focused on the small studio area where the guest and the interviewer will be sitting. Therefore, it is easier to concentrate on the subject in hand. However, while a surge of adrenalin helps some people to sharpen their performance, others can be stunned into mumbling incoherence.

There is no substitute for experience. Watch television and see how it works. See how people deal with questions. Tape as many interviews as possible and rehearse your own answers to the questions. Learn to identify the effective techniques, the irritating habits.

NEWS AND FEATURE PROGRAMMES

Become acquainted with the different types of programme presented. News items are highly condensed; feature items might be slightly more in-depth; while full-length investigative-type of programmes can often be hostile.

For example, many members of the Norfolk Broads' holiday industry in England co-operated willingly with a television company to help make a film about the industry. When it appeared, it turned out to be a critical view of the damage being caused to the waterways—much of it, the programme claimed, by leisure boats. Several sequences featured what the broadcasters considered to be good television. The participants were very criticial of these, including shots with dead fish in the foreground, the use of a telephoto lens to foreshorten perspective and make the waterways appear busier, and unidentified waste being ejected into the water.

In another case, a developer working on an imaginative new shopping centre in a provincial university town provided facilities for a television company, but was later horrified to find that the finished film used footage of attractive existing shops (implying they would have to close) which were not even in the development area, and avoided any shots of the derelict, characterless properties that were due to close.

SPECIAL-INTEREST PROGRAMMES

Both radio and television present special-interest programmes. These tend to be less aggressive because the broadcasters are working in the same industry week after week. The programmes are dependent on the degree of co-operation they get from people who work in the special-interest sectors, such as gardening, antiques, motoring, or leisure.

This does not stop such broadcasters from being hard hitting, but it does ensure that they are reasonably accurate and fair in any criticism. Be sure that you know what the broadcaster is aiming at before you or one of your executives agrees to co-operate. Insist on knowing how your contribution is to be used, and in what context.

LOCATION INTERVIEWS

There are a number of ways in which interviews can be organized. With major news events, a participant may be stopped in the street and a camera or microphone thrust at him or her. Be sure your spokesman is not caught out by such situations. If the organization has been in negotiation over a proposed plant closure, consider the possibility of an interviewer standing on the steps of the offices when your personnel director comes out. Think beforehand about what is to be said. If this is limited by the negotiations, construct something that will still give the broadcasters a piece of useful television or tape. However, remember that *you* are in charge: it is quite acceptable for you or your spokesman to politely excuse yourselves and break away after making a short statement.

TELEPHONE INTERVIEWS

On occasions, your organization will be asked to give a telephone interview. This should be resisted if possible. The quality will be bad, and you have no control over the editing and the usage of the material. Furthermore, the viewer or listener may get the impression that it was not important enough for your company representative to go to the studio.

An executive in a studio interview may well have a down-the-line interview (talking to a studio monitor) but will have to look as though he or she is having a real-life conversation with the interviewer. The best advice is to ignore the electronics and talk to just one real person. The same principle applies on down-the-line radio interviews, where that 'real' person may be a microphone in front of the studio guest.

PANEL DISCUSSIONS

Advanced preparation here, as always, is helpful. Consider the points you would like your executive to get over. It is not always a good idea to be the first person into a discussion; equally, the discussion should not be allowed to go too far before your spokesman starts to make points. Make sure your organization's views are put over effectively but not over-extensively.

You or your spokesman should be quite prepared to put normal politeness quietly to one side. Do not allow yourself to be brow-beaten by the chairman, but answer the question in the way you would like. Do not try to be too clever by turning the question into the one that you would have liked to have been asked—this can only be done by *very* professional interviewees.

SYNDICATED RADIO INTERVIEWS

In the UK, there are now several organizations that will produce an interview on tape, syndicated to local stations. The above basic principles still apply. However, as your organization is paying for the service, you will receive more help in the preparation. Remember that the final radio tape has to stand up to broadcast standards or it will not get used. The syndicating companies will not allow the interview to become soft; they want—and you want—good usable material.

STUDIO INTERVIEWS

Face-to-face interviews are invaluable because your speaker is not competing for attention, though he or she is competing for the time. If the interview is live, then the amount of time available will be known beforehand, and there is likely to have been more discussion beforehand about the areas to be covered. If the interview is to be filmed and edited, its length might depend on the amount of interest that the speaker is able to generate. Never agree to a five-minute interview that will be cut down to 30 seconds on-screen.

Consider carefully the points you or your spokesman want to put over. You may need to identify the questions that are to be asked in order to weave these into your answers.

Always treat interviewers as professionals trying to do a professional job. Their only major advantage is that they will have more experience. Do not try to challenge them on their own area of professionalism; but remember that they are extremely unlikely to know as much about the sector under discussion as you or your spokesman.

Never bluff. Handle naive questions politely. If the interviewer is asking a simple question, it is because the viewers or listeners would like to ask the same simple question. There are many ways of presenting the truth, but avoid misrepresentations.

Listen carefully to the stance that the interviewer is taking. Quite often he or she is representing the public at large. This is perfectly fair; you need to judge whether he or she has got a better measure of public feeling than you yourself.

SOME BROADCAST TIPS

Put adequate preparation into what you or your spokesman is to say. Do not rely on being a spontaneous speaker. Concentrate on the good news and avoid temptations to justify yourself. Do not allow the interviewer to get on top of the situation. Keep your cool; concentrate on the essentials. Do not be diverted. Learn to convert technicalities into simple lay language. Do not say anything on-air or off-air that you might regret later. Prepare for yourself or your executive a brief of the main points you wish to cover.

Do not, under any circumstances, drink before the interview. Wear clothes appropriate to the situation. Avoid annoying mannerisms. Concentrate on what *you* want to say, not on what *they* want to say. Think of interesting ways of illustrating your points. Keep it enthusiastic. Avoid jargon. Talk through the interviewer to the audience. Do not allow yourself to be interrupted. Correct any inaccuracies in the questions.

Look honest, sound honest, and be honest—then you and your organization might be believed.

How to work well with journalists: a check-list

1. Make your story factual, and never write anything that would embarrass a journalist if it appeared in print and were challenged.
2. Use the most effective way of getting the copy in front of the journalist. This may well dictate whether it should be a conference, a news release, or a telephone call.
3. Write in the style that you would like to see used when the material is published, resisting superlatives and assertions.
4. Respect the journalists' independence and never expect favours or special treatment.
5. Respect the journalists' professionalism and expect them to respect yours.
6. Get to know the journalists with whom you are most likely to be in regular contact and learn what makes them tick.
7. Never allow your non-PR colleagues to dictate what should go into a news story unless you are convinced that it is right.
8. On everything that you are researching or writing, constantly look for the fresh news angle.
9. Never knock the competition, either in the written or the spoken word—

if journalists want to know what they are up to they will have to ask them directly.

10. Handle the bad news as positively and confidently as you do the good.
11. Avoid embargoes if at all possible and use them only where they are strictly necessary.
12. If there is the slightest possibility that an incident could create bad news, have the courage to release this before the enquiries begin.
13. Have a contingency plan for dealing with the problems that can be reasonably expected—and PR machinery for dealing with those that cannot be expected!
14. Prepare standby statements on issues and incidents where journalists may require comment, and be sure that these are issued to all personnel who may need to talk to the media.
15. Be certain that all news stories are also issued internally and to professional advisors (such as the organization's advertising agency, accountants, marketing consultants, and so on).
16. Treat any aggressive or unsympathetic journalist calmly and evenly— you will never win an argument with a journalist.
17. Do not allow yourself to be bullied by the media, and remember that you represent not their interests but the organization that is paying your salary—*they* will never forget it!
18. Try to tailor as many stories as possible to individual publications or key commentators on your industry.
19. Do not allow any of your non-PR colleagues who are not properly trained to talk directly to the media without your close involvement.
20. Regularly check your news by discussing your PR angles with colleagues from other organizations or non-competitive companies.
21. If you find that you cannot give journalists the complete story, always explain why this is so and when you will be able to fully up-date.
22. Always keep every promise to the media—not just the big one ('I'll let you have an exclusive on this when the acquisition is finalised'), but also the small ones ('I'll ring you back in five minutes').
23. Look for good picture angles to support the written word—particularly when dealing with television.
24. Never assume that a journalist understands the background; always find this out by asking the right questions.

Building broad company credibility on strong media relations

Obviously, media relations will be only part of a broader public relations programme. However, this element will often be one of the most effective ways to reach the audiences upon whom the organization depends.

Certainly there is much research that shows the credibility of messages that reach the public through the editorial media in comparison with, for example, advertising, where the reader (or listener or viewer) balances the information against the fact that it is a bought message. Even some of the most sophisticated PR campaigns will be built on a base of good media relations. Certainly there can be no general PR practitioner who can claim to be effective unless he or she is a master in media relations.

Further reading

GENERAL

Adair, J., *Effective Decision-making* (Pan, London, 1985).
de Bono, E., *de Bono's Thinking Course* (BBC, London, 1983).
Drucker, P., *Effective Executive* (Heinemann, London, 1967).
Goodworth, C. T., *Effective Speaking and Presentation* (Business Books, London, 1980).
Hart, N. A., *Business to Business Advertising* (Associated Business Press, London, 1983).
Hart, N. A. and Waite N. E., *How to get on in Marketing* (Kogan Page, London, 1987).
Jones, N., *Strike in the Media* (Basil Blackwell, Oxford, 1986).
Kennedy, G., *Everything is Negotiable* (Arrow, London, 1983).
Rise, A. and Trout, J., *Positioning: The Battle for Your Mind* (McGraw-Hill, Maidenhead, 1980).
Townsend, R., *Further up the Organisation* (Coronet, London, 1985).
Wells, G., *How to Communicate* (McGraw-Hill, Maidenhead, 1979).
Wells, G., *So You Think You Can Manage?* (Video Arts, London, 1984).

PUBLIC RELATIONS

Awad, J. F., *Power of Public Relations* (Praeger Scientific, New York, 1985).
Black, S. and Sharpe, M., *Practical Public Relations* (Prentice-Hall, Englewood Cliffs, NJ, 1983).
Bowman, P. and Ellis, N., *Manual of Public Relations*, rev. 2nd edn (Heinemann, London, 1984).
Center, A. and Walsh, F. *Public Relations Practices*, 3rd edn (Prentice-Hall, Englewood Cliffs, NJ, 1985).
Coulson, T. C., *Public Relations Is Your Business* (Business Books, London, 1981).
Cutlip, Center & Broom *Effective Public Relations*, 6th edn (Prentice-Hall, Englewood Cliffs, NJ, 1985).
Fraser, P. Seitel, *The Practice of Public Relations*, 2nd edn (Charles E. Merrill, Columbus, Ohio, 1985).

Haywood, R., *All About PR* (McGraw-Hill, Maidenhead, 1984).
Howard, W. (ed.), *Practice of Public Relations* (Heinemann, London, 1982).
Jefkins, F., *Public Relations for Marketing Management* (Macmillan, London, 1983).
Jefkins, F., *Planned Press and Public Relations* (International Textbooks, Glasgow, 1977).
Kopel, E., *Financial and Corporate Public Relations* (McGraw-Hill, Maidenhead, 1982).
Lesly, P. (ed.), *Lesly's Public Relations Handbook*, 3rd edn (Prentice-Hall, Englewood Cliffs, NJ, 1985).
Mendes, N. (ed.), *This Public Relation Consultancy Business* (Mendes, Halesowen, 1984).
Newsam & Scott, *This is PR: The Realities of Public Relations*, 2nd edn (Wadsworth, Belmont, Cal., 1980).
Ridgeway, J., *Successful Media Relations* (Gower Press, Farnborough, Hants, 1984).

MARKETING

Davidson, H. J., *Offensive Marketing* (Penguin, Harmondsworth, 1987).
Hart, N. and Stapleton, J., *Glossary of Marketing Terms* (Heinemann, London, 1987).
Goldmann, H. M., *How to Win Customers* (Pan, London, 1980).
Wilson, M., *The Management of the Marketing Function* (Gower Press, Farnborough, Hants, 1980).
Wilson, M., *So You Think You Can Sell?* (Video Arts, London, 1985).

12.

COMMUNICATIONS RESEARCH

Chris West

The contribution of research

Surprisingly, in this age of communication, the business world is still populated by some poor communicators. In the main, these are individuals and companies who feel that staff, customers, owners, and others who can influence the fortunes of the organization, can be left in partial or complete ignorance of corporate objectives, strategies, needs, and methods without any ill effects. However, in the main, the days of successful autocratic management have passed, along with the 50-hour working week and child labour. T. J. Peters and R. H. Waterman (*In Search of Excellence*) have shown that successful companies are distinguished by frequent and intense communication between managers, but for complete success this practice must be extended to all groups that are involved in the operations of the company. It must be recognized, however, that it is one thing for a small group informally to understand one another's requirements and motives and quite another for this to be achieved among much larger groups, where a formal communications strategy is required.

No strategy can be planned without information, and good communication, like good marketing, will be achieved only if communicators understands the real needs of their target audiences. Many corporate executives feel that they obtain such information automatically, either from their own experience or through the corporate grapevine. This may be true to an extent, but experience indicates that it is rare for an executive to be made party to the whole truth or the unvarnished truth, especially when dealing with subordinates or others with positions to defend. Strategies based on half-truths or folklore are unlikely to be well conceived. The need for action, the objectives of the communications campaign, the methods by which the campaign should be conducted, and the specific messages that are likely to produce the desired result can be decided only by reference to factual and unbiased information on the current awareness, perceptions, and requirements of the audiences that the corporation wishes to reach.

Sometimes the background is obvious. A new company knows that it has to work hard to gain awareness of its existence and objectives. A company entering a take-over battle knows that it has to fight to persuade shareholders to support the present management. A period of intense labour difficulties must be followed by a period of bridge-building with the workforce. But more often than not, the need for a communications strategy is far from obvious, and, even when it is apparent, recent data that will determine the type and structure of campaign are rarely available to management.

A national building society with a London head office, regional offices, and hundreds of branches used a company newsletter as a means of passing on information on corporate developments, changes in policy, and personnel and social news. The intention was not only to create a family feeling but also to ensure that staff were sufficiently knowledgeable to answer questions from outsiders. The system appeared to management to work well, but when probed by research, this proved to be a false impression. The newsletter was seen as an instrument for distributing official propaganda, designed to conceal the truth rather than enlighten the staff. Issues of major concern to staff, such as salary policy, were carefully left out of the newsletter. In response, an unofficial newsletter had been started and was widely circulated. This covered the real issues and had gained considerable credibility, but it was totally outside the control of management. The dangers were obvious and real. The research also showed that the communication needs varied considerably by grade of staff. Those in responsible positions required more detailed information to be communicated in personal briefings. The more junior staff also required personal contact from their managers, who deal not only with matters directly affecting the staff but also with the general progress of the company. Written communications were seen as a means of providing supporting information, but not as the main method of communicating. A video of a statement by the chairman or managing director smacked too much of 'Big Brother' and was generally counter-productive. Not surprisingly, these findings stimulated the company to concentrate on the oral flow of information down the management chain and to attempt to re-establish the credibility of official written communications. The cynic would say that the research showed only what any half-competent manager knows already, namely, that people must be made to feel that they matter in an organization. It is nevertheless amazing how often this simple fact is overlooked in corporate communications strategies.

The communications planner must be in a position to answer seven key questions:

1. Does a communications problem exist?
2. What is the nature and extent of the communications problem?
3. What new or corrective messages need to be transmitted?
4. Who should receive the messages?
5. How can the messages be most effectively (or cost-effectively) transmitted?

6. What is (or has been) the effect of the communications programme?
7. Is there a requirement for further action?

In order to answer each of the above questions, the communications planner requires reliable, objective information drawn from the relevant audiences within and outside the company. Without such information, the strategy will be based on feelings, guesswork, and prejudice. As with all areas of marketing and planning, data to support decision-making can be made available using market research techniques; to ignore this facility is to increase the risk of failure unnecessarily.

THE COMMUNICATIONS PROBLEM

All companies have to communicate effectively with a variety of publics. Their staff, customers, shareholders, and bankers form part of a body of stakeholders who in one way or another, and to varying degrees, can influence performance. Whether a problem exists or not depends on how well the communications task has been performed in the past and on external factors over which the company itself has no direct influence. In a dynamic environment there is bound to be a continuous stream of events that threatens corporate performance unless a correct response is made. In addition, the company's own actions and policies can create images and attitudes that impair performance. Examples abound. Over the years, countless British companies have carefully crafted an image of being poor on delivery and unreliable as regards the service they offer. In reality, their performance may be no worse than their foreign rivals, but it is the image that counts rather than the performance. Mercedes owners are quite used to placing the order for their next car when they take delivery of a new model, to ensure that the car is available when they require it; but who accuses Mercedes of poor delivery lead times?

A communications problem exists if the perceptions of target audiences are at variance with the truth and are detrimental to the performance of the company. At its simplest, the problem can arise from the circulation of inaccurate information. Labour relations are plagued by the circulation of rumours and half-truths masquerading as firm corporate policy. Share prices are a perennial victim to rumoured take-over bids or changes in profit expectations. Misinformation is eagerly latched on to in the absence of an adequate flow of reliable information from authoritative sources, but it soon comes to light when it is fed back to the corporation as supporting evidence for some corrective action. The more subtle problems are more difficult to cope with, simply because there is no mechanism by which they automatically come to light. How does the company discover that a lacklustre stock market performance is due to the chairman's lack of charisma and his consequent inability to project enthusiasm for the company and its business? How does it discover that the real reason for lost business is that the accounts department has pressed too hard for payment in the past and the company is therefore perceived as being totally unsympathetic? The answer, in both cases, is research. The real attitudes and perceptions of the company's publics can be probed and explained in considerable depth by the use of survey techniques.

Research can go further than just showing the truth of the current situation. Knowing current attitudes and perceptions is only part of what is needed. To formulate a strategy the company must also know what impressions its publics should hold in order to act in the company's best interests. In other words, it needs to have a model of the ideal image profile which it can aim for; pulling the actual image profile as far as possible into line with the ideal image profile then becomes the task of the communications strategy. Obviously, the information that is to be communicated needs to be truthful, and therefore the same research observations may initiate operational changes within the company. Jaguar Cars' advertising programme to convince customers that its products were reliable would have soon foundered if this had been exposed as untrue.

The reasons why unfavourable attitudes and images persist are to some extent of academic interest, but they need to be explored if repetitions of the problems are to be avoided in future. This is particularly true if the cause lies in some inadequacy in the company's communications process or programme. Companies may create problems by providing too little information or by using the wrong communications methods. Long silences and insufficiently detailed information releases generate vacuums that are liable to be filled by speculation. The frequency, the depth, and the methods of communicating need to relate to the requirements of the audiences, and research can establish what these requirements are.

DETERMINING THE MESSAGE

In order to define a solution to the identified problem, research can be used to pinpoint the precise messages that will result in a change in attitude. All publics have an ideal image profile, which is conditioned by the business in which the company is operating, the publics' objectives and needs, the company's past performance, and comparisons with other organizations. Most of these requirements can be defined and measured by research. Attributes such as friendliness, efficiency, concern with customer problems, and reliability are readily recognized by customers and others and are often used to describe organizations. The importance of each attribute in determining whether, for example, customers are willing to do business can be rated, and the actual performance of companies on these factors can be scaled.

These measurements are vital in determining communications strategies. To an extent, companies can educate their publics on what they should be looking for, but inevitably they hold their own opinions as well. The messages that should be transmitted in the communications programme are those that are likely to cause the target audiences to abandon beliefs that are unfavourable to the company and adopt new favourable opinions repositioning it either closer to the ideal or in an appropriate position relative to competition or peer groups. As indicated above, the messages must be supported by fact in order to be credible, but when dealing with people facts are much easier to establish than perceptions. A pound of image is worth a ton of performance, but it is harder to establish and more difficult to remove.

IDENTIFYING TARGET AUDIENCES

The target audiences for communications strategies can be defined quite simply in macro terms: employees, shareholders, customers, and media are all easily identifiable groups. However, the communications programme may need to be more narrowly focused on sub-segments of the total audience or on groups that are particularly influential in shaping opinions or affecting performance. Rifle shot strategies aimed at the specific trouble spots or opinion leaders and opinion formers may prove to be far more cost-effective than broadcast approaches covering all members of the groups. Identifying such individuals is a key research task.

SELECTING THE OPTIMUM COMMUNICATIONS CHANNELS

Just as the communications needs of an audience may be far from obvious, so are the methods of communicating effectively. Communications methods and media are well defined, but their role in a specific communications strategy needs to be determined by reference to the requirements of the audiences. There is an ever-present danger that approaches are adopted because *management* finds them acceptable, and what is acceptable to management may be very far from the real requirements of the audience. Only the audience itself can define what is acceptable and appropriate, and there is little doubt that the effectiveness and credibility of the message can be influenced by the means by which it is communicated. The gravity and degree of confidentiality of the message and the size of the target audience should all influence the communications channels. Few employees would wish to hear of their salary review by means of an advertisement, but shareholders do not require a personal meeting with the chairman to be notified of movements in the share price—indeed, were such a meeting to be called, they would fear the worst.

The effectiveness of a communications approach can be influenced by fashion, by the extent to which it has been used previously for similar purposes, by the message itself, and by the extent to which it reaches the target audiences. Judgements on each of these require research-based information. An overworked approach may blunt its effectiveness, but there is no means of assessing whether it has been overworked other than by reference to the audience at which it is to be aimed. Previous use, or abuse, of media may well have undermined its credibility. Staff newsletters may be perceived as too frivolous, too closely allied with a particular segment of management, or simply too dull to be of value as a serious method of communicating future policy. Only research among staff can establish the true position.

Applications

There is a tendency to regard research as a one-off exercise designed to fill obvious gaps in knowledge. This assumes that, once acquired, knowledge rarely requires updating or amending. In the corporate environment, it also assumes that the actions of the company do not result in change. Although it is true that some information becomes obsolete only slowly, most situations involving people can prove highly volatile. Opinions and perceptions can certainly change, and if this is to be tracked, the research process must be continuous.

Communications research is most appropriate at four stages of the programme:

1. To assist in the formulation of the strategy.
2. To test whether the proposed campaign meets the objectives of the communicator.
3. To test the effect of the campaign.
4. To monitor developments following the commencement of the campaign and, if necessary, to initiate a new strategy.

STRATEGY FORMULATION

The use of research for strategy formulation is commonly accepted. This is the point at which the communicators' ignorance is most noticeable and where the need for objective data is greatest. Unless the company is already engaged in a monitoring programme, research itself will not highlight the need for a communications strategy. The cycle is most commonly initiated by events, changes in policy, or deterioration in performance.

Basic research to prepare the strategy fills the secondary purpose of establishing a benchmark against which the success of the strategy can be measured. It is just as important to know where you have come from as to know where you are going.

Research to assist in the preparation of a strategy needs to be wide-ranging, covering all aspects of the communications process and all actions that will result in an improvement in the company's situation. This commonly involves research among samples of the target publics themselves.

PRE-TESTING OF CAMPAIGNS

Once a strategy has been devised, complete with target audiences, messages, and media, some form of testing is essential in order to ensure that it will produce the required effect. To launch a campaign without testing its effectiveness risks not only wasting all or part of the campaign budget but also compounding the problem. However well intentioned, a bad campaign may prove worse than no campaign at all. A pre-test is a modest insurance policy.

POST-TESTING OF CAMPAIGN EFFECTIVENESS

Success of the campaign can be judged only by measuring the changes in attitudes and perceptions that have resulted from the campaign. This is achieved by means of research carried out after the campaign has been completed.

TRACKING STUDIES

Tracking changes in attitudes among audiences by means of continuous research or periodic surveys is a refinement of the process which is not always necessary but can certainly contribute to the maintenance of a correct profile. Continuous monitoring should be considered during periods of rapid change or when it is essential to have up-to-date information ready to hand, for example during a protracted labour dispute or a contested bid. For the most part, management can be kept adequately informed on attitudes and opinions by means of occasional surveys. If undertaken, these may signal the need for a new or revised communications strategy.

Research techniques

The quality of the information provided by the research programme is a function of the quality and volume of the research techniques used. Research is a highly specialized activity, and it is difficult for the non-researcher to determine how the research should be undertaken, let alone actually do it. Furthermore, it is sometimes difficult to judge the quality of what is being offered by a specialist research supplier, unless there is some means of independently checking the results. Although this may be possible for quantitative market surveys, it is rarely so for qualitative research into opinions and attitudes. The user of communications research is therefore heavily dependent on the supplier of services to ensure that the approach and techniques are appropriate and valid. The purpose of this section is not to provide a detailed review of communications research techniques, but to offer readers sufficient preliminary insight into the mysterious practices of the researcher to enable them to understand what they are being offered.

In general terms, information can be collected from secondary and primary sources and can be acquired by means of a variety of research techniques. Secondary research involves the collection of data that have already been published in reports, the press, and other generally or privately available sources. Secondary data are normally obtained by a literature search. Primary data refer to original data obtained directly from participants in the business, normally by means of sample surveys. The nature of communications research is such that primary data are required to solve most problems; secondary data may be available, but the communications problems of companies are generally so specific to their situation at a particular time that specially tailored research is essential to obtain any real understanding. Primary data collection involves the use of personal and telephone interviews, group discussions (field research techniques), and special analysis routines in order to capture relevant information from a sample, which can then be extrapolated to represent the entirety of the target audience being considered. The types and volume of research techniques to be used depend on the information to be collected and the respondents who will provide it. Research has its limits in terms of the types of information that can be collected; some information is too sensitive or confidential for respondents to release.

In communications research, the most commonly encountered techniques are:

- The communications audit.
- Published data search.
- In-depth personal interviews.
- Telephone interviews.
- Mail or internal questionnaires.
- Group discussions.
- Media research.
- Advertising assessment techniques.

THE COMMUNICATIONS AUDIT

The communications audit is a means of describing and assessing the tangible and intangible communications resources of a company that are available to the communications planner. The resources comprise the communication skills of the staff, the media available to disseminate information, the value placed on the media by information recipients, and the information base that the company holds on the publics that it needs to reach. The purpose of the audit is to determine whether the company has sufficient resources, whether it is making adequate use of what exists, whether what is there is properly planned and organized, whether there is untapped potential to be exploited, and whether there are gaps in resources that need to be filled. The audit is carried out within and outside the organization; it is based on contacts with key staff responsible for initiating communications and among the recipients of communications both within and outside the company. The latter is needed to place values on levels of communications skills as perceived by the recipients, and on the values attached to the media available to the company.

A typical audit of staff communications could involve the following steps:

1. A critical review of the communications objectives and policies of management.
2. An appraisal of the staff responsible for internal communications.
3. An assessment of the information held on staff attitudes and information needs.
4. An examination of the methods by which information on staff attitudes and information needs is collected.
5. A detailed examination of staff journals, newsletters and other formal methods by which information is distributed to staff, covering content, format, and frequency.
6. A study of the informal communication channels through which staff receive information
7. An evaluation of the value placed on each communication channel by various grades of staff.
8. An assessment of the credibility of the messages disseminated by each communication channel.

Such an audit would show whether the resources were adequate and the types of changes that should be instituted in order to improve communications. Similar programmes could be undertaken in most other target audience groups with refinements reflecting their particular status and structure.

PUBLISHED DATA SOURCES

Published information can cover a wide range of communications and marketing topics, and, although it is rare for it to relate directly to a corporate communications problem, it may provide useful background. The most widely available data relate to the numbers of individuals and organizations in specified target groups; descriptions of communications programmes undertaken by similar organizations; evaluations of the effectiveness of comparable communications campaigns; the readership of journals; and, in some cases, expenditure by competitors on specific communications programmes. These data are generally available from official statistics, private surveys, academic publications, marketing journals, and the marketing and communications trade press. Expenditure data may be deduced from statistics on media advertising.

Although they are of indirect use, it is well worth searching for published data, not so much because they will provide answers, but because they may assist in directing the more expensive field research. Obtaining the share register of a company that is the subject of an acquisition bid is an obvious and essential preliminary to communications aimed at them, but it can also be used as a sample base for shareholder research. Information on how rivals have improved their labour relations may well provide some interesting guidelines for research among the company's own staff.

A significant advantage of published research is that it is generally inexpensive to acquire. A few days in a good business library can pay worthwhile dividends.

FIELD RESEARCH

The communications audit, image and attitude studies, target audience identification, message testing, and the evaluation of alternative communication channels will normally be based on direct contacts with samples or censuses of target audiences. This is the essence of survey research, and it can be as usefully applied to communications research as to market evaluations. The principle is that, if a company wishes to know what its publics think, what they would like to think, how they would prefer to receive information, and the types of information they would like to receive, the simplest way to find out is to ask them. It is normally impossible to ask all of them; nor is it essential to do so. A survey carried out among a sample will provide all the information that is required, provided that the sample is representative of the group as a whole.

The major techniques for making contacts with samples of respondents are personal interviews, telephone interviews, questionnaires sent through the post or the internal distribution system, and group discussions. The major difference between the techniques is the method of making contact with the respondents and the length of the contact, but this obviously affects the volume and depth of information that is obtained. It also affects the cost of the research programme.

Personal interviews

Face-to-face interviews are the workhorse of the research business. They may be totally unstructured, meaning that the direction of questioning is evolved during the interview in the light of the answers given, or they can be partially or fully structured so that predetermined types of information are collected. Their main advantage is that they can probe respondents' attitudes and feelings in depth and can seek explanations as to why respondents feel the way they do. The main disadvantage is that they are time-consuming for both the researcher and the respondent. However, in the more sensitive areas of communications research, that can be a small price to pay in order to ensure that the data are adequate and that the respondents feel that they have made a full contribution to the research programme.

Telephone interviews

The questions asked in face-to-face interviews can also be put by telephone or in the form of written questionnaires which are completed by the respondents themselves. These techniques cannot be used to obtain in-depth understanding, but they are quite suitable for obtaining structured information. They are useful where time is limited or where it is necessary to allow respondents to provide the information in their own time. The telephone has gained ground as a research technique because it enables the researcher to obtain rapid responses from samples of respondents. Its usefulness in this respect has been further enhanced by computerization. CATI (Computer-Aided Telephone Interview) systems display questionnaires to telephone interviewers and also capture the data. Edit checks can be built into the program so that the answers are tested as they are entered. CATI systems will also manage the sample by displaying telephone numbers remaining to be called to interviewers as they become free, and even organizing recalls. Analysis can be almost instantaneous as the survey is completed or at any stage during the interviewing process.

Self-completed questionnaires

Self-completed questionnaires have fallen out of favour for general reseach but are retained in communications research, largely because the respondents have some interest in providing a reply and the response rates are therefore sufficiently high to provide valid data. Self-completed questionnaires are particularly suitable for obtaining information from respondents who are travelling frequently or are otherwise difficult to contact during the normal working day. They are also useful when it is necessary for respondents to think at length about the questions before replying.

Group discussions
The depth of understanding provided by a survey can be radically improved by using the group discussion as the means of collecting information. This technique interviews groups of respondents simultaneously so that they hear each others' views and provide a reaction to them. Normally, six to eight respondents are brought together, sometimes in special rooms with recording facilities. The discussions may last several hours and the topics are explored in great depth. The added understanding is provided by the interplay between respondents, and the role of the interviewer (or moderator) is to guide the discussion, rather than ask specific questions. However, the cost of recruitment and the need to provide some form of incentive, plus the heavy calls on the researcher's time, mean that the technique is very costly and must therefore be used sparingly. Fortunately, the data yield from a single group is considerably more detailed and informative than individual interviews with an equivalent number of respondents. Group discussions therefore play an important role in the types of qualitative research required for communications planning, despite the fact that they are relatively expensive.

Questionnaires and check-lists
The single most important input to all four techniques is the questionnaire or check-list that is used. If this is inadequate and omits essential topics, the data yield will be incomplete; if it misleads the respondents, the answers will be wrong. Designing questionnaires is a major research skill often under-valued, and it may well take a number of attempts and a pre-test of the questionnaire before a satisfactory document is finally produced.

MEDIA RESEARCH

As the name implies, media research is designed to provide data on all aspects of the media by which information is communicated. For national, local, and trade press it covers the numbers of readers of specific journals, the structure of the readership, and readers' comprehension and retention of the information they have taken in from journals. It can also provide reactions to specific copy and messages. Similar types of data can be collected for all other media types such as posters, direct mail, and even sponsorship. Its uses are wider than corporate communications, but obviously the techniques are of value in assessing the usefulness of channels and the effect that they have on recipients. Media research is largely undertaken by the media themselves for their own planning purposes, but the corporate communicator needs to be aware of its existence since it can be a useful information source.

ADVERTISING ASSESSMENT

Advertising research is another specialization that can be directly and indirectly useful to the communicator. It is of direct use if advertisements are to be used as part of the communications mix; it is indirectly useful in that some of the techniques may be of value for assessing other methods of communication.

Advertisers have developed an armoury of sophisticated techniques for the pre- and post-testing of their output. These concentrate on identifying the messages that have the greatest impact and recall among their target audiences and therefore are communicating effectively. Corporate communicators have an idea to sell rather than a product, but their requirement is the same: they need to know that they are getting through in the best possible way. Therefore they can borrow some of the advertisers' research technology. Ratings of messages, recall tests, association tests, and recognition tests (such as Starch) are all worth considering when evaluating a corporate communications campaign.

INTERNAL AND EXTERNAL RESEARCH

Since communications can be either internal or external, the research must also be directed at audiences within and outside the company. This does not have a major effect on the techniques to be used, but it can influence the ways in which they are deployed. Internal audiences are more likely to co-operate but at the same time will be more sensitive, since they stand to gain or lose directly. The fact that the research is being undertaken may be perceived as a threat. It may also be used as an opportunity to pass messages back to management. The results are therefore prone to biases which must be recognized in advance and neutralized. Sampling internally may also raise problems. Participation may be seen as a status symbol, and management is sometimes at too much pain to ensure that certain individuals are given a chance to express their views. This process can impair the representativeness of the survey.

Research among external audiences may be dogged by a reluctance to co-operate and relatively low interest on the part of respondents, but it is unlikely to encounter more than the normal research biases. The researcher is also free to construct the method and sample on normal research principles.

Obtaining and using the information

Once the information required has been specified, the communications planner needs to initiate the research process by which it will be obtained.

The major decisions to be taken are:

- Who will obtain the data?
- What resources will be deployed?
- How long will the survey take?
- How much will the survey cost?

Communications planners need to devote as much time to determining how their information is to be collected as to deciding what information is to be sought. It is reasonably evident that the quality of the information obtained will depend on the skills of the researchers. However, the efficiency with which they are employed will also effect results. Badly organized surveys generally produce poor data. There is also a cost implication. Research is rarely inexpensive, and in budget-conscious organizations planning is needed to ensure that surveys are carried out as cost-effectively as possible. In any survey, time, resources, and cost are almost inseparable. Long, complicated surveys requiring high levels of skill cost more than short, simple exercises. As in all services, the main input to a research programme is time, and the more time that is spent, the higher the cost. Costs are sometimes disguised if the research resources are internal employees, but they are present nevertheless, and in today's financially driven organizations, research services are more than likely to be cross-charged between departments.

In all types of research involving interviews, the number, type, and length of interview are generally the major determinants of cost and are therefore a common cost yardstick. Because they take longer to complete, personal interviews are generally more expensive than telephone interviews. In corporate research, interviews with senior staff require more skill than interviews with junior staff or members of the public, and are therefore more expensive. At 1986 prices, interviews can cost between a few pounds each to over £100. Thus, a large sample survey, even if it covers respondents that are easy to locate and uses a short questionnaire, is likely to cost between £5000 and £10 000. Where executive time is required, for example for desk research and analysis, this would be charged at £200–£300 per day. Group discussions currently average £750 per session. Research bills are unlikely to be low, and so when budgets are limited, as they invariably are, the communications planner must plan the execution of any research exercise carefully in order to ensure that maximum value is extracted.

INTERNAL AND BOUGHT-IN RESOURCES

Most communications planners will have little choice over whether they use in-house or external resources to collect their data. Relatively few companies employ market research staff, and of those that do, few employ enough to carry out major research surveys. However, it is worth examining briefly the merits of the alternative approaches.

Internal staff are close to the business of the company, are thoroughly familiar with its structure, and generally have collected information about the business on a regular basis. They are well up the learning curve and need minimal preparation before commencing any new survey work. Their major disadvantage, particularly if the research is to be undertaken among staff, is that they are part of the organization that is itself the subject of study; their objectivity is therefore liable to be questioned. For research among external groups this is less of a disadvantage, but even then there is some risk that the information given may be biased by the respondent because it is sought directly by an employee of the company.

The independent view offered by external consultants has value, though the price is paid in the longer learning time that will be required before they can commence. There is some truth in the jibe that 'a consultant is someone who borrows your watch to tell you the time, and then runs off with it!' Perhaps more importantly, consultants can provide skills and resources that are infrequently required. Communications research is unlikely to be a constant feature of corporate life, and a standing team would hardly be justified unless they had other tasks to fulfil. As described above, some of the research requirements are highly specialized and can be fully employed only if the researchers are working for a number of clients. This of course enables them to observe a wide variety of communications problems, and what they lack in industry or company knowledge may be more than offset by their ability to cross-fertilize from similar situations in other environments.

PROPOSING A SURVEY

Whichever resources are to be used, there are a number of stages that planners must go through in order to ensure that they get what they want at a price they can afford. These are:

1. To prepare a clear brief describing their requirements.
2. To obtain a proposal from the research team.
3. To select the best approach on the basis of the proposal.

The brief is the most important step in obtaining the information required. If it is incomplete, the survey will not provide all the data the planner requires. If it is over-elaborate, too much information will be collected and the survey will be unecessarily expensive. The brief should contain the following information in order that the researcher can make the most appropriate proposal:

• Background on the company and the problems it is experiencing.
• The reasons why information is being sought.
• The uses to which the information will be put, or the topics that need to be addressed in any recommendations arising out of the research.

- Information already held which will form a basis for the new research.
- The geographical scope of the survey.
- The information that is required.
- The publics that should be covered.
- Guidance on the research methods to be used.
- The time available for the survey.

The brief is not intended to provide a complete blueprint for the survey, but only a statement of what the planner requires. It is the researcher's task to convert the brief into a formal proposal or offer. The proposal will use the material contained in the brief to show the precise information that can be collected, the methods that will be used, the time needed and, if relevant, the cost. In making the proposal, the researcher should seek to guide the planner by eliminating objectives that are impractical and suggesting additional approaches or information that can be collected without adding to the overall cost. Once accepted, the proposal provides the guidelines for the research (not the brief) and is the basis of the contract between planner and researcher.

Where competitive proposals are sought, they also become the basis for the selection of the researcher. The quality of the proposal is a significant indicator of the quality of the organization making the offer, but it is not the only factor to be taken into account. The proposal shows whether the researcher has understood the problem and is capable of making a cost-effective response. However, the planner should also consider other factors that will indicate whether the quality of the project will be adequate. Some of these may be covered in the proposal, but if they are not they should be asked for. They include the previous research experience of the research team, the biographies of the staff that will be working on the project, the physical resources available to the research team (such as computing hardware and software), data bases available to the research company, and any specific research techniques in which the team is particularly skilled. In making the final selection, remember that the lowest quote is not necessarily the best. In research you generally get what you pay for, and wide discrepancies between quotations generally mean that you are being offered different surveys. Be certain that the quote you accept is going to provide you with the information you require at levels of accuracy that are acceptable.

RUNNING THE SURVEY

Once the survey is commissioned, the planner's task is far from complete. Sitting back and waiting for the researchers to report is inviting problems. It is essential to keep in regular touch with the research team in order to ensure that the survey is progressing on time, that any modifications in approach or data yield suggested by the research are agreed upon in time, and that any early findings are acted upon. The planner should also review and agree on the questionnaires that are to be used and should consider the results of any pilot work along with the research team. Research expertise is not essential to make an intelligent contribution.

Close involvement does not mean subjecting the research team to a constant third degree. They have to have room in which to manoeuvre, and additional meetings are wasteful in time and resources; on the other hand, the results have to be used by the planner, and once the survey is complete it is too late to make good any deficiencies that have arisen during the research process. No research team objects to regular reporting meetings and they will normally cost for them. Such meetings are vital.

GETTING VALUE FOR MONEY

The value of the research project will be determined by the actions taken at all stages, from briefing to reporting. Detailed specification of requirements, careful selection of the research team, and close involvement during the survey will all help to ensure that the planner gets value for money; but there are a number of further actions that will improve the ultimate value of the project.

Planners should disclose their requirements to the researchers as soon as possible. By doing so they can make use of any previous experience that the researchers have had and will probably be able to design a better brief.

Relevant information known to the planner should be provided to the research team and not held back as a means of checking the results. There is little point in paying twice for the same information.

The project should be large enough to generate valid and convincing data, and no larger. Small samples might be quite adequate in certain circumstances and there is little point in paying for more research than is needed. The researchers' guidance should be sought on what is adequate.

The information yield should not be extended so far that interesting but unactionable data are collected. If the results cannot be acted upon within six months of collection, they are not worth having.

Finally, the information must be used. This sounds obvious, but there are far too many instances of surveys languishing on shelves rather than providing the background for action.

Further reading

Chisnall, Peter, *Market Research*, 3rd edn (McGraw-Hill, Maidenhead, 1986).

Broadbent, Simon (ed.), *Market Researchers Look at Advertising* (Sigmatext, London, 1980).

Hague, Paul, *The Industrial Market Research Handbook* (Kogan Page, London, 1985).

Henry, Harry (ed.), *Readership Research: Theory and Practice*. Proceedings of First International Symposium, New Orleans, 1981 (Sigmatext, London, 1981).

Wilson, Aubrey, *The Assessment of Industrial Markets* (Associated Business Programmes, London, 1973).

Worcester, R. and Downham, J. (eds), *The Consumer Market Research Handbook* (North Holland, Amsterdam, 1986).

13.

CORPORATE RESPONSIBILITY

Len Peach

The philosophy

'Corporate responsibility', 'social responsibility', 'social accounting', 'the responsibilities of business', and other phrases have all been widely used in speeches by businessmen, politicians, trade union leaders, and others in our society who are looking for evidence of change. Alongside mounting attacks on many of the leading institutions in our society, there is a growing awareness within these institutions that a response is needed not just to criticisms, but to the genuine demands of a rapidly changing social, political, and economic environment.

Because thinking on this subject still tends to polarize between those who, rightly believing that the business of business is business, consider that this must lead them to eschew activities that are unrelated to the short-term results of their organizations and those who indulge in a number of social activities for a variety of moral reasons but without much business rationale, two things are necessary for any firm embarking on such an undertaking. First, the subject of responsibility should be defined in a way that reflects more than an indulgence in good works. Second, it should be accompanied by a rationale that puts corporate responsibility within the mainstream, instead of on the periphery, of business activity.

In arriving at a definition that does not conflict with the need for a rationale, it is necessary to discard anything that smacks of an appeal to the heart of a busy executive. One approach to this problem is to start by classifying corporate responsibility into three distinct, though interrelated, levels. In doing this, it is useful to liken the environmental impact of a business organization to a stone dropped in a pond: the ripples go outward.

This first ripple, or circle, corresponds to the first level of the suggested classification. This level relates to the basic responsibilities of any company generated by the very fact of its existence. It pays its taxes, observes the law, satisfies the basic needs of its employees and shareholders, and has honourable dealings with its suppliers, customers, and creditors. If these responsibilities are not fulfilled, then it will not be long before the company finds itself in trouble.

At the second level, the size or technology of a company will cause it to look further in scope and time than at the first level. Because it will have an effect on the environment around it, it must take on certain organizational responsibilities so that it not only satisfies the needs of all its stakeholders but also minimizes the negative effects on them of its activities. Thus, steps will be taken to contain pollution, avoid product misuses and, in short, pay heed to the spirit rather the letter of the law, act in anticipation of new legislation, and anticipate the changing reactions of its stakeholders. It is at this level that the bulk of thinking on corporate responsibility is concentrated. It can, of course, be argued that actions at these two levels are not really signs of corporate responsibility, but that, rather like failing to pay income tax, it is simply irresponsible not to take them. Failure to meet these levels of responsibility is short-sighted, but there are still many to whom the message must be preached.

The third level, or circle, relates to the societal responsibilities of the company, and represents the stage where the interaction between business and other forces in society is so strong that individual companies are inevitably involved in what is happening as a whole. In summary, the argument for 'third-circle' activities is that the healthier the environment, the better the chances of success for the company. Conversely, if the 'fabric' of a community is not sound, then the activities of any section of that community are in jeopardy. The company must be aware of the effect of the wider community on the organization and activity, not just of itself, but on that of all other organizations. It will therefore be concerned in helping to remove the ills that constrain the healthy development of society as a whole.

The distinction between actions at the different levels is fundamental. At the first and second levels they are company-oriented, relating to the direct impact of the company on individuals and groups in society. Actions taken at the third level are society-oriented and are related to the impact of social issues of the company. An understanding of this distinction is crucial.

The definition of corporate responsibility that now follows this analogy is in two parts:

1. The responsibility to plan and manage an organization's relationships with all those involved in or affected by its activities, or those who can affect the ability of that organization to operate effectively.
2. The planned and managed response of an organization to social and political change.

Defining corporate responsibility in these ways does not run away from ethical and moral considerations. It makes conscience the quality, rather than the objective of what is done; it analyses responsible actions as part of a company's survival kit; and it ensures that the deeds in which it engages may still be 'good' but are more likely to reflect the priority needs of society.

From this classification, we can conclude that corporate responsibility in this sense is not a fringe activity touching on one or two functions in an organization. It is a whole new way of thinking and acting which has to be built into everything an organization does. Whether in the R & D function, manufacturing, finance, marketing, personnel, distribution, or public relations, a company must look closely at the effect of all of its activities and decisions on all of its relationships with all of its stakeholders, and must at least try to manage change.

It must also seem that the normal interpretation of 'social responsibility' is not altogether adequate in describing what is involved. 'Total' responsibility would be a more accurate description, since this covers the responsibility of an organization at all three of the above levels—basic, organizational, and societal.

Nevertheless, it is at the third, societal, level that the least thinking has been done and where the most controversy takes place. Yet, it is at this level that business management today is facing new and urgent pressures, pressures that tend to be beyond the traditional experience of management. They arise from urban and environmental problems, pressure groups and minorities, inadequate institutions, and so on. It is these factors that are having an increasing and dominant effect on the climate in which we can do business, and which, if not controlled, make the efforts of even the best company management of marginal effect, thus militating against its long-term profitability.

To say that business must be involved in public and social affairs does not mean that it should cease to carry out the legitimate tasks it has always done. It simply means that, in the light of the new variables affecting its activities, it must review its investment mix so that a portion of its resources can be invested in building and maintaining the national fabric on which it, and all other sections of society, must depend. Investment in this way can be equated with money spent in research and management development: money spent today to protect the future.

Although these other investments often require an initial act of faith, it has been demonstrated retrospectively that a failure to invest in such areas has caused firms to cease to be profitable. The realization often comes too late. It is my suggestion that a failure to invest in the solution of societal problems will in the long term contribute to the ineffectiveness of business organizations. Why? Because the fabric of society on which we all depend will have itself failed. 'Third-circle' activities are not a drain on or an alternative to profit: rather, the long-term profit-making potential of every individual company, and of free enterprise as a whole—and indeed, their very survival—will be jeopardized unless all companies substitute for their token handouts, often made from muddled motives, heavy investments in this third level of total responsibility.

This is why it is relevant to consider the subject at a time when many businesses are fighting for survival. To maintain that this is a time to cut back or delay a stake in the future is tantamount to denying the future itself. We are talking about seed corn, and the organization or nation that neglects its seed corn is short-sighted indeed.

The impact of these arguments on personnel management

What is the relevance of these arguments for management? Certainly, personnel managers have been acutely aware of the basic responsibilities of the company. These have been spelled out to them in the legislation of the last 20 years. The various acts relating to industrial relations, employment protection, health and safety, sex and race discrimination, and the establishment of enforcement bodies leave them in no doubt about the minimum responsibilities in these fields of industry. The good practice of today becomes the legislation of tomorrow. So those companies who pioneered the field of organizational responsibilities, or the 'second circle', find that their standards have become the basis of legislation and so have become 'first-circle' activities. Companies that practised equal pay and anticipated the changing reactions of women and of the legislators have seen their advanced practice become law. Those who are seeking today to disclose more information to employees or to build industrial participation within their companies may in the next few years see legislation that will establish new norms.

In some cases legislation has the effect of creating attitudes that produce 'second-circle' activity. There have long been guidelines on the employment of disabled people. All personnel managers know how difficult these are to fulfil, and yet a number of companies, in addition to attempting to discharge these responsibilities, have taken the initiative to establish sheltered workshops or to identify and foster new areas of employment for the disabled. In the computing industry efforts have been made to train and recruit the blind into programming; and, recognizing the impact of new electronic switchboards on a major occupation of the blind, work has gone into the production of switchboards for blind operators. There is no legal requirement to do these things. It is recognized that companies must consider the impact of their products and changes on all stakeholders.

The field of employment has seen the greatest focus on the wider social responsibilities during the past few years. The tragedy of young people without employment is one that has probably appeared on the agendas of most boards of directors during that time. There appears to be a real conflict here. With falling order books, reduced profitability, and low levels of investment, the business decision is not to recruit; yet I suspect that research would find that, helped by various subsidies and government encouragement, industries have not cut back to the levels dictated and, instead of eliminating the apprentice and graduate programmes, have maintained a recruitment of young people—at a reduced level, but a level higher than that which a purely financial judgement would have dictated.

It is at the third, or 'societal', level at which there will be most disagreement. The call to divert resources to community ventures at a time of economic constraint may seem improbable, and the thesis already propounded may seem to smack of a political message since it is concerned with the survival of private enterprise and it is argued that there are some people in our society who are committed to the downfall of capitalism. However, the vast majority of our population is committed to a mixed economy, and the survival and prosperity of the individual businesses that make up the private sector is of the prime importance to all of us. It was the failure of Karl Marx to appreciate the ability of the capitalist system to adapt to change that prevented his prophesies from being realized. The requirement to adapt to and anticipate change has never been greater than it is today.

Meeting societal responsibilities requires anticipating the full range of social, political, economic, and technological trends and changes in the community that can affect the future of the organization, and taking steps to minimize the constraints or to benefit from the opportunities generated by these trends and changes. It therefore requires both a strategic plan, devoted to, in this case, 10 years, and an operating plan, normally between one and two years but probably in this case between two and five years because of the long-term nature nature of the trends and solutions to problems. It also requires a long-term approach to problem prevention. The decision to build small factories with an optimum size of 1000 employees in a number of locations rather than one large factory will reduce the substantial social disadvantages for the community if a need to contract the labour force occurs.

A subject to which managers may address themselves in the 'third circle' is the present credibility gap existing between government, academics, and business. On the relationship between government and industry on personnel matters, how many of us have sought to organize exchanges of personnel with the civil service in, say, the Department of Employment, to ensure that there is a wider understanding of the industrial viewpoint and, equally, that industry has a knowledge of the civil service view? The exchange of employees between institutions can have a major impact on the thinking of the respective organizations. How many civil servants have attended management training courses of industrial companies and vice versa?

One skill that business has in abundance and that voluntary and charity organizations lack is that of management. Those involved in charitable institutions usually have the motivation but not the discipline that experienced management engenders regarding the planning, implementing, and controlling of projects against objectives formulated in the light of resources available or resources forecast. A major contribution that business institutions can make to 'third-circle' activities is to second experienced managers and professionals to community projects. These assignments may be part-time or full-time. In some cases a trained accountant spending half a day a week may be able to reorganize the finances of an institution or provide the financial guidance and leadership that is lacking. In other cases the need will be for a full-time secondment of one or two years. There will not be a shortage of volunteers for the latter, provided the assignment is seen to be part of an individual's career progression and without any financial loss. In other words, the manager's salary is maintained, usually with the donor organization paying a 'make-up' to the salary paid by the receiving organization, or meeting all the extra cost, and with the donor company maintaining salary progression and benefits responsibility.

Such secondments can also be used as a transition to another career. Undoubtedly, there are a number of people in industry who, after substantial service, become disillusioned with their company or their industrial life and would like to undertake a second career in, for example, government or education or social service. To divorce oneself from the company or profession to which one has given one's whole working life is, however, a major step, and few people dare to take it. A secondment offers the opportunity for some of these employees to test the waters outside and to return to industry with a different perspective, or to pursue a new career with the confidence that experience brings.

Discharging social responsibility: one company's experience

THE RESOURCES AVAILABLE

So corporate responsibility is neither charity nor an indulgence in good works. It is in industry's own long- and short-term interests that it play a more active part in helping to solve some of society's problems. Our prosperity depends on the prosperity of the communities in which we operate, and the economic and social problems throughout Europe in the 1980s are increasing in both scale and complexity.

Changes in the attitudes and expectations of society mean that private enterprise organizations are increasingly expected to justify their existence, both by their economic contribution to society and by what they are doing to contribute specific skills and resources to the needs of society. Static public expenditure on social welfare throughout Europe only underlines this fact.

Corporate responsibility encompasses the actions of a company that recognizes that its continued acceptance in society—even its survival— depends to a very great extent on its demonstrating not only an awareness of the problems of society, but also a willingness and capacity to do something about those problems. The bigger the Corporate Citizen and the greater its commercial success, the higher will be society's expectations of its contribution. A planned and managed response to social change is therefore essential for leading-edge companies in the 1980s and beyond.

A company's resources are cash, management, and professional expertise—that is, the skills of its employees—plus its technology or products. Companies have been making donations of cash to charitable organizations for many years, often without any sense of strategy. Ideally, money should be used as seed corn to develop new ideas. A proportion of each donation should be designated for leverage, that is, to ensure that there is a multiplier effect in successful projects and to make widely known the lessons learnt and the experiences gained. Cash donations, however, while important in themselves, on the whole buy little visibility, since donations are mere drops in a sea of social welfare funding. Corporate responsibility is much more about involvement and participation than just signing a cheque.

Companies frequently claim that their greatest assets are their people—their employees. It is therefore logical that people have much to offer the community. Industry is recognized particularly for its management and technical skills, and these are the very skills needed to ensure that community initiatives are successful and are run on business lines.

IBM United Kingdom makes it employees available to the community in two ways: first, through its Secondment Programme, its single largest contribution to the community, loaning the equivalent of 26 man-years of employee time to external organizations; and second, through a 10 per cent scheme which enables employees to take a half-day off per week with the approval of local management to make a contribution to the community, whether as a Justice of the Peace, the leader of a youth club, or a prison visitor.

The focus of this help is external to IBM, but equally important, management must ensure that the company's internal procedures reflect the good practice and objectives it seems to achieve externally. It is hypocritical to help youth training schemes, particularly for ethnic minorities, if a company does nothing to recruit young people; it is short-sighted to second staff to help small firms, if an organization cannot settle its own suppliers' invoices promptly.

Finally, in many companies the organization's third resource—its equipment or products—is increasingly in demand in educating and preparing the young for work, retraining adults, improving the management and administration of community organizations, and maximizing the potential of people and organizations. For example, as a leader in the information technology (IT) industry, IBM must also take a lead in identifying the positive role that IT can play in helping not only life's high-flyers, but also the disadvantaged and the disabled.

In the UK, since it is essential to incorporate computer literacy across the whole range of education and post-experience education, the IBM Institute is focusing on the use of information technology by non-IT professionals, that is, in disciplines ranging from architecture to engineering and from economics to medicine. Computing equipment is also being used in curriculum development in schools and in the integration of the disabled into society.

So cash, people, and technology or products are the resources IBM can contribute. The company is not unique in these resources: all organizations have them to a greater or lesser degree.

The ways in which social problems are tackled and agencies are involved differ from one country to the next. Whereas the Church may take the lead in one country, responsibility for social programmes may rest purely with government in another. And in the UK we have 150 000 charitable organizations playing an active role.

The common factor, however, is the static level, in relative terms, of government spending on social problems, and this is unlikely to change in the foreseeable future. In fact, we are witnessing a slow, but very real, shift away from purely government or public funding for social programmes to a situation where the private sector is expected, and to some extent encouraged, to step in and fill the gaps.

Filling the right gaps in the right way is the challenge facing all of us, and resources will always be in short supply. The demands are many, and scarce resources facing overwhelming demand are easily dissipated. Their utilization demands management discipline.

ISSUE MANAGEMENT

Although the rationale for corporate responsibility is enlightened self-interest, the motivations for getting involved in one particular project can range from pure altruism or do-gooding to pure self-interest, and from self-interest to enlightenment. Major corporate donors are always inundated with appeals for help and therefore must give very careful consideration to the corporate responsibility criteria they wish to apply to all the projects they support.

Corporate responsibility programmes should be issue-driven. By that I mean that a company should select a few major national social problems in which its management believes that the company is particularly qualified to help. In this way, it can develop an in-depth knowledge and understanding of each of these issues and learn who are the key players and prime movers. Such knowledge helps to ensure that the programmes finally supported are the best of their kind.

The three issues chosen by IBM are the complex social and economic problems of unemployment, education for life, and community welfare.

Unemployment among young people is a problem throughout Europe. In the United Kingdom, through work creation, the company is addressing the need for real, permanent jobs in both the inner city and the countryside. It is focusing on the creation of wealth, the maintenance of jobs in existing firms, and the creation of new jobs in new small companies.

Education for life is very much an umbrella title for a range of educational programmes which not only introduce information technology to education, but also build permament bridges between industry and education. IBM is as interested in preparing the young unemployed for working life as in retraining adults, and the company places great emphasis on curriculum development in schools as well as on special programmes for the disadvantaged.

Under the heading of community welfare, efforts are concentrated on the disabled, as information technology has so much to contribute towards the integration of the physically and mentally handicapped.

Each of these three issues has an 'issue manager' in IBM UK in the Public Affairs Department, who is responsible for the necessary research on the subject and the preparation and implementation of an action plan. To ensure that the programmes stay on course, the Director of Corporate Affairs holds quarterly issue review meetings of the External Programmes staff. There is such a large measure of interrelationship between the issues that there is a need to focus on these in terms of geographical spread as well as with a view to achieving a fair balance across the issues. In this way management is able to identify any gaps that may exist in the total contributions package and improve the overall effectiveness of the programmes as well as their internal and external promotion.

PROJECT CRITERIA

Within the domain of issue focus, there are some basic projection selection criteria that are essential to ensure the success and visibility of the programmes. These criteria are leadership, multiplier effect, innovation, partnership, and quality.

IBM UK selects projects which it hopes will maintain a leadership position. Not only is the company's leadership beneficial to its external image among opinion leaders in government and industry, but its employees too feel a sense of pride in working for a company that is recognized locally and nationally as a good corporate citizen.

Obviously, to reflect the company's own ethos, its management is looking for 'quality' external projects: those with the right ingredients for success; those that will meet real needs in society and not unnecessarily duplicate the work of others; and those that can be adequately funded and staffed by able people. One aim is for a large proportion of these to be 'pioneering' projects, developing new and successful methods of addressing social problems. Such initiatives also provide the biggest challenges for employees on secondment and reflect the pioneering nature of the computing industry.

Having seen an innovative scheme through from embryo to successful adulthood, the company should seek to encourage its replication elsewhere, whether driven by the initial sponsors or, more commonly, by other agencies, including government. One example of the successful multiplier effect is in projects where IBM UK has acted as a catalyst, bringing together key organizations from the public, private, and voluntary sectors. One of the most noticeable trends in recent years is the emphasis placed on working in partnership with other organizations—'The Great and the Good'. Companies have always joined forces with voluntary and statutory agencies, ultimately responsible for the provision of services to the community; but more recently enterprises have also been in collaboration with one another, pooling skills and ideas jointly to bring more resources to bear on social issues. Sharing the responsibility in this way has resulted in a greater commitment and longer-term support for community projects and further integration of each company into the fabric of society.

STIMULATING EMPLOYEE INVOLVEMENT

To issue management and project selection must be added the management task of stimulating employee involvement, and here it is essential that executive management take the lead.

Without the involvement and commitment of executive management, corporate responsibility programmes will not achieve success. The chairman and directors of the company should frequently make their commitment to these programmes known, both inside and outside the organization. At the beginning of each year, executive management should review the selection of issues and the programmes proposed to address them. And throughout the year, senior management should be involved at a local level through appropriate committees.

Members of External Programmes staff naturally sit on a wide range of committees externally, but directors also should be encouraged to represent the company on external organizations, and senior management at the regional level. Committee memberships have proved to be a very effective means of influencing policy, particularly in the education field.

Through IBM UK's Resident Director Programme, the country is split into three, each region with its own resident director, acting as the chairman's deputy in the region. Apart from location and some personnel duties, the resident directors are responsible for overseeing corporate responsibility initiatives in their regions. They may play an active part in important regional organizations, such as the Scottish Development Agency, which attracts inward investment to Scotland, or the Area Board of the government's Youth Training Agency. They represent IBM at official civic functions as well as at local community events, and they chair the Regional Contributions Review Committee in turns.

External Programmes staff make presentations on the philosophy and practice of corporate responsibility and its importance to the future success of the company as often as possible at branch and divisional meetings, trying to stimulate support for programmes and to encourage the active involvement of as many employees as possible. From time to time they have been invited on to management development courses, and have developed a management development module on corporate responsibility for middle manager training, which places corporate responsibility firmly in the mainstream of everyday business.

Secondments and IBM's 10 per cent scheme have already been mentioned. Many employees are also very active on their own account in their spare time.

Even the skills and expertise of early retirees are harnessed—is there no escape?—through a newly launched network called 'Earlynet', which facilitates communications between IBMers in early retirement. The network is owned and run by its members and is a forum for the sharing of knowledge, skills, ideas, and common interests to aid the successful transition from employment to early retirement. Earlynet is not a social club. It is a promoter of the opportunities and challenges of retirement, and this includes details of paid and unpaid jobs in business and in the community. For instance, recently Earlynet was asked whether it could recommend an early retiree for an £18,000 + car post as director of a national educational charity. As a top-up to pension, it has to be attractive to a group of very active former employees, who are already engaged in a wide range of activities, from running their own businesses to full-time study, from writing to community work.

Altogether, the range of employee involvement is vast.

MANAGEMENT SECONDMENTS

IBM UK was one of the early leaders of the secondment movement in the United Kingdom and helped establish the Action Resource Centre in 1973 to encourage all companies to take a more active part in the community through the secondment of their staff. From 10 secondments from business in 1973, the numbers have grown to over 1000 secondments from business and industry annually a decade or so later. Industry's successful efforts (as of 1983) to persuade the UK government to free companies from corporation tax on the salaries of personnel seconded to charitable organizations has undoubtedly provided an extra incentive.

IBM UK has seconded 130 men and women full-time to projects of benefit to the community since 1972. The current annual target level of secondments is 1 per 1000 employees for social issues and a further 10 man-years for secondments to government and professional bodies, making a total of 26 man-years, or 1.5 secondees per 1000 employees.

One of these employees described his secondment experience to me in these words:

> It's like getting off a luxury liner in mid-ocean and stepping into a towing board of uncertain seaworthiness with enough food and rudimentary charts. You know you will eventually be picked up again, although you're not sure where you will be. You hope that the skipper will remember your name and be sufficiently impressed by your exploits to offer you a good job back on the crew.

This one short quotation sums up very clearly the problems, and the rewards, of secondment. It also highlights the need for very careful selection of candidates—self-motivation, flexibility, and sensitivity are essential qualities when moving employees out of the relative cocoon of their company world into a very different environment. This excludes low performers; one should try to ensure that the average performance rating of secondees is better than the average for the company as a whole.

In most companies, the average level of a secondee is at middle management, and although many of them have taken mid-career secondments and one or two a pre-retirement secondment, there is a need to recognize the immense value of the programme that industry and commerce should seek to grow in the future. When one of IBM's young secondees to the government's Invest in Britain Bureau was promoted from commercial director to head of the agency in his first year, the value of the programme in career terms was more readily perceived by sometimes sceptical line management and ambitious employees.

It must also be emphasized that one can regularly test the climate of opinion outside the company through secondees and learn from them to keep pace with changing values and good practice, to ensure not just that the company does not fall behind the accepted norms of behaviour, but that it keeps ahead.

For instance, a personnel officer who spent two years helping to pioneer the work of a new organization in equal opportunities training, particularly in the race relations field, for public and private sector organizations has used his very broad knowledge of this field on IBM's own internal courses, ensuring that the equal opportunity policy that has been in place for many years continues to be effective in practice.

THE FUTURE OF SOCIAL RESPONSIBILITY

In the 'third circle', the most obvious example of the developing social responsibility of major companies has been in the growth of secondments to charitable enterprises and to those organizations concerned with generating employment opportunities. The organization Business in the Community (BIC) is now a powerful force in the field of entrepreneurial initiatives and employment creation, and has both benefited from and created substantial opportunities for the loan of those whose managerial experience provides the missing factor in harnessing the goodwill that exists within well-meaning institutions and making it an efficient and effective force in achieving social objectives. BIC itself provides an institutional model for the future. Set up in 1981 by major companies, government, trade unions, and voluntary organizations, it acts as a focus and catalyst for the greater involvement of industry and commerce in the local communities, where they are based, where they trade, and from which they draw their employees. It now has more than 200 corporate members, and has formally agreed objectives based on the premise that for business to flourish it needs a healthy environment. It acts as a catalyst in involving the corporate sector in its various communities. It helps develop mechanisms such as partnerships and alliances as well as secondments, traineeships, local sourcing policies, development trusts, and enterprise agencies.

The launching of the Per Cent Club in December 1986 marked another step forward in the commitment of corporations to the principles of social responsibility and community involvement. The Per Cent Club is a group of companies that have promised to give 0.5 per cent of their pre-tax profits or 1.25 per cent of their gross annual dividend to benefit the community. The Per Cent Club's definition of charitable or community activities is broad enough to include donations in cash or in kind, including equipment, services, secondment of staff, use of facilities, premises expertise, and advice. It also includes sponsorship—of education, training, and arts, music, and literature—but would exclude activities where the objective is primarily commercial.

The future of social responsibility fulfilment, therefore, probably lies with institutions such as BIC and with an extended secondment programme. Cash or equipment in the form of donations will always be available and will be welcomed, but in the end, it is the quality of management and the professionalism of the institution which supply the multiplier in efforts for success. IBM provides secondments on the basis of 1 in 1000 of its employees; a similar attitude on the part of all large and middle-size companies would probably increase the number of those on secondment from 1000 to 10 000. Through their efforts, ideas would be transposed, new initiatives would be realized, and results would be enhanced both for the recipient communities and organizations and for the loaning companies. Secondment at an appropriate stage in a manager's career provides the width of viewpoint and understanding that the insularity of a career in one company or industry inhibits, while retaining the individual secondee's loyalty to the organization that permitted the secondment to take place.

As long as the current state of unemployment exists within Europe, there will be a substantial requirement for major companies to loan their best to aid the creation of new industry and to provide the training for those for whom the future looks bleak. As mentioned earlier, the success of capitalism and its survival have been founded on its ability to adapt. At a time when the gap between those in work and those out of work grows wider, it will be important for companies to use a small but effective proportion of their resources and their manpower to mitigate the worst effects of unemployment and to keep hope alive for those who have suffered most. It is in this spirit that the future of social responsibility lies.

INDEX